QUEER
AND
Catholic

MARK DOWD

DARTON · LONGMAN + TODD

First published in Great Britain in 2017 by
Darton, Longman and Todd Ltd
1 Spencer Court
140–142 Wandsworth High Street
London SW18 4JJ

ISBN 978-0-232-53309-5

A catalogue record for this book is available from the British Library

Front cover: The author on First Holy Communion Day, June 1967.

Designed and produced by Judy Linard
Printed and bound by ScandBook AB

In loving memory of my parents,
Patricia Reynolds and Edward Patrick Dowd

Acknowledgements

T he cover of an autobiography suggests there is but one author. This is the first book I have ever written but until recently, I had little idea of what a collective effort is required to bring such a work into being. I owe a debt of gratitude to many, many people. In truth, there are many such 'authors', the hundreds of you who have helped me mould this story and become a part of it over the decades. I can´t mention you all individually, but as the cliché goes, 'you know who you are'.

The following have specifically helped me revise sections of the book (indeed, some have been key characters in at least three of the chapters), while others have been 'a second pair of eyes' over historical stages where one's memory and judgement can often be blurred by time, so thanks to: Mark Broadbent, Brenda Carter, Michael Daly, Antony Dowd, Helen Dowd, Julian Filochowski, the lately departed and much missed Sarah Hann, Paul Harnett, Joanne Hinchliffe, Stephen Hough, Christine Hogg, Martha Kearney, Bernárd Lynch, Joe McMurray, Marion Milne, Fr Timothy Radcliffe OP, 'Pablo' (of chapter eight, not his real name), Carolyn Shearman, Sam Snape and Brendan Walsh. Special thanks too to Peter Stanford whose idea this book was in 2014 over a boozy and animated lunch at the Bleeding Heart Bistro in London EC4, and to Frank Cottrell-Boyce who especially loved the tale which forms chapter six of this volume and who told me to just write the book! Broadcasters and former work colleagues have been exceptional in their agreeing to read and recommend, so thanks in anticipation to Fergal Keane, Matthew Parris and Nick Robinson.

Literary agents Annette Crossland and Bill Goodall took all of two hours to respond to my initial pitch to them, when the industry average can often be three months, so both are to be commended for their decisiveness and for always believing in the project. The same can be said of David Moloney and the publishing team at Darton, Longman and Todd who embraced the manuscript straight away and have been a delight to work with throughout.

Finally, he arrived too late in the writing process to make it into the final manuscript, but very special thanks to Stephen Gingell who could certainly have made at least a compelling footnote, or even a very decent chapter eleven. But no, let´s just go the whole hog … and let's hope he merits a substantial mention in *'Queer and Catholic … Continued'*.

Mark Dowd, Manchester,
Autumn 2017

Preface

Channel Four TV headquarters, Horseferry Road, Westminster. October 2000.

'If I was to give you *carte blanche* and a budget of two hundred grand for a ninety minute documentary, what film would you make?' asked Tim Gardam, Director of Programmes. My answer came straight out, without a hint of hesitation. 'I'd like to show why the Roman Catholic Church is so anti-gay.' 'And why is the church so anti-gay?,' came the rejoinder. 'Because,' I said, 'because it is so gay.'

A furrowed brow appeared on the TV executive's forehead and so I took him through the logic of my argument. The young gay Catholic had, in the celibate priesthood, the perfect excuse for his enquiring parents, as to why those wedding bells might remain elusive. He inhabits a distinctly uneasy space. A Catholic blessed (or cursed) with same sex attraction is rather akin to an orthodox Jew who cannot get the smell of sizzling bacon rashers out of his head. Or a fervent Muslim with an irresistible devotion to single malt whisky. 'A Queer Catholic' might on the surface appear like a classic oxymoron, commonly cited as 'a figure of speech that juxtaposes elements that appear to be contradictory.' My church teaches me that this desire is an 'objective disorder.' And yet … the church environment can, at times, be the gayest place on the planet. At times, all the talk is of 'Lavender Rectories', if you will.

We made that film. And one of our contributors came up with the following observation:

'Imagine if a Martian landed on planet earth and his

spaceship allowed him to peer in through a stained glass window of a Catholic cathedral during mass. What would he register? A man, dressed up in clothes normally associated with the female of the species, carrying out maternal feeding tasks with bread and wine – and all under the image of a muscular, near-naked man.'

This is my story of being Queer and Catholic – a story that at almost every stage of the bittersweet slalom of some fifty years features the influence of the 'F' word. Father. First, the lifelong task of making sense of 'God', conceived of all too readily as masculine and parental. 'Ground of all being' or the biggest con trick of all time? Second, the craving for unconditional acceptance from my progenitor who, early on, realised he had a clever wee son who was decidedly unorthodox in his sexual tastes. And finally, the nagging question that refuses to go away. Will that restlessness persist until such time as you embrace what was there from your earliest infant years, the conviction that you too should become a 'Father' – a Catholic priest, conforming his life in the service of the marginalised and downtrodden?

It's the question we often run away from. What was I put on this planet to do? It was all right for Jonah in the Old Testament. He resisted his 'vocation' but when a whale turns up on his doorstep and spits him out in Nineveh, the Almighty has not left much room for ambiguity. Or take the man shortly to assume the name 'Paul', a first century oppressor of Christians. A blinding light, followed by a booming voice 'Saul, Saul, why dost thou persecute me?'

They were handed their lines.

But where were mine?

1

*My father ...
and the Persil advert*

You open the door and it's the first thing you see. An altar boy on the steps of a Catholic Church. In a frame. His cheeks heavily rouged due to the clumsy intervention of a hand that does not do deft touches. The equally heavy graphite strokes of a HB pencil have made his fingers look unnaturally distinct through his snow white gloves. He looks anxious. No wonder. This is, after all, Autumn 1939 and the world is now at war. This disturbingly beautiful boy is my father aged eleven years. It is an image bequeathed to me more than twenty-five years ago by my grandmother, his mother, for safe keeping. Now it greeted and bade me farewell on every entry and exit from my Fleet Street flat.

Now my father is gone. But he is also still very much around.

'The owl of Minerva only spreads its wings with the falling of dusk,' is Hegel's elliptical way of telling us that the pattern and sense of life's meaning are never fully revealed in the present. Now that Edward Patrick Dowd is no more, I sense something with increasing certainty – that my life is caught up between two poles, two extremities of yearning for acceptance and chronic fear of rejection in which he will always play a leading role.

The eldest of a family of six children raised in Salford, my father was never given to grand displays of emotion. He was the kind of man who would have responded to the alert of a nuclear war by checking there were enough tea bags in the kitchen supply to get us through those first few days of atomic hell. All the more astonishing then, his behaviour on the night of 29 May 1968. We had just moved into our new modern council house in Clifton, barely two hundred metres up the road from where I was born eight years previously. As the European Cup final between Manchester United and Benfica approached ninety minutes, my father was on the edge of his seat with the game tied at one all. Then, three late goals from Best, Charlton and Kidd in extra time made us the first English club to lay our hands on the trophy. 'Ted' went into raptures. He jumped up and down on the sofa, picked up my mother, Patricia, and ran around our front room in a sequence of movements that was half dance, half pole vault. This was not a man usually given to tactile embraces. Yet here he was, for just a few minutes, a man transformed. Hugs were given as though we were all about to be sent off in exile to Botany Bay. He led us on a celebratory mission to Hart's corner shop for bottles of dandelion and burdock and smoky bacon crisps. Even better, we were given the next day off school. To this day, when Manchester United lose, I feel a weird irrational sense that the fragile anchoring of my world is becoming unhinged. Through all of our ups and downs, talking about and watching football was always the safe lifeline of communication with my father. And on this night, I sensed even as a young boy, a man who was liberated, released to be who he really could be if only he could throw off the shackles.

Sadly, such moments were rare. The man who would sit there in silence browning slices of Warburton's sliced bread on a toasting fork on the gas fire for me at 6.30am before I sauntered off to St Mark's Church for altar boy duties, was, I suspect, dogged by anxieties that always stayed below the surface. He suffered constant migraines and missed months of work as a bus conductor with Lancashire United Transport. On occasions, when he was ill in bed, I was sent to pick up his beige brown pay packet from the local depot in Swinton. When his sick pay entitlement ran out, the figure denoting his earnings displayed in the small cellophane window often reduced my mother to a tight-lipped silence. Tears in front of any of her three sons, I suspect, would have been seen as 'weakness'.

On a handful of occasions at the other end of that spectrum of footballing ecstasy, my two brothers and I would know the sting of his brown leather belt across the back of our legs. It was normally for 'giving lip'. The punishment was nothing unusual for the time, the place. My father was not cruel, unkind or malicious. I think he was 'trapped'. He was exceptionally intelligent, but education had provided no passport to a world where his talents could flourish. There was a chasm between what might have been and what came to be. And one event stays with me to this day as the nadir of father–son relations, an event that can still make me tremble. And sob.

At the local Catholic primary school, I was having a spot of bother. You see, I stood out a bit. Well – a lot. The signs were there for all to see if only they had looked more closely. How many eight year old boys wept incessantly that year when Cliff Richard, singing 'Congratulations', was defeated in the 1968 Eurovision Song Contest by Spain's Massiel singing 'La La La' – by a mere point? How many young boys, bored to death at a family wedding, learnt the steps to the old time sequence dance, the Veleta, and within months went on to be a sub-standard Billy Elliot on the ballroom dance floor? My father was conflicted on this one. It might have compromised his masculinity with the neighbours, but it had its pluses. On one summer holiday at the Butlin's holiday camp at Pwllheli, I took to the dance floor in the Regency Ballroom with my mother, Patricia, while my father stayed back in our chalet and played cards with my younger brother Antony. Two hours later, my mother and I arrived back with a fistful of fivers – tips and donations from onlookers who had admired the twinkle-toed youngster foxtrotting like a gazelle under the sparkling silver globes with his proud mother. I like to think Pat and I set the precedent for the later generation of pole dancers.

All this might have helped make up the occasional shortfall in the family coffers, but it was not going down too well with some of the rougher elements at school. They dubbed me the

'Prof'. They said they'd stick my head down the toilet when we got to 'big school'. (St Ambrose Barlow in Swinton, the dreaded Secondary Modern.) My cousin David also started to get the flack and for weeks, a gang of around seven ruffians would grab us after school, hold our hands behind our backs and thump us in the stomach. I began to run for the school gate at 3.50pm in the hope of getting back home to safety. I hid stones in the ground which I'd hurl in self-defence. I even recall lodging cans of aerosol behind boulders ready to spray in their faces if need be. But more often than not, the assailers prevailed. My mother ran a ladies outfitters near Bolton and could not meet us at the school gate. And my Dad was either on the buses or out for the count with one of his blinding headaches.

It all came to a climax one Tuesday night. I simply dreaded the idea of facing those boys any more at school. I had told my parents about them and they had responded by asking an elderly next door neighbour to occasionally meet us at the school gate. Mrs Berry, all four feet and eight inches of her, bless her, made little difference. My mother sent me to bed early. My sobbing only got louder and louder. Then the bedroom door was flung open by my father. He was on an 'early shift' next morning at 4.30am, had gone to bed at 8pm and I had woken him up. He was furious. I can't recall exactly what he said, but all I recall is that *now, at this very time of desperation*, my father had turned on me. Didn't he understand what it was like to bite your tongue in your sleep, to wake up with your hands sweaty and clenched? When he left the room, I stifled the sobbing with a pillow and hardly slept.

The following day, I took it all into my own hands. Unable to face another beating, I slipped out of the school gate after the 2.10pm playground break and ran like the clappers for home. I had expected to do my usual latchkey child act and let myself in, light the gas fire and make a pot of tea with some bread and Hartley's blackcurrant jam. But this was Wednesday, a day my mother did not open her shop. When she saw me at home, ninety minutes early, she demanded to know what was going on. I told her I had to run away from those boys.

But instead of backing me up, she rounded on me for causing a scene. 'What will those teachers be thinking now? They'll be worried sick about you'. We still weren't connected by phone to the outer world, so she told me to stay put while she went round to explain it all to Mr Moss, the headteacher.

This was bleak. I felt there was *no one* I could turn to. No one who would take my side. Alone. So alone. When she went through that front door, I grabbed one of my toy cars, a yellow and silver Dinky model, and began to snap it all to pieces. I thrust a large metal bumper plate into my mouth and swallowed it. I had half hoped I would choke on it, but it went straight down, so I repeated the process with another piece of the silvery car frame. Not satisfied with that, I then wandered into the kitchen, stood on a chair and extended my hands out for a large bottle of Dettol. I unscrewed the plastic top and drank about a third of its contents. I spluttered and choked but, for the time being managed to keep it down. Reflux surged up through my nostrils but through force of will, I kept most of it in. Anything to avoid being thumped and thumped again. Then it got even worse.

The five bullies from school now appeared out of nowhere outside our house with their faces pressed against the lounge window. Their heads were distorted as if they were in some grotesque hall of mirrors. A voice yelled through the letterbox: 'if you tell on us we're gonna bloody knock your head in. Mossy's onto us. If you don't keep your gob shut, you're dead.' I ran to lock the back door and for a moment I thought they might force the front door open, so I scuttled upstairs and locked the bathroom door behind me. There I stayed until it all went quiet and the next sound I heard was the key turning in the front door lock. It was my mother. When I stole back into our front room, I saw her looking at my dismembered Dinky car. Then she clocked the now part-empty Dettol bottle with the cap off. Her eight year ballroom dancing prodigy now started to throw up all over the carpet. 'What's happened to your favourite car?' she asked. As my eyes welled up, I pointed to my mouth. I will never forget that look on my mother's face. Part horror and part self-reproach. Within minutes we were with Dr Bhanji, the local GP. She explained all the day's events to him and he prescribed me a large bottle brown of liquid – in effect a hefty tranquiliser. It seems odd now that we weren't sent to the Accident and Emergency for X-rays. Instead, my mother was given the unpleasant task of 'number two duty' – to check that the two pieces of metal I had swallowed were accounted for safely by natural means in the hours and days ahead.

I didn't attend school for two weeks and I've no idea what was in that brown liquid. All I know was that it made my Gran's bottle of liquid cod liver oil taste like nectar. It was foul. I slept for twelve hours at a stretch and even when I was 'awake' I was floating around in a haze with the fairies. Back at St Mark's primary school there was an inquest. Mr Moss, the headteacher, sorted out the thugs. They never laid a finger on me again. During all this period in time, my father was withdrawn, preferring, it appeared, to leave all the officiating to my mother. I wanted some reassurance from him, some sense that it was all OK now. But nothing followed.

Which is not to say that he was always unattentive. There was one time I was deeply aware of his scrutiny. It was during one Sunday afternoon while I was watching TV. I had acquired a new best friend – the boy from the Persil ad. My viewing habits were the majority's in reverse. *They* would put the kettle on during the ad breaks, whereas when I heard the Granada channel music sing, signalling the commercials, I would scamper back into the front room to the alluring presence of the new Rediffusion colour TV set. My new best friend had short blond hair and he was great at sport. But his athleticism, said the voiceover, was a real challenge to his mother – how would she ever get all the mud off that rugby kit? As he strutted into the house, he was instructed to strip off – all the way down to his white underpants. I can still see him, at the top of the stairs, throwing his dirty sports kit down to his mother who would lovingly get his gear 'whiter than white'. I stared and I stared. Of course, I didn't know what it 'meant,' but I had a sort of 'Ready Brek' glow inside of me whenever he appeared. He was the picture of innocence. I couldn't take my eyes off him and made no attempt to hide my fascination with this angelically cute apparition. Why should I? Did my father cotton on? Hard to say, but he certainly saw me watching. And more than once. What seemed odd was that, almost overnight, his viewing preferences seemed to take a distinct lurch to BBC1 and BBC2 – where there were no commercials.

The eleven plus exam approached. The binary options were clear: pass and a one way ticket to liberation at grammar school, away from the bullies. Exodus. Fail and it would be non-stop torment at St Ambrose Barlow where the taunts of 'Prof' would end up with me hauled on to the school roof and left to be mocked. My mother had already savoured eleven plus success with my elder brother Christopher and now she reverted back to her tried and trusted formula – the *General Progress Reasoning Papers.* No matter that she worked all day selling frocks, cooked the family tea when she came home and had dozens of alterations to work on with her Singer sewing machine. She committed herself to hour after hour of it – 'Black is to white as truth is to...' (four choices.)

The big day came. The omens weren't good. While twenty per cent or so passed the eleven plus nationally, at St Mark's Primary it had been several years since more than one child had passed out of a class of thirty. I'd found it easy enough. Easy, that is, until I got home and faced my mother's: 'were there any you were unsure of?' There had been a series of questions in which one had to combine two short words from columns A and B to make a larger lexical unit. I told her I had combined 'rope' with 'let' to make 'ropelet' – a surely a short rope? 'What were the other words in the first column?' 'Ring' had eluded me – but how was an eleven year old boy to know what a 'ringlet' was? This omission seemed to convince my mother that I had failed. Weeks of anguish followed, before the dreaded brown paper envelope arrived from the local education authority. They never used the words 'pass or fail' – they simply listed a series of schools to which one was now eligible to apply. All mine were grammar schools – Thornleigh, Stand Grammar, St Bede's and so the list went on. My parents wanted me to go to De La Salle. It was three miles away in Weaste, near Eccles and the competition for places was fierce. It was renowned for its formidably difficult entrance exam which had certainly proved too much for my elder brother who had had to settle for Stand Grammar, a *Protestant* school, if you will. (This involved my mother being summoned to the local Bishop who granted his permission for this tribal disloyalty, only on condition that Christopher take weekly Catholic instruction from our parish priest, Fr Sweeney.)

The De La Salle exam was a killer. My composition essay on 'Bonfire Night' had been constructed with no paragraphing. Worse still was the maths paper. I knew nothing about fractions. To my parents' despair, I came home and proudly showed them how I had added one fifth and one quarter to make two ninths by adding up the numbers above and below the lines. (I can still now break out in a sweat if I hear the term 'common denominator' used, even in the most colloquial of contexts.) But I was saved by the following question, the answer to which possibly was one of those classic life-changing moments.

> '*In a local street you view trees planted outside houses on both sides of the road. On one side, there is a tree every fifteen houses. On the opposite side, there is a tree every fifty houses. The only time when two trees face each other directly is at the end of the street. How many houses are in the street?*'

I think 300 will be forever my favourite number. It got me into one of the best schools in the north of England and guaranteed that, from September 1971, I would run the risk of looking like a prat in my maroon and yellow school uniform. I was the only boy to pass from primary school and I did not know a soul at the new place. But who cares? The clever boys wouldn't put me on the roof or flush my head down the toilet.

Would they?

2

Talking in my sleep

The note that never made it to its intended recipient in Romeo and Juliet. Or maybe, 'Eeny meeny, miney'... the impulsive thrust with the biro to fill in that sixth and ultimately winning lottery number. Or maybe the overly hasty signature on the contract without checking the small print where that 'devil in the detail' costs you thousands and thousands of hard earned pounds. There are whole lives that dramatically change course like carriages going through points on a train track. Mine was one simple word scrawled on a piece of paper. That word was: 'Yes.'

March 1973. I was in my second year with the teaching brothers at De La Salle College in Salford and doing very nicely thank you. Top of the class in 1X and now in 2X doing fractions in my sleep (yes, with common denominators, don't you know?!). I had proud parents who could now relax and focus their minds on getting their youngest, Antony, to accomplish an eleven-plus 'hat trick'.

One Tuesday afternoon, our Religious Education class played host to a surprise visitor. Brother Dominic Green was a portly, charismatic type with the gift of the gab. He was shaped like a barrel – one of those 'weebles that wobble but that don't fall down'. He bustled purposely between our wooden desks and handed out pieces of paper which posed a most interesting question 'Do you think God wants you to become a De La Salle brother?' I pondered for several minutes before reaching for my biro. I was one of five pupils in our year of a hundred who answered in the affirmative. This can hardly have come as a shock to my mother and father. From the age of five, I got used to answering the question, 'what do you want to be when you grow up?' My contemporaries had answered with 'footballer, train driver or fireman,' but my answer had always been consistent: 'teacher or priest'. There was more than a little logic to my 'yes'. The order of St John the Baptist De La Salle, founded by a Rheims-born cleric in the latter half of the seventeenth century, had been established with the intention of educating the children of the poor. In my day it had become a pretty middle class affair, with well to do kids travelling from as far as Glossop in Derbyshire to attend, but its Direct Grant Grammar School status had meant that the less well-off still had a chance of a first rate education without the crippling fees. I looked up to the brothers. They knew their academic subjects, were single-minded and were mostly decent men. As role models went – they were not bad at all. Enough for a 'yes' on that scrap of paper – and a subsequent visit of Brother Dominic to the family home.

The Dowd residence at 20 Wyndham Avenue was exactly halfway between Bolton and Manchester. Five years previously, just after that ecstatic father–son bonding European Cup Final, our former house at 70 Manchester Road had been the subject of a compulsory purchase by Salford Council whose planning department wanted to flatten a small number of solid Victorian houses to make way for a whole new swathe of functional redbrick council houses. My parents loathed the idea of losing their home on the whim of a local bureaucratic committee but the council always got their way. They were offered a measly six hundred pounds in compensation and a one way ticket to the sunlit uplands – a three bedroom council house, *with an indoor toilet!* The stale aroma of the chamber pot under the bed was banished forever. New items appeared. Hot wax lamps on the new Rediffusion colour TV set. A rent book. And, at last, we were connected to the outside world via an olive green coloured handset that was placed strategically on the piano in the lounge thus making any private phone conversations impossible.

You always knew when we were expecting guests because

that was the only time the hoover came out. And Brother Dominic got the royal treatment. The Pledge was applied to every available surface. My mother and I went through almost a bottle of disinfectant in the kitchen and bathroom. The tubby, gregarious brother caused an eyebrow or two to be raised when he dunked his Rich Tea biscuits in his cup of Mantunna. He then revealed the 'why and wherefore' of his mission.

'Your Mark, it would appear, may well have a vocation to the religious life with De La Salle,' he said. 'And to test this, we have a special school called St Cassian's. I'd like to ask permission for him to visit us on a 'Come and See' weekend – to see if he likes it.'

'Where is it?' asked my father looking a trifle worried. 'Berkshire,' came the reply. 'In the countryside. A lovely quiet spot,' assured the vocations director.

Berkshire could have been in Outer Mongolia for all we knew. For eight consecutive years we had been to the same Blackpool boarding house for our summer holidays (that trip to Pwllheli had been well off our beaten track.) As a family we were a fairly parochial lot. All of my twenty aunts and uncles were still living within six miles of where they had been born. 'Down south' really did mean, beyond Stockport.

Brother Dominic had sparked my interest in this place called St Cassian's. I went to check the place out one weekend in May with the other four boys who had expressed an interest. We were driven down in the school minibus by Brother Gabriel and took in exotic places like Evesham and Hungerford, before we merged on the outskirts of Kintbury, later home to Terence Conran of Habitat fame and the author Robert Harris. It would go on to be named later as one of the ten most attractive villages in the UK.

On arriving at St Cassian's, we were each assigned a 'companion'. It sounded innocent enough, but as I came to discover, these carefully selected seniors were to be Brother Dominic's 'eyes and ears' during our weekend stay. The person who had been assigned to keep close tabs on me was an agreeable sort, Peter Parsonage. On arriving and taking my dormitory bed, he took me quietly to one side. 'You're a marked man,' he said. 'Why?' I said nervously. 'What have I done wrong?' He laughed. 'Nothing. It's 'Dommo'.' He came in this morning and gave me this.' It was a white sticker with my name on it, which he then peeled off and placed on the headboard over my bed. 'I shouldn't really tell you this, but Dommo gave me instructions. "I want that boy," he said to me. "He's a good 'un"'. I blushed.

But 'Dommo' got his wish. I fell in love with the place – and a lot of it was down to 'Cedric'. Not a man, or a boy, or even a pet dog. 'Cedric' was the name of the biggest tree I had ever seen in my life. More than two hundred and fifty years old, this gargantuan cedar dominated everything around it. It was like a stunning, reassuring arboreal octopus. That weekend I stood in front of it for what seemed like hours on end, marvelling at the sound of the rasping wind rustling through its tentacles. It swayed and moved as the clouds flurried through the pale blue sky above. It was so *other*. You couldn't imagine Cedric anyway near Lowry's chimney stacks and factories. Clearly there was some deeply felt pastoral 'thing' stirring away in my sub-conscious. You almost wanted to be enveloped by its sturdy, solid branches.

Indeed, it wasn't just 'Cedric' – the whole place was captivating. Every corridor and hall had a solid and comforting smell of beeswax. The school site was based on the Wallingtons estate, an impressive stretch of land purchased by William Waynflete, the Bishop of Winchester, in the fifteenth century. The redbrick manor house which accounted for much of the school building had been remodelled after a huge fire had eclipsed the original in 1784. As a contrast with industrial Salford, it could not have been more stark. Cedar for cement seemed a good swap. But why was I not daunted at leaving home? I still don't honestly know. But I signed up. And that meant 'Dommo' had got his man. My parents seemed to accept it as the 'will of God'. (Some thirty five years later I would get a different account from my mother following my father's death: 'He never liked the idea of you going off down there. He thought you were too young to be away from home like that. But what could he do? You were so keen and if it's what God was asking you to do…?')

At this point in the tale, the Catholic 'misery memoir' warning siren is possibly sounding. If you've been brought up on a diet of *Angela's Ashes*, *The Magdalene Sisters* and *Philomena* the scene is now set for a tale in which innocence and aspiration is cruelly crushed by the evil machinations associated with the horrors of institutionalised religion. It's a perspective shared by many a 'recovering Catholic' but that's not my tale. My time at St Cassian's played a huge role in defining many of the emerging themes of my life and was overwhelmingly positive. First, I was in a class of only twenty pupils. We got a first rate education, ranging from the erudite and elderly Brother Augustine (French and English), via the wet behind the ears youngster Brother Stephen (chemistry), through the wily and paternal headteacher Brother Joseph (maths and physics) to the witty and teasing Brother Aidan (History and RE). At a time when boarding school fees were requiring parents to take out small mortgages, this would cost Edward and Patricia Dowd not a penny.

Moreover, we were taught responsibility and care for one another in a way that day school simply cannot fashion. Each boy was allotted a 'manual labour' task: that meant half an hour of polishing, sweeping or washing pans in the kitchen after breakfast and before classes. We'd be assigned in groups to prepare the veg for the head chef, Mrs Appleford, while others were deputed to head off to help out Brother Herman on the farm for longer stints at a time. There were very few food miles in this establishment as much of what we ate was cultivated, prepared and cooked from the acres of land around the house. Boarding schools have their detractors, but the business of having to live and adapt to people twenty four/ seven made huge demands of character. Back in Salford, if you had major differences with a fellow student, you could somehow sweep it under the carpet it in the nine to four,

Monday to Friday regime. On the other hand, when you're in community, there's nowhere to hide. If you chipped in, carried out your tasks and helped others, you were deemed 'a good kid'. If not, you were the target of the crowd. It was social reinforcement of a positive kind. Since I had always craved approval and acceptance, I moulded myself to fit in. (Ever since I can remember, even the slightest reprimand had the effect of reducing me to inconsolable tears. I was once caught chewing a pencil in primary school and singled out by Miss Smethurst for a very public scolding. It was as though my world had fallen apart. I had never learned as a child, that frowning on an action did not mean root and branch rejection of you as a person.)

My time in deepest rural Berkshire was passing serenely. The brothers insisted on a weekly letter-writing session, which guaranteed a steady stream of correspondence to and from the family home. Once a month I'd get what we referred to as a 'red cross parcel' from my folks. This often contained a specially baked coconut cake, a hastily written note from my mother on pale blue Basildon Bond notepaper and press cuttings from my Dad. Love of Man United was the lifeline of contact between us and he'd dutifully cut out reports from the Saturday evening 'Football Pink'.

I returned home for a Christmas break and told my parents of my new school and how Brother Joseph, the head, had cottoned on to my burgeoning interest in classical music to such an extent that he let me choose records for playing during 'reading hour' at weekends. The school report was glowing. Top of the class again. What could possibly go wrong?

In early 1974, I returned to Berkshire to begin the Spring term and that is when the ghost of the Persil advert began to reassert its presence. That experience of gazing warmly as an eight year old at that beautiful boy on the TV had happened six years ago. There'd been many a change since. First the facts of life. My father had never dared broach the subject, so it had fallen to Father Kevin, the school chaplain, to do the honours shortly after I had begun grammar school back in 1971. My introduction to them had been a tad controversial. The priest at De La Salle had taken small groups of us to his study to take us through a small pamphlet called 'Sex Education for Boys'. It had looked innocent enough on the outside with its brown and white cover. But the only way we could all see this publication simultaneously was by standing in a small circle around his chair as he took us through the increasingly detailed drawings. That morning I had done two paper rounds between 7am and 8am and was so late for school that I'd skipped breakfast. Then, after a fifteen minute bus ride, I'd run about a mile down Claremont Road just in time to avoid the dreaded 'late book'. By 9.15am, blood sugar levels were hitting the danger zone. What happened next was excruciatingly embarrassing. I was already feeling light-headed, beginning to sweat and getting the sound of ringing in my ears. Father Kevin then coaxed us all into positions. 'Don't be shy,' he had said. 'There's nothing to be feeling awkward about here.' He turned to page eight. Out of nothing, a quite startling picture of a large droopy penis appeared. My legs gave way and I fell to the ground, unconscious. The rest, as they say, is history. 'Dowdy', it was said gleefully in class 1X, couldn't handle sex.

How prophetic they were. Every boy had been loaned a copy of the sex manual to take home and show his parents. Mine stayed hidden inside my geography atlas all week, the offending penis making an appropriately snug fit alongside the coastline of Chile. Three years on, there was now considerably more testosterone coursing round my adolescent body and it found a focus rather more immediate than a washing powder advert. Suddenly, this pleasant boarding school felt like it was becoming an incubator for a desire which my church would, a decade later, go on to describe in an authoritative teaching document as 'intrinsically disordered.' When did it all start? Mornings after rising and evenings before bedtime in our dormitories, we'd line up in the washrooms, stripped to the waist, to carry out our customary ablutions. The incarnate object of my attention was Duncan. All I now recall is manoeuvring myself into position to stand behind his washbasin and admire the outline of his rather body-defining maroon-coloured corduroy trousers. I looked at his unclothed taut, muscular torso and then, whenever he turned round, I quickly averted my gaze and pretended to be captured in sacred thoughts. 'Lord make me chaste but not just yet,' wasn't half of it.

As the weeks went by, the pressure cooker effect intensified. As fate would have it, 'Dunner' as he was known, was also from my Salford school and I often wondered why he had elected to sign up for this place. I knew deep down that there was more statistical likelihood of Ronnie Biggs becoming Pope than of him becoming a teaching brother. I assumed he'd come here to get away from home, enjoy a change of scene. But everywhere I turned, he was there in front of me. Our huge dormitory of St Benildus, whose sturdy windows looked out directly out to the imposing presence of 'Cedric' housed twenty beds. My luck (or misfortune) was that mine was a stone's throw away from Duncan's. As I became overloaded with this strange and compelling desire, I'd sneak discrete glances at him over the rim of my wooden headboard and hope no one would spot me. When the lights went out at 10pm on the dot and the dormitory senior proclaimed: 'Live Jesus in our Hearts', the resounding cry that came back was 'Forever'. Then I'd feel sad. Jesus seemed to be anywhere but in my heart. And it would be another eight hours or more before I could lay my eyes on Duncan again at morning mass in the chapel.

That dormitory became the venue for some unusual antics. One boy was a chronic sleepwalker. On one occasion, several of us switched a couple of beds round so that when he returned after his somnambulant promenade, he ended up climbing into bed with another lad who was, to put it mildly, rather startled to find he was sharing a bed with a potential suitor. (We'd switch all the lights on for maximum scandal effect – a move I have since learned was potentially very detrimental to our nocturnal rambler.) For a short while I did seriously countenance faking my own sleepwalking, hoping that, as Duncan was a heavy sleeper, I might, if the beds fell into the right positions, get an unexpected bonus of climbing into bed with him. But I desisted. I was afraid I would draw attention to my state of arousal and excitement.

On another occasion, it was I who provided all the midnight entertainment. At the end of one indescribably bitter January night, long after the feeble radiators in the huge room had ceased working, I was finding it impossible to get off to sleep. My body was a block of ice and no amount of adolescent lust could get the temperature gauge to flicker upwards. My feet had lost all sensation, save for a dull and persistent ache. I dived down, snorkel style, to the bottom of the bed and began to use what scant warmth remained in my hands to nurture the blood capillaries in my feet back to life. At first the action was gentle and discrete, but little by little, encouraged by the returning warmth into my toes, the action became ever more vigorous. This must have carried on for a good two or three minutes. Then, out of nothing, from under the deepest recesses of my woollen blankets, I was suddenly aware of the dormitory lights being switched on. An authoritative voice bellowed out: 'You. What *are* you doing down there?'

My dormitory companions were now awake and all they could see was a semi-inert lump under the bedclothes which was making the strange (or perhaps not so strange) sound of flesh on flesh. Mole-like, my head popped out from the darkness. The lights startled me. I scrunched up my eyes and pleaded: '*But Brother, I'm only rubbing my feet.*' Cue hysterical laughter, a laughter which brought the headteacher Brother Joseph, wandering along the corridor with his torch. We were all sentenced to the Gulag – an extra afternoon of manual labour on the farm with Brother Herman. And the 'rubbing of feet' entered into the boarding school lexicon as a euphemism for self-abuse – a subject that figured all too unhealthily and obsessively in our laddish discourse.

I wasn't especially interested in the solitary expression at this point. I was on fire, rather, for another human being, a boy I didn't even especially like as a person. Duncan was seen as arrogant, aloof and stand-offish, qualities that only fanned the flames of physical attraction. Make no bones about it, this was pure and unadulterated lust and it manifested itself in some strange ways. In chemistry and physics, Duncan was my lab partner. This brought with it thrilling opportunities for physical contact. Experiments on focal length with lenses, kinetic energy with moving objects or caressing test tubes of potassium permanganate all had ample scope for body to body experience. Sparing the gory details, this had some fairly dramatic impact on my young body as I struggled to keep the lid on. Towards the end of that Spring term, I could bear it no longer. This was getting to be torture. It was a huge risk, but if there was even the slightest chance of reciprocation, I had to go for it. The evenings were now getting longer as 'Cedric's' shadows extended all over the school grounds. Somewhat out of the blue, I suggested to him after supper and before night prayer that we go for a walk on the rugby pitch. He looked puzzled. 'What for?' he asked. I put my hand on his shoulder and felt an immediate response downstairs. 'It's a big secret,' I said excitedly. 'And you're the only one who'll know.' His ego seem flattered. He didn't have many friends and had been the target of some taunting of late. 'OK, then, let's go,' he said.

I wanted to get to get as far away from the school building as I could in case we were overheard. When I felt it was safe, I took a deep breath and out it came. I didn't know the word 'gay', and though I had heard of the very medical sounding, 'homosexual,' that all sounded too clinical. So I focused on him. I knew he was full of himself so I told him he was handsome and the best looking boy in the school. He looked at me puzzled. 'Why are you telling me all this?' Then the penny dropped. He looked neither horrified nor interested. Maybe flattered, but that was it. My gamble had failed. Duncan, it seemed, was not a fellow traveller. For a few moments I felt downcast and then I knew there was more urgent business. If he blabbed on me about this, living in this place would become intolerable. I'd quickly become the wonky feet rubber from Salford and the butt of merciless banter about 'benders and bum chums'. The truth was I had very few cards to play. I had nothing to threaten him with and little to offer either, save my continued friendship and loyalty. And Duncan must have felt unnerved, not by me, but by the increasingly loud jibes from the older boys who were beginning to pick on him, because this pledge of mine to stand by him seemed to placate him. To his eternal credit, he never did rat on me.

My hopes had been dashed. But this was not love which had floundered on the rocks, just an inconveniently forceful carnality and I suspect it helped prepare me for my first sexual encounter which occurred just a few weeks later – not with a fellow schoolboy. This was to happen – with Brother Dermott.

In between terms I had been asked to stay on and help out at a special event. Teaching brothers were arriving from all over the country for a kind of 'religious order congress'. 'Dommo' had sold it well. I had been specially picked out with half a dozen others. There'd be some top up pocket money for waiting on the two dozen or so visitors at mealtimes, preparing the vegetables and making sure Mrs Appleford was not short of hands in the kitchen. If I had a vocation to the religious life as a brother, I had to learn to chip in and be a team player. It's what God wanted of me I was sure. So I signed up (I knew Duncan would not be selected and I thought it better to begin the painful process of cold turkey. It would be good to be free from what one Dominican priest later on referred to as 'the tyranny of genitality'.)

The prestigious visitors arrived and I helped take their bags to their rooms. One brother spotted I had a northern accent and told me he taught at the De la Salle School in St Helen's and we exchanged pleasantries. What were my favourite subjects at school?, he asked me. 'French and English,' I responded swiftly. His eyes lit up. 'Aha, a fellow linguist. I'll be keeping an eye out for you young man.' In this post Jimmy Savile landscape that would be enough to send anyone running for cover. But this was 1974. And sure enough, three days later,

Brother Dermott stumbled, or rather, *appeared* to stumble across me talking about languages other than French with a fellow pupil. 'Mark, do you know any Russian?' I shook my head. 'It's so exciting. It has all these amazing declensions and strange exotic sounds.' He gave me a couple of examples, took a piece of paper and started sketching out Cyrillic characters such as Д, Ф, and Щ ' Of course, they look a lot better in text books, but they're all in my room. Shall we go and look at some more?'

I love languages and am adept at them, but have never been able to force myself to handle Russian. This following incident may explain why. Off we went to Brother Dermott's room and he prepared to show me his declensions. Lest anyone reading this think that what happened next 'caused me to be gay', please bear in mind a certain apparition in that washing powder ad six years ago and months of ungratified lusting over Duncan. Indeed, if anything, this encounter with the teaching brother should have made me straight. Dermott was no looker. That's being kind. He was hideously ugly. Aged about thirty five, he had a greasy auburn mop with a basin-cut hairstyle. His freckly face was part hidden by heavy, thick-rimmed spectacles. He was part man, part reptile – I have often thought of him when I see Woody Allen. Except Woody Allen made me laugh.

What dexterous footwork he used. He started with Russian and languages and got on to parents' evenings and demanding mothers and fathers. 'And do you know what subject came up last week with one of them?' he asked me. I shook my head. 'Masturbation.' My pulse quickened. 'This mother, she said that we had no business raising it in RE classes and that it should be left to the home.'

He paused. 'What do you think? Do you think it's always wrong?' Cripes. What a question. We seemed to have moved a fair bit away from Russian datives and pronouns. 'Er...I just think it happens. If it is a sin, as Brother Aidan told us in RE, I guess there's a lot worse ones.' In hindsight, this was not an especially adroit answer. Green light. He drew himself closer.

Then very close until he lowered his trousers and began 'rubbing his feet'. All he wanted me to do was to hold him around his genitals until the inevitable moment which was a matter of a couple of minutes at most. I simply froze on the spot. But he was like a wounded creature in pain. He couldn't look me in the eye and his face was taut. He was fighting himself. When he reached the point of climax, instead of a rousing groan of relief he let out a pathetic melancholy whimper. It was one of the saddest things I have ever witnessed in my life.

I should have just run out of the room, but suddenly I had become the adult. He looked across at me so forlorn. No doubt some will say this was also part of the manipulation, but to this day I just think he was a lonely guy who'd got trapped. However, more shocking was what came next. He recovered his composure and got onto the floor to reach for something under his bed. It was a newspaper with the words *Gay News* emblazoned across the masthead. What was he going to do now? Show me indecent pictures?

'Do you know about the personal ads section?,' he asked me. 'You can put a notice in here and then go and meet people in London and places and stay in hotels with them.' Was this guy mad? I was fourteen and I said as much. 'Well, you'd have to say you're twenty one in the ad, but of course when you got down to London, they'd have quite a nice surprise.' Or an instant coronary and on possible recovery, a half decent chance of a long stint in Reading gaol. When I look back now, I still think this was far worse than the physical misdemeanours. He was encouraging a child who was legally seven years under the age of consent to take up with total strangers in seedy Earl's Court hotels. 'Now all this is our secret, you know that Mark? There are some people who simply wouldn't understand our kind of special friendship.' I made my excuses and left.

Why didn't I go straight off to the headteacher and blow his cover? Maybe I'd made some illogical assumption this would let unravel all the previous few months of sexual tension over Duncan. There were undoubtedly feelings of pity too that were factored in. What I did do was find myself a confidant: my best friend Chris, another Salfordian. I related the whole thing from start to finish. He was outraged and insisted I spill the beans, but I never did. In fact this all remained under wraps until a TV documentary about the whole subject of Catholic sex abuse which aired on Channel Four in 2003. What the incident did *not* do was dent my hopes and ambitions to become a teaching brother. Dermott was a bad apple but I had plentiful examples of role models in front of me who could keep my aspirations alive. It would take me many years to question whether the barrel itself might have been the real problem.

St Cassian's existed principally to foster and nurture vocations to the religious life but by May 1974, the order of St John the Baptist De La Salle was beginning to have other ideas about how best to keep up the 'flow of labourers into their vineyard'. The fact is that out of sixty or so pupils, only one or two would ever go on to make solemn vows and enter the order. It must have been costing them a fortune (and we were the beneficiaries.) The institution was what was known as a 'juniorate' – a college for educating young boys aged 11–16. But serious questions were being asked as to whether this was wise. Could a young man really discern a vocation to the religious life at this stage in his life? Was there a danger in being over-protected from the world and making unrealistic decisions which he may later come to regret? The brothers had come to a decision: St Cassian's was to be transformed into a retreat centre. The fourth and fifth years among us would stay on and complete their 'O' level exams, but we third years would return back to our feeder schools. My rural idyll, 'Cedric' and all that I had come to cherish in verdant Berkshire was over. No more cross country runs along the wonderful Kennet and Avon canal. An end to hikes on Hungerford Common and in Buttermere Copse. Back to Lowryland and Salford smoke stacks. I imagined the taunts from our soon to be, 4X classmates: 'Did they not want you then?' When Brother Joseph broke this news to us there were stifled tears that went on for days. It was like having your family broken up. I was not a little angry. I had put myself on the line for all this and here were the brothers changing all the rules, but this was the Catholic Church after all – what was I expecting, a MORI survey?

So in the summer of 1974, I packed my bags for the last time and made the six hour journey north by coach. Our north west contingent was dropped off at our respective schools: West Park in St Helens, De La Salle Liverpool, Cardinal Langley in Middleton, North Manchester, and finally Weaste Lane in Salford. I discovered much, much later that my parents were more than pleased to have me back in the family ranks, except strong expressions of feelings were not the norm. So in fact, I ended up feeling confused because life just appeared to carry on much as before. I had been through a lot in the space of ten months, but life at home seemed to pick up pretty much from where it had left off. My father was on the buses and my mother was selling frocks and doing alterations. Elder brother Chris was now a minor soccer star at the 'proddy dog' grammar school and my younger brother was getting ready for the assault on the dreaded 'eleven plus'.

Then – out of the blue – the 'love that dare not speak its name' erupted like a volcano.

It was about 9am in the middle of the summer holidays. I shared a very small room with my younger brother, but Antony was already up and about and I was dozing in bed. I felt a hand prodding me. It was my mother. 'Wake up. Come downstairs.' I rubbed my eyes and turned over. 'No school,' I said. 'Having a lie in.' She didn't buy this. 'Get downstairs,' she said in an uncommonly unfriendly tone. 'There's something we have to talk about.' Whatever was the matter? I knew it was serious since as a family, we had a tendency to brush most things under the carpet. Confrontation was not our favourite pastime, but clearly something had risen to such a level of concern and alarm that it had to be tackled head on. My school report? No way. Had I missed mass? Negative. What then could it be?

I meandered downstairs in my stripy beige and maroon cotton pyjamas and made sure the waistcord was tight and secure before I went into our front room. I didn't want to be an inadvertent flasher with my own mother. 'Sit down,' she said, pointing at the sofa and reaching for an Embassy Regal. 'What's this all about?' I asked outright. She took a deep breath and pursed her lips. 'Your Dad and I just want to say … just want to say that…' She was struggling for the right formula. And did it help that Dad was not there but doing a split shift on the number 14 en route to Patricroft? She continued. '… just want to say that if there's anything troubling you, you can tell us about it.' What did this mean? Brother Dermott? Who had spoken out of turn? No, surely not. Something else maybe?

'Thank you,' I replied. 'Is that it? Can I go back to bed now?' A shake of the head and a long puff on that ever so important cigarette.

'There is something troubling you – and you know it.' I had no idea. What *was* she going on about?

'*Who's Duncan? … You've been talking about him in your sleep.*'

Is this the most original example of coming out in modern history? I flushed like a Guernsey Tom at the idea that my secret was out. Then a terrible picture came into my mind that made me go even more crimson. That image was of my mother, bolt upright in bed in her curlers, covering the ears of her husband and trying to insulate him from the stream of lewd invective piercing the paper thin walls of our shabbily constructed council house. In a more spacious dwelling I might just have got away with it, but not at 20 Wyndham Avenue M27 6PY. My parents' room was a decent enough size, about fourteen by ten feet, but the other two rooms were effectively small singles. What's worse, each of the three bedroom doors opened out on to the landing area which was a mere strip of turquoise carpet measuring nine by three feet. Cheek by jowl wasn't half of it. It wasn't quite battery farming, but it was not far from it.

Good God. What had I been saying? It was the love that most certainly had dared speak its name – at three in the morning. It's a miracle that the holy water downstairs in the porch hadn't evaporated and the statue of the Sacred Heart wasn't in a thousand pieces. What about my little nine-year-old brother in the bed next to me? No wonder he had got up early and was nowhere to be seen. He'd scarpered.

My mother was a supremely practical person. Nothing would defeat her, certainly not a spot of unwelcome male homosexuality. Within minutes she was revealing her strategy for nipping it in the bud. 'Hello, this is Mrs Dowd. I need an urgent appointment to see Dr Bhanji.' Dr Rahimtulla Harji Bhanji, was a Kenyan immigrant of eastern Indian, Gujarati, descent and the father of Krishna Pandit Bhanji, more commonly known as the Academy Award winning actor, now, Sir Ben Kingsley. That afternoon, my mother and I strolled purposively along (well, she with more urgency than I), to the GP's surgery at 119 Station Road, Pendlebury, a large terraced building next door to the former home of the celebrated painter, L.S. Lowry. My mother's instinctive reaction to seek out a medical opinion may appear eccentric and unorthodox from the giddy heights of twenty first century gay emancipation, but a little context is required here. It was not until the following year that the American Psychological Association would withdraw its labelling of same sex attraction as a mental disorder. Homosexual acts had been legalised by the Westminster parliament seven years previously, but only then to consenting adults of twenty one years. Moreover, the only 'role models' that existed were the likes of John Inman on *Are You Being Served* or haunted, dysfunctional cinematic figures such as Dirk Bogarde's Melville Farr in the 1960s film, *Victim* (the first English language film to employ the word 'homosexual' in a script and which was also banned initially in the United States). Working class Roman Catholics in the industrial North West were hardly going to be trailblazers and I was by no means the only male adolescent frogmarched off to the GP's surgery in that era.

The session with Dr Bhanji was a total farce. 'What seems to be the problem?' he began in textbook fashion. My mother Pat, now seemed suddenly overcome with embarrassment and was perhaps regretting her earlier impulsive decision to pick up the phone. She nodded to me. 'You tell him, love.' I was not going to play ball as I had a very strong feeling deep down that a crash course of antibiotics wasn't going to flush this out of my system. 'No, you tell him,' I said, and I folded my arms. And it went on like this for some time. Poor Dr Bhanji might have been watching a tennis match as his neck muscles twitched back and forth, until he lost his patience. 'Please, tell me what is the problem or are you wasting my time?' My mother inhaled. 'Our Mark, he likes his best friend at school.' The doctor's brow tightened. 'And what is the problem with liking your best friend at school?' A long pause and then my mother leaned forward towards him. 'Well Doctor Bhanji, when I say like … I mean *like*.' As she had moved towards him, I was suddenly unable to see her face as she faced him, but a Carry On style wink at this point cannot be ruled out. Dr Bhanji stared at me. I felt as though I had robbed the local Barclays Bank. 'Well,' he said. 'This is nothing to be worried about.' I stared back triumphantly back at my mother. But then his next words wiped the smile off my face. 'Mark is a good-looking boy and it is certain the girls will be having an eye for him before too long. It is a passing phase. Tell me about your friend, Mark.'

'Well he was good at sport,' I said 'and tipped to be captain of the rugby team.' Dr Bhanji relaxed. 'Ah, a classic. Hero worship among insecure young males. Mrs Dowd, Mark dotes on his friend because he inwardly aspires to be a hero, like his classroom companion.' No I didn't. Bollocks. I just fancied him to bits, wanted to rip his clothes off and do unspeakable things with him, but I was hardly going to go public with this. The doctor's surgery was, after all, located straight opposite our parish church of St Mark and if I wasn't careful, it would be a case of next stop Father Caulfield. I opted for silence. This was the same doctor who had seen me in a terrible state after that spate of bullying five years ago. Then he had prescribed me a large bottle of foul tasting brown medicine, a powerful tranquiliser that had doped me up for weeks on end as I missed school and sought to calm my nerves. Had any of this played a part in his deliberations I wondered?

So that was where we left it. We departed the consulting room with no prescription this time round. There were no daily capsules or tablets, just a slow wait for the inevitable stampede of women to come knocking at my door, banish all those memories and turn me into a rampant heterosexual. But it had been my mother who had taken all this on, at no uncertain personal risk to herself. My father had been at work and was no doubt briefed on the outcome. He and I never discussed it. And it's not as if my mother was an unquestioning agent of the Vatican, simply putting into practice Rome's teaching. My parents could be assertively independent when it came to their attitudes to the Church and its clergy. The five year gaps either side of me and my brothers Christopher and Antony was evidence (later confirmed by my mother) that the papal ban on artificial contraception was never a defining feature of the Dowd household. 'What would they know about bringing kids up?' my mother would ask rhetorically. 'I mean married life – they've no idea.' In more general terms, her generally suspicious view of men in dog collars yielded my favourite: '*I'll tell you one thing love – you never see a thin priest.*'

But desperate times required recourse to succour. The following weekend, at mass, my mother whispered in my ear as the altar servers processed out ahead of Father Caulfield and Father Sweeney. 'Don't forget to pray to God about your problem.' I shook my head. 'I don't think it's a problem,' I answered. If we had not been in church I am sure I'd have got a clip around the ear, but she let it pass and, no doubt, stormed heaven on my behalf. But to little avail.

My nocturnal mutterings about Duncan had been totally involuntary. Unlike other acts. My poor mother. No sooner had she adapted to one eruption than she found herself walking headlong into another. It was barely a week after the GP visit and I was at home on my own. It was late afternoon and a spot of test match cricket on the box was keeping me engaged as Derek Underwood scythed through the Pakistani batting to reduce them to a hundred and thirty for nine on a rain affected wicket. Out of nowhere (was it those tight cricket whites?) I suddenly felt incredibly aroused – the kind of excitement that will not go away unless it is dealt with. Then an image of Duncan crept slyly into my head and I was done for. It was around a quarter past five. Dad was on the buses. Mum would normally get home around a quarter to six and my brothers were both out. A small window of opportunity to kill off temptation. And how best to swat it? By succumbing to it, of course. It was a Thursday, so as long as I confessed on Saturday I'd be OK for communion at Sunday mass and no one would be the wiser.

Self-abuse was frequently talked of in school as 'mortal sin' – an offence so grave that it could cut you off from the love of God. This was why confession was essential before receiving communion. Young Catholic boys and girls had to be 'in a state of grace'. As a regime it tended to work OK, unless you gave into temptation in that small timeframe between Saturday lunchtime when the priests took confessions and Sunday morning mass. If that happened, you absented yourself from receiving the host of bread, running the risk of drawing attention to yourself. Once or twice I had told my mother I was not going up to the altar rails on account of swallowing a piece of meat that had been caught between my teeth as this technically broke the one hour fast we were obliged to observe before reception of Christ's body and blood. The advantage of this little canard was a classy double whammy. Not only did it provide a handy excuse, it also made one look particularly devout.

But masturbation as 'grave sin?' This seemed total nonsense to me – I mean what kind of Creator would it be that we worshipped who could be so easily piqued by something so common among young boys? On the other hand, there was a tiny chance I could be wrong and therefore the sacrament of confession was my 'Pascalian wager'. Pascal, an eighteenth century French philosopher was not at all sure about God's existence, but he had reckoned that the stakes for ignoring God's statutes and then finding out after you died that you had got it all wrong were so high, that the best option was to assume a divinely constructed world and adjust accordingly. It was a classic 'lesser of two evils'. You lost out much less that way than doubting God, getting it wrong and buying a one way ticket to damnation.

I was so sexually excited that I knew this wouldn't take long. I got up from the sofa to lock the back door (everyone always used the back door) and got down to the practicalities. The bell went for the final lap. It was like a bit of David Coleman commentary, 'and there goes Juantorena down the back straight, opening his legs and showing his class.' Then a sizeable complication interrupted my effortless progress to the gold medal. Oh no! What's this? My mother coming up the garden path with her shopping bags. My first instinct was to fixate on the back door. Only a Catholic could write the following logically flawed proposition:

I locked the back door.

I am wanking.

Therefore, if my mother turns the handle on the door and it is locked, she will know I have been abusing myself.

I quickly pulled up my flared wranglers, zipped up and wobbled to the back door. The key was quietly turned in the lock, hopefully out of her earshot as my mother eased towards the door. Then, calamity. I had been so near to that finishing line that the final movements across the floor of the lounge had … well, set it all in motion. As I opened the back door to help her with her bags, we both crossed our respective thresholds.

'Are you all right love?' she asked as all around me went blurred. I could barely focus on her tartan-covered shopping bag. 'Have you got one of your heads coming on?' she inquired. 'You don't look your normal self.' I pirouetted round with her bags so she could not see my face and took an eternity to place them on the kitchen table. 'We're having Bird's Eye cod in butter sauce for tea ... you like that don't you?'

I'd just about got away with it. But that back door key and lock were never the same again.

I suspect my mother did continue to seek divine intervention, but if her prayers were to be answered, it was not in the form of a cure. Up to now this had all been about uncomplicated lust and an outbreak of this unwanted condition, had it become public, could have been hugely embarrassing among our tightly knit Catholic community. But lurking around the corner was something so transformative, something of such overwhelming beauty and poetic power that it brought me to the brink of feeling that same sex love might give my soul a glimpse of infinity.

3

First love

Doctor Bhanji's predictions turned out to be surprisingly accurate, at least for a while. Now aged fifteen and approaching the first major examination hurdle of 'O' levels, I was now so desperate to cover my tracks and not be discovered that I began to date girls.

There is nothing like the acute pain of adolescent self-consciousness. Thrice daily trips to the mirror to examine a facial spot that has erupted, seemingly because of nothing more than glancing at somebody's Mars bar on the bus. Even worse, that constant preoccupation with what people think of you and whether you have a thrilling social life. Against this backdrop, I didn't dare prise open that closet door. For the best part of a year to eighteen months, I took a succession of girls to Hallé Concerts in Manchester's Free Trade Hall. Ever since the cheesy *Mozart 40* by Waldo De Los Rios (a sort of Spanish James Last) had hit the charts in 1971, I had been ripe for classical conversion. Now, years of piling up my 88 pence Classics For Pleasure LPs came to the fore. After luxuriating in Elgar, Ravel and Mozart at concerts, there'd be a repeat pattern. A gentle start with discrete dating and then several weeks in, a suggestion (not from me) that we take things a bit more seriously in the physical department. I could just about manage the transition from the peck on the cheek to a tentative french kiss to render my 'goodnight' farewell, but serious nooky was an altogether different kettle of fish. Those who pity Catholics for their generally screwed-up approach to sex occasionally fail to see how this yoke can occasionally be put to expert use in reverse. Cue sexually harassed male:

'Look, don't get me wrong, I'm really glad you like me so much in that respect, but the Church really does have a point about sex outside marriage and … well … I just feel you're rushing me.' Lines, normally the preserve of the female came easily enough to me. And it generally worked. That was always my cue to break things off and dabble once more in the Catholic dating carousel – which in our case meant copping off with girls from Adelphi High, the Salford grammar equivalent for girls. Monthly dances between the two elite institutions were heavily patrolled by the vigilant nuns and they were eager to snuff out the slightest trace of overt sexual desire. I was the only one in the hall who was egging the holy sisters on.

Looking back, I shudder to think now how desperate I was to appear 'normal'. If anything more than a few weeks went by without having a girl in tow, I become morose and paranoid that those in 5X would start to put two and two together. My peers were heading off to weekend parties at a frighteningly successful rate. Every Monday morning it seemed, conversations in class figured on new names, conquests. Girls as trophies. On one sodden Salford evening I crept out to the phone box at the top of Rake Lane Industrial estate kitted with a healthy supply of 10p pieces. Inside there was the stench of stale urine that almost made me throw up. Fag ends were peppered around my Timpsons brogues, while rain dripped in from a leak in the kiosk roof above. It didn't help that the Yellow Pages directory had been half torn to shreds, but fortunately the 'D' section was still largely intact. I rang the number for a Manchester based dating agency which promised to answer all calls up to 8pm. As the heavens opened and rain began to ooze into my less than watertight red 'Tardis', I spoke to a woman called Sally.

'And what are the ideal qualities in the person you're looking for,' she asked.

'Er…' Long pause. 'Not really sure about that. You know … someone to go out with, go for long country walks … and all that.'

Sally seemed a little confused, but we meandered on. I begged her not to send any literature in the post as I was 'just about to move house' and then after twelve minutes or so, she wised up to the fact that the repeated interruptions of pips before silver coins were slotted in to prolong our conversation meant that this was no ordinary phone call.

'Can I ask you how old you are, *James*?'

A deep breath ushered in the first truthful grain of content in this entire encounter.

'I'll be … I'll be sixteen on my next birthday.'

I thought I heard a stifled laugh at the other end of the phone, before Sally briskly stated that if I hadn't found a girlfriend by the time I was twenty one, I was to call back and see if we could 'progress things'. I departed the phone box in the driving rain and traipsed back home having used up six of my eight 10p pieces – about 20 per cent of my weekly paper-round money. It was an investment that had produced zero returns. I was no nearer to securing that elusive next girlfriend. And without that, anyone could start up the rumour mill that I was 'one of them.' Even being suspected as 'one of them', bracketed with the Johns, Curry and Inman, would have been a one-way ticket to social pariah status. It had to be avoided at all costs.

That sodden, dog-eared telephone directory up the road was soon put to further use. This time the target letter was 'H,' as I scoured it for any organisations with the word *Homosexual* in the title. 'Homosexual: See C.H.E' Casting aside images of Latin American revolutionaries with berets on, I came across a number for the 'Campaign for Homosexual Equality' and spoke to a chap called Phil who told me they met on Wednesday evenings in central Manchester above a pub called the Thompsons Arms next to the Chorlton Street National Express Coach Station (why are so many provincial gay bars and clubs within a two minute walk of the city bus station? A coincidence or handy for all those refugees from small towns and villages?)

'Where you off to now?' asked my Dad who tucking into

his bacon and egg, fresh from his late afternoon shift on the buses. I went through the motions of packing a sports kit into my Man United duffle bag. 'Football. But it'll soon be dark,' my mother pointed out. I lied about some new all weather, floodlit footy pitch in Salford and took the Number 8 bus into town. Outside the Thompsons Arms, the gentle drizzle trickled down out against the surrounding street lights. A succession of men arrived, each on their own. Their heads were either pointed downwards at the pavement or occasionally, one or two of them would look from side to side as if they were concerned about being spotted. I knew exactly where they were coming from. I was beginning to wish that 'Phil' (if that indeed was his real name) had made an arrangement to meet me to help calm my nerves rather than let me climb those stairs and face the rabble of total strangers that lay beyond those closed wooden doors. As I got nearer, the sound of male voices got louder and I thought long and hard about turning round and just going home (and beginning to worry about how I would explain the presence of a totally pristine football kit to my mother – a far cry from my muddied childhood heart-throb in that Persil advert.)

When I pushed the doors apart, all eyes turned towards me. Every one of the thirty of so men in that room were at least twice my age and they looked mortified. I was at least five years below the legal age of consent and their nervousness can be explained by the dreadful legacy of decades and decades of prejudice – a post Oscar Wilde trial assumption that all gay men wanted to do is 'corrupt youth'. The last thing they wanted was to be seen chatting up a 'piece of chicken' (a new phrase I had picked up, overhearing two men close by as I had walked in.) I might have been game for a bit of corruption if the truth be told, but no one would engage with me for what seemed an eternity. Finally a lone voice punctured the leaden silence. 'Mark?' said a man, who I took to be Phil. He gestured towards an empty seat next to him and I sat down, he shuffled sideways away from me. Then the meeting began. A dreary discussion about a new constitution dominated by man who bore more than a passing resemblance to Ronnie Barker. A man with his hand permanently raised. A man whose baptismal certificate must surely have borne the five separate names: Point Of Order Mr Chairman. At the end, most of them stayed around for tea and coffee but I was left on my own, clutching a mug of Tetleys and anxiously caressing my Wagon Wheel. I pretended to be enraptured by a series of posters on the wall about Gay Pride and their forthcoming meetings but I was reading nothing. My heart was going like a pneumatic drill and my head was spinning. My face was hot and flushed. I felt like a total wally, drowning in a corrosive and acute self-consciousness. I hated that room. Piercingly bright overhead striplights, a series of very sober-looking men in ill-fitting dark grey and brown jackets and not a smile or a laugh conjured up between them. When you think of the current vogue in some gay circles for confident dressing, smart, occasionally daring clothes and arch, witty humour – good God, meetings of the Soviet Central Committee must have been a laugh a minute compared to this. If this was a future vision of liberation, I dreaded to think what the alternative looked like.

As I exited toward the wooden doors, hoping no one would clock me, Phil's voice echoed across the room, 'see you next week?' I nodded and left. Never to return.

It was now lashing down as I made for home. On the walk back from the bus stop, I seized my football shirt and shorts and dragged them through a huge puddle on the Manchester Road and threw them in the laundry basket in the upstairs bathroom. My mother never did receive a satisfactory answer to her question as to why my football socks had remained totally unblemished.

Around this period, the summer of 1976, I must have been looking fairly confused and miserable. Everything around me at school was holding up a straightjacket into which I could not fit. O level Biology offered male and female gametes, sperm and ova combining effortlessly to make new life. Elsewhere, Portia offered a little more hope as she temporarily dressed up as a bloke in her pursuit of Bassanio in *The Merchant of Venice* only for 'boy meets girl' to win the day in Act Five. Did no one write scripts for someone like me? Was I destined to spend my life hanging around public toilets and giving hand jobs to older men like hundreds of thousands of people before me?

It must have been getting to me. I was approached by the new school chaplain, a young member of the Servite order called Father Martin, who asked me if I needed to have a chat. Following double maths late one Thursday afternoon, we went to his room. Under the watching gaze of an image of Pope Paul VI high up on the wall above his desk, it all came out. Not just the gay thing, not just the fake girlfriends, but something altogether more revealing. It's a term I used that I will never forget and one that set this fresh faced priest just nodding sympathetically and non-judgementally.

'*I feel as though I am only half living.*'

The malaise I had identified went deeper than any residual awkwardness about being gay and what people might say if they knew the truth. Essentially I was telling this man I had a human heart and so much love to give, but there was no one remotely on the horizon. This was not the confession of someone steeped in self-loathing. No, this was a young man expressing from the depths of his being that there was a force, an energy inside that was going to waste because it had no target, no focus to fasten onto. In this exchange of just under an hour, there was no condemnation, no knee-jerk recourse to church statements or the party line. It might have taken nearly another forty years for Pope Francis to come up with his 'who am I to judge?' line if a man is gay, but here was a member of the clergy essentially doing just that. At the end of our session, he said he would pray for me – and this guy must have had a hot line to the deity because within weeks, I was in the grip of a force of such power, such soul-splitting intensity that '*half living*' suddenly seemed a distant landscape from the shores of early manhood. This – undoubtedly – was the real thing.

This was no *coup de foudre*. Paul had been sitting three metres behind me to the left, on and off, since September 1971. Maybe it was the desk layout in that class that explains this long, ticking fuse. The seating arrangement in class ran from names 'Bardsley to Haniak' and we had been allotted our study stations in alphabetical order. My bad luck was to end up right in the front, constantly under the vigilance of the teacher with the result that, unless one screwed one's head round, one had hardly any idea of what was happening behind. Paul was not really in my social circle since pop music, a natural focal point of shared interests among teenage boys, had us light years apart. Paul was Hendrix to my Chirpy Chirpy Cheep Cheep. My big thing of the time had been amassing endless pop 45s with my paper round money. Swinton precinct was a hideously ugly shopping complex of 1960s graffiti-ridden concrete that sucked in streams of kids on chopper bikes with too much time on their hands. But its saving grace was – Rumbelows. Here I built the foundations for what would become a fairly decent 1970s pop collection, with purchases of 'My Brother Jake' by Free, 'Devil's Answer' by Atomic Rooster and 'This Town Ain't Big Enough For The Both Of Us' by Sparks. Sometimes my taste slipped and 'Me and You and a Dog Named Boo' by Lobo was by no means the worst of the kitsch singles that made it into my burgeoning collection of 45 rpm vinyls. But I knew Paul was into a bloke called Bob Dylan and from what little I knew of this artist, he was a long haired hippy who couldn't sing in tune and, if given the chance, would have crucified such irresistible classics as 'Seasons in the Sun' by Terry Jacks.

How do people 'creep up on you' after years and years? It's a telling question and one I still don't know the answer to. Of course Paul had no idea he was 'creeping' anywhere or up on anyone – I was just that kid at the front of the class who had that faintly annoying habit of coming top of the form every summer. Yet this did not make me a discredited 'swot', because I was in endless exam combat with the less preferred Polish boy – the geeky Henryk Feszczur and I was popular by default (essentially, the 'stop Feszczur' candidate). But as we moved into the sixth form, new horizons opened. We were now allowed out of the school complex in the long lunch break to play footy in Buile Hill Park, a huge relief after five years of compulsory scrums and line outs in our rugby obsessed grammar school. The park was a huge Grade II listed space off the Eccles Old Road, a former military base in the second world war and a one time favourite strolling spot for L.S. Lowry. Wedged between the Soviet style concrete jungle of Salford Shopping Centre and Eccles, Buile Hill was a green oasis. After the intense academic claustrophobia of mornings studying French grammar and the poetry of Thom Gunn and Ted Hughes, the acres of verdant space over the road from Weaste Lane were irresistible. Paul was one of the twenty or so of us who'd run themselves into the ground every lunchtime. There was no rhyme or reason to the team selection. Sometimes he'd be on my team and sometimes he used his superior footballing prowess with the opposing team. Paul was boyish and fresh-faced, of mildly ruddy Irish complexion. His ears were ever so slightly jug-shaped, an endearing element in an otherwise open, intelligent and ever so slightly rebellious face. The succession of light blue shirts he wore were frequently unbuttoned down to his belt, revealing a tight, gently scrawny torso that was lean and agile. When he moved with the ball, you could see the muscles rippling ever so gently next to his ribs. Moreover, he ran with an intensity and focus that often eluded the others. When most of us were flagging after forty minutes or so, Paul's dynamo just kept on and on. After these first few weeks of footy combat, when Friday afternoons came, a cloud of melancholy began to descend on me. A whole weekend would now elapse before I would see him again. I didn't even have his home telephone number.

Bob Dylan now became my unlikely knight in shining armour, long long before he was made Nobel Prize winner for Literature. I still hated all that whining, but at the local library, I began to read his lyrics as though they were exotic

poetry. I near as damn it memorised *Hurricane* and *Highway
61 Revisited* and tried as deftly as I could to share with Paul
my new found passion. And it worked. I could really have
done with *Coles Notes* or *Dylan For Dummies*, but within
weeks we were buddies and the more we spoke, the more I
became hooked. Those long weekends now became slightly
more bearable as I was soon being invited to go on occasional
outings with his family (who, unlike us, had a car), to places
like Bolton Abbey in Yorkshire and Bakewell and Buxton in
the Peak District.

And it was essentially events within Paul's family that
became the springboard for an acquaintance that rapidly
transformed into something much more deep, something
solid and substantial. It's well noted that boys in their late
teens can be fairly hopeless communicators when it comes
to talking about feelings, anxieties and vulnerabilities. Later
on, Paul would come to talk appreciatively of my 'emotional
intelligence' as a key element in our bonding. The fact was
that here was a sixteen year old under huge pressure at
home. The eldest of three children, Paul was caught between
his mother and his father. The latter, all charm and jokes in
public, as soon as the family door was closed, was reported
to occasionally turn volatile and demanding. Paul talked of
mental health issues and having to fend off his father against
his mother. Things got so serious that the school chaplain
was drafted in as a confidant and go-between. Paul entrusted
more and more of this to me, a development that only served
to make me feel ever more attached to him. As a throwback to
that rural release and freedom in Berkshire three years earlier,
I now suggested lengthy hikes in Derbyshire where I knew
we would be safe to talk privately, away from the prying gaze
of fellow sixth formers. And boy, did we rack up the miles –
always on the same route. Train to Dove Holes on the Buxton
line from Manchester Piccadilly with our packed lunches and
then about thirteen miles in a rambling loop to Chapel-en-
le-Frith, come rain or shine, followed by two or three pints
of under-age Robinson's bitter before the last train home.

On the third of these excursions, I told him about Brother
Dermott and even took the risk of coming out to him – but
I needn't have feared rejection. It was like water off a duck's
back to him at this stage. Paul was mature, dedicated and not
going to jettison months of hard earned trust and ease over
having a gay mate at school, however weird that might be in
the summer of 1977.

What I could not do, of course, was fully declare my hand
about how he had become the most definite object of my
affection. I was terrified of losing him, but the overwhelming
sensation at this stage was relief. Why relief exactly? Because
after all the burning lust of 'Duncangate' here was something
so wholesome, so good, so selfless. Make no mistake about it,
this was true love – the real thing. For the first time in my life I
felt utterly focused on 'the other,' a development I experienced
as liberation from myself. Listening to his tales, his domestic
ups and downs and his progress with his Economics A level
was all I wanted. If craving is the source of all suffering in the
Buddhist way of things, this was most definitely deliverance.
My mind flipped back to some striking images in our physics
classes, Newton's laws of motion and the differences between
centripetal and centrifugal forces. In the former, all action
and motion gravitates towards the centre from the periphery.
As an essentially 'arty' type, I always want to apply such
scientific concepts to more interesting human dimensions.
Selfish, inward-looking egoists became 'centripetal types'. In
contrast, the centrifugal effect essentially conjured up images
of brightly coloured liquids in test tubes whizzing round
and round inside a bowl and their contents being drawn to
the outward extremities of the circular container. In more
accessible everyday terms, it's the force that propels you off a
park roundabout when the circular motion gets too much and
you can't grip the central axis any longer. In my worldview,
it was about people who looked outwards and resisted the
indulgences of adolescent self-obsession. I knew I was all too
inclined towards the latter – until Paul came along and freed
me from myself. All too often as human subjects we tire of

listening to others as we, rather like a chess player with his eye on the clock, await our own dedicated time. It's so often a case of that delightful quip, 'anyhow that's enough about me, how do *you* think I am?' The human animal, so often it seems, is a self-made creature who worships his creator. Observe any four year old and turn-taking skills are often poor. Many adults, it seems, never really improve on their ability in infancy. But with Paul, there was release from this tyranny. This was nothing I had manufactured from within. I experienced love as grace, as gift from without. It was, for this young soul, a delicious and rare glimpse of infinity as it felt intensely like a force that pointed beyond itself to another plane. And all this, thanks to bloody Bob Dylan.

I wish it could have remained this way. The fact is that after several months of this, the cravings began to kick in. I began to want Paul for myself. As a 'sixteen going on seventeen' my 'gaydar' was hardly well-developed, but I sensed little if any encouragement that he felt remotely the same way about me. He began to date girls and I listened patiently as tales of at first Nina, and then Aileen featured in our conversations. We were studying Othello for A level, and I was now getting practicals in the gut-churning horrors of being exposed to the 'green-eyed monster' of jealousy.

All this emotional power was beginning to do my head in. It felt like my heart was being ripped open by a can-opener of bewildering force. What was the *point,* damn it, of having all this amazing and wonderful life-transforming love if it just went nowhere, like torrents of water dribbling away through the cracks? This is when the plume came out. Sod you Ted Hughes, Thom Gunn, I would do better. In the space of two months I wrote dozens of poems and amassed them all in a discrete box wrapped in a soccer shirt under my bed. Most kids of my age had *Playboy* in some such setting, whereas I now preposterously fancied myself as Salford's gay answer to Keats.

The poems all centred on a major theme – that my unrequited feelings for Paul resembled all the finest things

in nature being caught in some monstrous, perverted
distortion. Roses 'unbloomed with creaking caution'. My
heart was affronted by 'swarming bees pollinating their
poison into defenceless ventricles'. Image after image came
into mind of an inner life that resembled one of those time
lapse nature movies in horrid reverse. Everything was
unflowering. Beauty was slowly being corroded by 'termites
of indifference that burrowgnaw leaving echoed emptiness'.
(I readily acknowledge the partial plagiarism of Gerard
Manley-Hopkins here.) On one occasion I even showed one
of these specimens to our A level English Literature tutor,
Steve Harrington, and introduced it as 'author unknown'.
His brow became furrowed as he read, and re-read. 'These
are extraordinary,' he said. 'Where did you find them? Who
wrote them?' I muttered something about coming across
them and copying them at Swinton library in the modern
poetry section and having forgotten to note down the author.
Then under his intense gaze, I scurried off lest he start to
ask me for more information. All I'd been seeking was some
acknowledgment that what I was writing wasn't total rubbish.
Finally, I plucked up the courage to show one to Paul himself
on an evening at a pub in the centre of Manchester. However,
I copped out and chose the most obscure and inaccessible
one of the whole collection. The theme of unrequited love
was far from obvious and to an interested but uninformed
eye, the panoply of images peppering my verses would
have smacked more of ecological disaster and post nuclear
holocaust than apocalyptic emotional ruin. In sixth form,
it was macro Economics and supply and demand that was
blowing in the wind for Paul. My stuff was hardly the kind of
thing that his hero Bob D would set to music. He looked at
the poem, nodded and handed it me back. I was an inch away
from clasping my hands, vice like around his handsome face
and yelling out amongst all the ale drinkers in the Rose and
Crown, 'It's you ... it's all for you. Because of you. Inspired
by *you*. Don't you get it?' But I didn't. I went home and crept
into my divan bed in my bedroom (a blessed development,

elder brother Chris was now at University, my kid brother Antony, alias 'Ginger', had taken his room and, at long last, I had some privacy.) Long after my parents had retired, I crept upstairs, switched the light off and wrapped my arms around myself. Just for a few seconds, centrifugal got the upper hand on centripetal and I really thought he was there alongside me and I had 'blended' – I had ceased to exist. I murmured. I stroked imaginary tousled chestnut brown hair and ached so hard that I thought the blood was going to explode and rip apart every fragile capillary in my body. So I switched the light back on and seized more pen and paper. As the stanzas seeped out, so another near literary masterpiece was pained into existence. Finally I 'burrowgnawed' myself wearily into slumber.

It couldn't go on like this. It was turning almost physically painful. For weeks on end I lost my appetite and picked in a cursory manner at my food. (My parents attributed it all to the oncoming A level exam anxiety.) What's worse, it was as though Paul and I, having travelled for seven years in the same train carriage were, at the end of the summer holiday, going to be separated. The whole business of our university destinations had proved quite controversial. Paul was heading off to Bristol to read Economics if his grades held up. In my case, the new headteacher, Brother Alexander, had decided that a small handful of boys would be entered for Oxford and Cambridge. This amounted to near academic suicide as the school had no history of preparing candidates for such prestigious destinations. I chose my college destination using the laws of supply and demand; St Peter's College, Oxford regularly came bottom of the Norrington Table, the league based on degree class results, so I worked out that no one would want to go there to read Philosophy, Politics and Economics. The written entrance exam was a killer…

'*With reference to at least three of Orwell's novels….*'

… and if you had only read two? And only one properly? And what the hell was 'modernism' in literary theory? The politics paper was even worse. So many of our studies had been about institutions and voting systems and here was Oxford asking me to plump for either liberty or equality as 'the essential and defining principle of political discourse.' To my amazement, I was called for an interview. Owing to the fact that my allotted slot was at 9.20am, the college asked me to travel down and dine the evening before and said they would provide a college room. I nervously checked in at the porter's lodge on New Inn Hall Street and within half an hour, found myself in a Harry Potter-esque dining hall. Portraits of former masters decked the walls and the resonance of eager confident young men boomed around the room. Candles flickered everywhere, catching the sides of faces. It was half-romantic and half-eerie. These people did not look like they had chosen St Peter's on the basis of Norrington league table relegation criteria at all. In fact, they looked horribly confident. Hands were used theatrically to emphasise a debating point. There were fierce nods of the head and not an inkling of self-consciousness. I half wondered if they didn't even own the place. I was petrified and said not a word to anyone during the starter (tomato soup with a dollop of yogurt in the middle, a confusing dish as I was used to seeing yogurt in 'Ski' cartons) and also the main course (*boeuf bourgignon* ... a real cut above Fray Bentos tins for sure).

When the dessert arrived, there was still a dizzying array of cutlery items on display and I had no idea what to pick up next, so I looked down the line and played for time. A rather solid piece of hazelnut parfait bearing a striking resemblance to an ice hockey puck was thrust under my nose on a white plate bearing the St Peter's coat of arms. I craned my neck to see which combination of metal implements I was supposed to seize next. It was like formation dancing with forks and spoons. Suddenly a voice diagonally across from me piped up. 'You ... over there. Mr Mysterious. Where are you from?'

I felt myself redden and then I cleared my throat since I knew I was now talking to not just this boy, but to all within earshot. 'Manchester.' 'Really,' said the well-fed chap opposite. 'MGS?' I was so nervous, I blanked on the acronym for

Manchester Grammar School and signalled my ignorance with a puzzled look and a slight shoulder shrug. One voice to my right muttered something about my dim chances of passing the interview if I came from Manchester and did not know what 'MGS' was.

'And what does your father do?' asked the boy who was now morphing into Billy Bunter. 'Mine's a company director – in Kidderminster.' All eyes were now fixed on Mr Mysterious and his face was burning. 'He's … he's a conductor,' I croaked back. Long pause. 'Really! Jazz or orchestral?' Even longer pause. Face now so hot that you could fry the proverbial egg at a metre away.

'Bus, actually.'

The ensuing roar of laughter – was it aimed at me or Bunter? I'll never know, but I hastily gulped down my water and left my half-eaten parfait and affected to be going to the gents. I should have returned for grace and the dismissal but I left that hall like a bat out of hell. (Most of the grown ups did indeed look like black winged creatures with their scary gowns on.) I went straight to my room and locked the door. It was only 7.20pm. There wasn't even a TV around to watch *Sportsnight with Coleman* and the FA Cup replays. I thought of creeping out to a phone box and calling home for a chat, but what would I have told them? I couldn't do the 'bus' thing with my Dad and my nervous tone of voice would have worried my mother sick, as ever since those eleven plus triumphs and my coming top of the class, she was used to non-stop exam success. Damn that bloody new headteacher with his unrealistic academic ambitions. Inevitably, my thoughts now turned to Paul during a very long night in which another poem eased its way into the world – the only one I ever wrote on Oxford college notepaper.

The ensuing interview next day was an unmitigated disaster. I have replayed it so many times in my head that it's possible I am still suffering from post-traumatic stress disorder brought on by that wretchedly deceptive Norrington table. First there were three of them all staring at me across the room. Three to one: that's an unfair fight where I came from. First up was John Kenyon, philosophy don. 'How would you prove that the picture on the wall and the clock on the mantelpiece exist at the same time?' I'd come a long way since common denominators, but *what?* I stood up and touched them both with my hands, almost clumsily dislodging some centuries old piece of art from its moorings. 'I know that's not proof for you, but it's proof for me,' I answered trying to look smart but feeling my legs were made of Rowntree's jelly. He muttered something about Barclay (or was it Berkeley?) and then a word I had never heard called 'sollypsism' (sic) or 'emperrycism' (sic). He then handed on the baton to the next sadist in the room, the economics tutor. 'Mr Dowd, how would you find out how much money was in the country at any one time?'

Beam me up Scotty.

'Er … I'd … I'd ring up … ring up the Bank of England.' They all looked aghast – or were they amazed by my utter brilliance? They hid it all under a sheen of ambiguous and aloof non-commitment. 'Why didn't you answer, "get everyone to tell the government how much money they have"?' asked Kenyon. 'People lie,' I retorted. It was probably the most intelligent and accurate phrase to have left my mouth in all my time in Oxford. The interview ended and I was shown the door. At least I didn't walk into the broom cupboard and refuse to come out like one terrified candidate had allegedly done on one occasion. Three weeks later came the inevitable letter. Fail. God how I hated Brother Alexander for putting me through all this.

My mother responded well enough, 'you can only do our best love', 'you gave it a try' and 'well it just wasn't to be was it?' My father was less engaged with all this university business, but he was now showing a healthy interest in helping me write speeches for a new found talent – debating. Acutely intelligent and quiet, my father would have walked into any university given a different set of conditions. Preparing speeches was a rare moment for him to flourish – a moment when he felt he could impress his academically successful kids. He'd study the motion before the house long and hard. He would then screw up his face. Then his dry wit would occasionally fashion a killer line, a *bon mot* which, when received well in public speaking auditoriums such as the Hotel Piccadilly, caused him no end of pleasure. On more than one occasion in the finals of the English Speaking Union, he cast off his normally reserved persona to stay behind after the final proceedings and question the judges' final allocation of marks if De La Salle did not win. Was he ever taken in by any of those 'beards'... the fake girlfriends? Maybe I had possibly gotten away with it. He did seem charmed by Christine, even if her request for a spot of blackcurrant jam in her home-made rice pudding had momentarily put the cat among the pigeons and forced him to scrape two months of mould from the top layer of the jar before passing it round the table. But if you look away, you can deny almost anything – that is until the evidence is staring at you in bold print right in front of your nose. How could I have been so stupid? Is what follows a classic tale of 'wanting to be found out?'

I blame Mary Whitehouse. In 1976 this middle aged campaigning puritan was on the warpath against Denis Lemon, the editor of *Gay News* for publishing 'The Love That Dares To Speak Its Name,' a poem by an English academic, James Kirkup. She wanted a prosecution for the ancient legal offence of blasphemy on account of a poem that narrated the lust and love of a Roman centurion for the dead Jesus. There had been no such successful prosecution for the best part of a hundred years. Acts of necrophilia were said to feature prominently in the text and her campaign was all over the press. I had never read the poem or even heard it quoted since the BBC news was wary of falling under Mrs Whitehouse's legal radar. I had bought a copy of *Gay News* and risked sending off a stamp addressed envelope for my own copy of the text so I could see what all the fuss was about. When the brown paper envelope arrived marked out by my own handwriting, I quickly whisked it upstairs and read it.

It was stomach churning. Each to his own and all that, but acts of necrophilia with *any* kind of cold, inert human body are bad enough, but with someone I believed to be the Son of God? Apart from the offensiveness, I had written enough of my own poems by now to realise this was not very good stuff. It was all over the place. It lacked structure, subtlety and cohesion. I wasn't sure if I wanted the editor of Gay News to lose a trial against that interfering woman who always displayed a prurient interest in all matters sexual, but it made me question why he had gone ahead at all. Perhaps it was a simple 'dare?' I tucked the envelope away under the bed.

But not well enough. A week later, my mother had been doing some hoovering and had pulled the bed away from the wall. I had failed to stuff the text properly inside the envelope and the enticing title must have been peeping out from the top. In a Catholic household this was ten times worse than being caught with a mucky mag under the deck. When I came home from school one Friday, briefcase stuffed with homework for the weekend, they were waiting. I have never, *ever*, seen my father so angry. No sooner had I stepped in through the door, than he brandished the poem in front of my nose.

'And what exactly, are you doing bringing this filth into the house?'

If I had been a Muslim, it was as though I had set fire to the Qu'ran in front of my own parents. Arguably this was even worse. 'Dad, it's a horrible poem, I agree, but I just wanted to see what all the fuss was about.' He stared back unconvinced. For once my mother, normally the chatty one, fell silent and hung her head. 'Don't you ever, *ever* dare bring this kind of stuff in here again. Do you hear? Well, do you? What would have happened if your little brother had read it?'

I'm not sure a twelve year old 'Ginger' would have entirely got it, but that was hardly a defence. I squawked something out about privacy and about how I wasn't expecting people to be rifling through my personal possessions, but this only got me a 'thick ear.' It was three years since that visit to the doctors and they had been hoping for a cure. Now, a horrid twist as it seemed they had a son who was getting off on some rather unorthodox material which involved a figure who was the cornerstone of their religious faith.

I stood there, my ear smarting and so much wanted to tell them about the good side of this, my love for Paul, my evidently superior poems which were not 'mucky', but noble, gallant, yes even 'spiritual' if you will. But I couldn't. I had been caught out. Big time. There were two unlikely positive outcomes from this wretched poem which had torpedoed its way into our family life. First, I think it put paid to any hope on my parents' part that I was passing through a 'phase' – Dr Bhanji had mentioned six months, not three years or more. But eager to salvage something from the rubble, it offered some semblance of reciprocity with Paul. For so long he had regaled me with tales of domestic tensions and now, I threw myself upon him and shared with him the horrors of 'The Love That Dare Not Speak Its Name'. I was so embarrassed by the actual content of the poem, I settled for paraphrasing it for him and thankfully he never requested to see it. The title, of course, could not have been more fitting for my own stifled passion for him. As our time together at De La Salle was drawing to a close and university beckoned, I decided it was now or never.

Oxford had closed its doors, but I was still destined to end up about an hour and a half from Paul in Bristol since my fall back option was political science at Exeter, some seventy five miles south west down the M5. We both secured excellent grades and as the summer of 1978 approached, the umbilical cord of sixth form life would no longer hold Paul and I together. If this thing was going to survive, it would now have to work on its own terms. And it was this prospect of separation that now made me take the plunge. It was time to 'come out' all over again. The stakes could not have been higher.

During the twelve months or more since Paul had known I was gay, I was so determined not to endanger what was so precious that I had attempted to be deliberately cool. I knew he was a bright chap, but with the exception of sharing an obscure poem with him, there was no reason for Paul to second guess that he was undoubtedly the very large apple of my eye. Another Peak District walk made it into the diary. We alighted at Dove Holes and began our cross country hike, a route that was now indelibly etched into our minds to such an extent that maps and compasses remained tucked away in our rucksacks throughout. As the butties and flasks came out, we settled down by a large stream high above Miller's Dale with views over the River Wye to our right. It was a dry, partially cloudy day – one of those days when the clouds race along at a dizzying rate, leaving a stroboscopic dappled dialectic of light and shadow across the fields and villages around. I told him I wasn't just gay, but that I had become 'very fond of someone' (talk about the art of understatement.) The look between us at that point needed no further interpretation. There was a long, but not uncomfortable silence. He was so cool. He made it clear that the feeling was not mutual, but that was all that needed to be said and that we were most definitely still 'best mates'. Relief. But of course, I could not throw my arms around him and tumble down the hill in a love-lock like they do in the movies. Once more I slammed the brakes on and stifled the torrent within.

What I know now that I did not know then, is that once you pass through this line of declaration, you go through emotional brake pads at a hellish rate. Before, when you're terrified of rejection, of it all going to pot, there's every reason to be measured, to conceal. But when the most important guy in your world basically says 'it's OK to be nuts about me but don't think I feel the same way,' you know that any declarations of passion are not going to terminate what you have. He's not going to like it especially, but you know it's not a deal breaker. It's like you're in a car doing a mad succession of jump starts. A few weeks after our hike, it all came to a head in, of all places, my parental home. We'd been to the local pub, the Windmill at the top of Station Road and we'd lost track of the time. Paul lived in Astley, a good seven or eight miles away along the East Lancs Road and his chances of getting the last twenty six bus home were zero. We staggered back to mine. My folks were still up, watching the late ITN news bulletin. They had always liked Paul – he was straight talking, unthreatening and had all the social skills you'd associate with a man with Irish blood in him. What's more, he was as nutty about football as I was, so even allowing for the heresy of his being an Everton fan, he always had plenty to chat about with my dad. 'Well love, you can stop over can't you,' insisted my mother, having first checked that Paul had phoned home to check in. 'I'll go and get some sheets. We can unfold the pouf and put it down in Mark's room.' Excruciating. I stared at the carpet so intensely I almost unthreaded it.

My parents went to bed. I switched off the piercing overhead striplight and substituted it with the soothing presence of a gentle table lamp. Then I went to the kitchen to find some suitable nightcap material. A bottle of Bell's whisky, last opened eight months ago at Christmas when the rellies had come round and all the aunties had doused it with those green bottles of Canada Dry Ale. I looked through my record collection and found *Mud Slide Slim* by James Taylor – not exactly Bob D, I grant you, but on the 'coolometer', definitely several notches ahead of Showaddywaddy and David Soul. As the guitar picking intro of 'You've Got a Friend' started up, I found myself unable to stop looking at Paul. First I just mouthed the words, and then I couldn't stop singing them to him:

'You just call out my name and you know wherever I am, I'll come running to see you again. Winter, Spring, Summer, or Fall, all you have to do is call and I'll be there … You've got a Friend.'

Paul intimated he felt the same – in a kind of way it became 'our song'. So intense. Deep inside the waterfalls welled up again and once more, they had nowhere to go. For the first time I made a physical demand of him. 'It would help me so much if I could just touch you, hold your hand, make contact … I'm really struggling here,' I told him. He was relaxed about it, but had an answer that effectively put paid to my request.

'We're not a very tactile, physical lot in our family. There's not a lot of touching and, well, it's just not something that feels right for me. I'm not being funny, that's just the way things are.'

What could I say? Love is about putting the other first, right? About not imposing yourself on the beloved. Except if this went on much longer I was going to have a haemorrhage of the soul. We called it a night. It was 2.30am. Lights were left off in the bedroom so as not to wake up the house and avoid any embarrassment when undressing in the vicinity of the pouf. That room was so small that the proverbial swinging cat would have issued a lawsuit for claustrophobic abuse. I was totally spent and lay down, knowing that Paul was on the floor about a metre away. It took all my self-discipline but I had nothing left in my tank to make any moves any more. He had made his position clear enough. I was resigned – and soon in a gentle sleep.

But there was more to come. In that very bedroom where, four years ago I had said, God knows what, about doing unspeakable things with Duncan and had startled my poor parents, I was awakened by a strange sensation. It felt like a hand – on my hand. I was still in half sleep, but as the moonlight strobed in through the partially drawn curtains and caught my poster of the 1977 FA Cup winning Manchester United team, a silhouetted figure clambered up, first towards the edge of the bed and then alongside me on my single divan. He lay there and was happy to be embraced. Two years of waiting, of wretched aching pain that was, in a stroke, dissipated. What moved me was the risk he had taken – here he was telling me about the problems with touching and embracing and half an hour later, I was holding him in my arms. Poor Paul. He had not opted for A Level English Lit. If he had, he'd have totally comprehended what I whispered next:

'*If it were now to die, 'Twere now to be most happy, for I fear my soul hath his content so absolute that not another comfort like to this succeeds in unknown fate.*'

Apologies to the Bard for the gender pronoun change. Paul was no Desdemona and I was even a less likely Salfordian Othello, but the words were spot on. As Paul drifted off to sleep, I knew I had a paper round to do at seven in the morning but there was no way I was going to waste these precious moments by falling asleep – they might never happen again. I'd known my Shakespeare. More still, I knew my Auden and this living creature was most definitely destined to lie 'mortal, guilty but to me entirely beautiful' in my arms till break of day.

Break of day in July 1978 saw me positively skipping down Manchester Road with my paper bag. 'Someone's happy,' said Mrs Stott in the newsagents as I bustled in to the shop and prepared to head off to offload my 'redtops', the *Sun*, the *Star* and the *Mirror*. It's a minor miracle that anyone in Clifton got their paper of choice that morning as my head was in the clouds. What did it all mean? Was Paul gay after all, pretty pretty please? Were we going to be a lifelong item and, if so, how would all this pan out at university and beyond?

It didn't take long for such wild daydreaming to be countered by a puncturing dose of horrid reality. After breakfast, Paul and I went for a walk. He was uncharacteristically strident and made it known, in no uncertain terms, that the events of the previous hours had been an aberration. I was not to raise my hopes and expectations. But of course such moments with him had given me a 'glimpse of infinity' and set a bar of such intensity that there would be a lifelong danger that no one or nothing would ever be able to even get near it. I wasn't to know that at the time. I contented myself with the thought that Paul was fighting himself, reacting to an experience he had not seen coming. Maybe one day? Away from home and the prying eyes of families and peers? At university?

So at the end of the summer, off we went, to our respective destinations: Bristol for him, Exeter for me. The distance helped me move on and dull the longing and the pining, though of course it reignited my feelings every time I hitchhiked up past Cullompton and Taunton on the M5 to stay with him in Leigh Woods at the western end of the Clifton Suspension Bridge. He reciprocated with journeys south – and the story of one evening during one such visit encapsulates perfectly the fraught *modus vivendi* we had managed to establish.

The Vietnam war film *The Deer Hunter* had opened to rave reviews and we'd both expressed a desire to see it. It went on to receive no fewer than nine Academy award nominations and tells the tale of a small group of steelworkers from the town of Clairton, Pennsylvania, who undergo physical and mental anguish at the hands of the Vietnamese. The central axis of the film is the friendship between 'Mike', played by Robert De Niro and his best buddy, 'Nick' played by Christopher Walken. The climax of the film revolves around Mike's desire to travel back out to the Far East to look for his mate who has gone missing in the war. Mike searches high and low and, to his horror, comes across Nick playing Russian Roulette for big stakes in a clandestine bar. It's obvious he has lost his mind and at first does not even recognise his one time drinking partner from the smelting factories of Pittsburgh. The revolver is passed back and forth. Blanks are fired and Mike pleads with Nick to stop. His intervention is hugely unpopular with the betting crowd as he is the only one who wants the horror show to stop. Mike racks his brains for something that may provoke Nick's memory and bring him back from the brink. He pulls his chair up to the table. He then casts his mind back to a catch phrase they employed during their weekends of deer hunting in the wilds of the rustbelt: 'One Shot.' Momentarily hope rises as Nick recalls the phrase and repeats it. He looks into Mike's face with a smile – then pulls the trigger and within seconds De Niro has his bloodied best mate dead in his arms.

The film was accompanied by a deft, melancholic soundtrack for guitar and orchestra by John Williams. Almost forty years on, 'Cavatina' still reduces me to tears within seconds because this film with its yearning music carried on its shoulders so much of what was precious between the two of us. After we left the cinema neither of us spoke for eight to ten minutes. In my mind, 'Nick' was Paul and not even the heroic interventions of a De Niro traversing the world in dogged pursuit could save him. It had been profoundly upsetting. The thought of life without Paul was simply unbearable even if he was not going to be my lifelong significant other.

We had walked all the way up Pennsylvania Road (more than apt given the location of the first hour of the film) and well into Prince of Wales Road in the heart of the Exeter university campus before we engaged in any real post-mortem discourse about the movie. To the left the entrance to Devon County Cricket Club drew nearer and nearer. I tapped Paul on the shoulder and beckoned him follow me. We legged ourselves up over the eight foot high gates and headed out towards the middle. On a chilly night under clear skies we lay shoulder to shoulder, hands touching and we marvelled at the array of stars in the night sky. The physical contact was discrete. Perhaps the single digit temperatures gave us permission. We said very little. *The Deer Hunter* had said it all – and yes, we knew we would go to the ends of the earth for each other if necessary.

We remain exceptionally close friends.

4

Friar

Occasionally shoulder to shoulder, but it had been two and a half years of largely unrequited love. But it had been time in which the urge to give and dedicate myself unconditionally to 'the other' had taken root despite all the scorn and disapproval of holy mother church. Rome had not stood idly by in the 1970s as news of post-Stonewall riots gay liberation swept through Europe and the USA. It had reacted with an authoritative teaching document, *Persona Humana*, whose unflinching language was designed to put us back in our boxes lest we get any fancy ideas of self-acceptance and, God forbid, *equality.*

> *In the pastoral field, these homosexuals must certainly be treated with understanding and sustained in the hope of overcoming their personal difficulties and their inability to fit into society. Their culpability will be judged with prudence. But no pastoral method can be employed which would give moral justification to these acts on the grounds that they would be consonant with the condition of such people. For according to the objective moral order, homosexual relations are acts which lack an essential and indispensable finality. In Sacred Scripture they are condemned as a serious depravity and even presented as the sad consequence of rejecting God.*

After all I held felt and known to be precious with Paul, how could a future relationship, yes even a sexual relationship based on self-giving and commitment be 'rejecting God?' It had been a divine gift – something that had made my spirit surge and which would have taken my soul off its hinges had it been reciprocated. 'A serious depravity?' Traditional teaching insisted that all sexual acts had to remain open to procreation, hence Rome's opposition to artificial contraception. Clearly two men or two women could not procreate, but what of heterosexual couples who were infertile, or beyond menopause? The church did not shackle these couples with abstinence. It just didn't add up. Would they have written any of their condemnation if they had experienced just a glimpse of the searing call to self-abandonment I had savoured? None of this, of course, was shared with my parents. I'd no need to as I'd soon be some two hundred and fifty miles away from home in the heady surroundings of Exeter University.

Why Exeter? Distance from roots? (Other applications included Kent, Southampton and Aberdeen. Spot a pattern here?) Was it a nostalgic throwback to a 1975 summer holiday with Auntie Winnie, Uncle Ged and cousin David in which a clunky navy blue Ford Anglia had graced Dartmoor, Buckfast Abbey and every possible cream tea outlet in Devon? The university's majestic setting, overlooking the verdant Exe valley certainly echoed my earlier boarding school escape to Berkshire. Maybe it's simply because I had starred in my interview and Exeter had reduced my A level offer to a mere two 'Cs' – a virtual open door.

Early September 1978. As Prime Minister Jim Callaghan struggled to keep his Lib-Lab Pact intact and agonised about a snap autumn election, it was time for me to leave the nest. How I hated those scenes of farewell at the family home. Most students these days get the benefit of loading up the family estate with duvets, toasters, and a dozen changes of clothes. But we had no family car. All my worldly belongings had to be crammed into a dark brown 1950s leather suitcase, the one that had faithfully made eight consecutive trips to the same Blackpool boarding house for the family holiday. Then it was the number eight Bolton to Manchester bus and to Piccadilly railway station for the five hour journey south.

That was arduous but manageable. The worst bit came before – the hanging around to say goodbye. An atmosphere would descend on the house. Why was my train not scheduled for nine am instead of one pm? Sitting around, sipping endless mugs of tea and dreading the moment when I'd have to find some way of looking at my father in the eye and managing a physical embrace. We both felt it – I know. A contagious awkwardness hovered around the house until I could handle it no more. I often ended up leaving an hour earlier than necessary and used my cumbersome load as an excuse. The young man who had ached for Paul to set aside his reticence for tactile embraces could, on these occasions, manage no more than a feeble handshake of 'adieu' – and even then our hands, like two magnetic norths, flinched apart as soon as they touched. Why? Was it 'Persil'? Was it the poem? Or was it something so deep down inside him that he was a stranger to his very self? It contrasted markedly with the hugs and embraces from my mother. But oddly, the more these lapped over me, the more it threw light on that unstated unease and fear of intimacy that dogged everything between me and my father.

None of this stopped me from throwing myself into university life. I excelled in my studies of political science, but leaving home was also the first time in my life when I became fully aware of trying to hold together the potentially uncomfortable bedfellows of Catholicism and same sex attraction. Falling in love with Paul had made me believe in 'the project'. I felt no need to choose between love of God and love of another man. Had not the awakenings of my own heart been a gift from beyond? By the end of my first term I had become President of the Gay Society (OK, there were only a dozen members – but if that was good enough for Jesus when he recruited the apostles…?) I was also an active member of the Catholic Society with responsibility for organising music in our weekly liturgies and running a weekly prayer group. The tectonic plates of queerdom and the Holy Roman Church nestled uneasily alongside each other.

At the start of our second year, I was called upon to represent both societies at the freshers' fair. This was the annual September jamboree in which a zillion student clubs and societies sell their wares in their bid to attract new members. The University Great Hall resembled the Henley Regatta and Glastonbury all rolled into one. A kaleidoscope of bunting, banners, and every coloured T-shirt you could name under the sun. It was an amazing spectacle – everything from men in goggles from the Parachuting Club, anarchists and lefties from Hunt Saboteurs to earnest young chaps in tweed and brogues brandishing their bibles on behalf of the 'CU' – the Christian Union.

But no one had a task quite like mine. I was called on to do stints on the Gay Society and Catholic Society stalls. It sounded challenging, but as the clubs were grouped thematically in the hall, I knew I'd probably be running large distances between the two stalls. Outside, I made a last minute check on the detailed plan of the table layout. I had to blink and do a double-take. I could scarcely believe my eyes. *They had been placed at right angles to one another and separated by barely two metres.* The Catholics were the last stall among the dozen or so religious societies grouped to the left and 'Gaysoc' had been placed at the end of a whole host of outfits loosely grouped by the term, 'sexual politics'. This novel juxtaposition almost gave our chaplain, Father Reg Riley, a nervous breakdown as he witnessed my slaloming from one stall to the next and back again. 'Latin mass? Yes, once a month and occasional retreats to the Benedictine Abbey at Buckfast…' (two steps to the left) 'We're hoping to go on our first Gay Pride march next June' … (two steps to the right). 'Confessions, well you can ask Father Reg here any time…' (and once more, a shuffle to the left …) 'there is just one gay pub in town called *The Acorn* and be careful crossing the road, as it's in the middle of a traffic roundabout.' (Maybe that explains why there seemed to be so few gay men around in Exeter?) Our chaplain reddened. He would not look me in the eye. To be fair to him, that had been a fairly consistent reaction ever since I went to confession to him in my second term.

It was, however, at Exeter that my faith came under its first serious test. Up until then I had been cocooned in a Catholic sub-culture in which the questioning of fundamentals had not exactly been encouraged. Indeed, I had naively assumed that most of my fellow students would be fellow left-footers like myself. It came as a total shock, then, to discover a key fact in an encyclopaedia in the university library. Only eight per cent of the UK population owed its loyalty to Rome. Suddenly the doubts began to chisel away at the foundations. It happened in seminars on Marx's critique of religion. It gathered pace during late drinking sessions in student parties when I was cornered and put on the spot. 'How can you believe in God when little babies die of leukaemia?' 'If there's one God, why did your God allow so many religions – what went wrong?' 'If God is infinitely merciful then no one will go to hell and everyone will be saved so what's the point of conforming to all these moral rules, if, in the end, the outcome will be the same?' Time and again I floundered and I'd fall back on those old chestnuts spawned by the De La Salle brothers, 'It's a very profound mystery,' and 'well these aren't exactly new questions are they, but the Christian faith has survived nearly two thousand years or so.' A canker of cognitive dissonance set in between my outer bravura and a gnawing corrosive doubt. I often trudged back home in a mist of semi-inebriation replaying these questions round and round in my mind. They were sabre jabs. They were *good* questions. They needed answering, or at least, they required some intelligent engagement.

And that is how I encountered the Dominicans, the 'Order of Preachers'. St Dominic, an astute thirteenth century Spaniard, established a community of wandering friars to combat something called the 'Albigensian heresy'. This was the view that matter was inherently evil and only the spiritual realm could be seen as good – a blatant denial of the goodness of physical creation and the incarnation – God becoming human in the figure of Jesus. This errant position had taken grip in southern France among a group called the Cathars and Dominic had assembled his own mobile bands of preachers to counter them. He was immensely successful. Soon his energetic efforts led to Dominican houses being founded in many of the intellectual hubs of Europe. The Dominicans arrived in England in August 1221, a mere week after their founder's death. During the suppression of the Reformation years and beyond, there had been no Dominican presence in these isles. However, the friars returned and had a discrete presence in Hexham, Northumberland in the late eighteenth century. By 1854 they had a toehold in Woodchester in the west of England and later they set up in Oxford where, in 1929, they established a presence in the very heart of one of the world's great centres of learning.

For me, the whole idea of religious vocation had never really gone away since my time with the De La Salle brothers. At university I'd powered my way through the works of Plato and Aristotle, Hegel, Rousseau and Thomas More and was getting the taste for this philosophy lark. Wasn't my intermittently floundering faith proof positive that the Church needed bright, smart types as chaplains who could hold their own in the jousting matches around the fundamentals of dogma? Moreover, most Dominicans were priests and unlike the brothers who were not ordained, they were charged with the task of carrying out the sacrifice of the mass. To a young man versed in the beauty of the Catholic liturgy, there could be no greater honour than offering up yourself in such a manner. Priests stood in as *personae Christi,* as representatives of Jesus himself, and none more so than at the high point of the Eucharistic sacrifice of the Last Supper when they cited the words, 'This is my body which will be given up for you.' This spine-chilling formula had another connotation as they'd been exactly behind the urge to total gift and self-donation that I had fleetingly felt with Paul. But if it was not meant to be, it left another route open to a different mode of self-giving – and this time not for just one person, but in service to humanity. I wrote to the novice master at Blackfriars, the Dominican priory in Oxford, and in the second term of my final Exeter year, I once more prepared for another potentially testing interview in the city of dreaming spires.

What a contrast with the nerve racking grilling in that tutor's quarters at St Peter's. This time it was a leisurely stroll around the University Parks. A kaleidoscope of azaleas and rhododendrons shimmered in a gentle breeze. Sunlight glistened on the River Cherwell and as I chatted away to Father Alban Weston, there was a comforting sound of willow on leather as the Oxford chaps in white took on Somerset County Cricket Club. For once I relaxed. There were no probing questions about transubstantiation and the doctrine of the trinity, merely an effort to establish some rapport, a process aided hugely by our joint encyclopaedic knowledge of football (even if he was a Liverpool fan, at least he was a believer.) At the end of our circuit of the Parks, he stopped strolling and looked me directly in the eye.

'Is there anything you'd like to ask us? Or are there perhaps things about you that you think we ought to know?'

Now one of my references for my start in religious life had been given by a priest in an order called the Servants of Mary, or Servites. He had told me, unambiguously, that I should be straight with them (so to speak) about being gay. The implication was that if I didn't mention it in my chats with them, then he certainly would in his letter of recommendation. This was something I wanted to avoid since I figured this would have made me look secretive and dodgy.

'Well, yes I suppose there is one thing...' I muttered. His eyebrows raised a tad. Our gentle pacing had now come to a complete halt.

'Yes...?'

'Er, well I'm not sure how to put this exactly.'

'You're a bright chap. Take your time. I'm sure you can find the words...'

'Well the thing is, I'm...'

'I'm???'

'I'm … I'm actually, you know.'

'Do I?'

I looked down at my shoes and noticed how scuffed and worn they appeared. Stead and Simpson circa 1976.

'I'm … I'm …'

'Yes?'

'I'm … gay.'

On saying the word, I raised my head again and now expected him to look away. But he didn't. He just looked straight back at me. And relaxed into a smile. Had it been *that* obvious? Didn't he want to march me off to the GP then for some tablets?

'What?' I said, a little too brusquely perhaps.

'Put it this way,' said Father Weston, 'I don't think you'll be the only one.'

I wasn't.

In late September 1981, I pitched up with that hefty brown suitcase once more, to my new home at Blackfriars, the Priory of the Holy Spirit, 64 St Giles, Oxford OX1 3LY, a mere hundred metres from the front door of the Ashmolean Museum and opposite St John's, one of Oxford's premier colleges.

This was a radically different person who had trembled like jelly under the spotlight of those Oxford academics three years earlier. I arrived, not only spurred on by the confidence of excelling in my studies with a first class degree in political science, but also with more inner steel, a resolve borne out spending three months in the summer of 1981 in the University of Bethlehem teaching Palestinian students on the West Bank. It had been my first proper independent trip abroad and no amount of debilitating cholera and dysentery sustained on an overland trip to Cairo at the end of my stay could dim my spirits as I looked ahead to joining one of the Catholic Church's elite orders. I sauntered along Oxford's Cornmarket en route to the Dominican HQ. It was the nearest I'd ever get to Fraulein Maria's 'I Have Confidence,' en route to the Von Trapp residence in *The Sound Of Music*.

The door was answered by an exceptionally camp and

friendly man dressed in a rather coffee-stained white habit. He introduced himself as Brother Kevin. His black rosary beads swished from side to side on his belt as he led me to the first floor of the priory. Within three minutes I was being introduced to Nigel: not the prior, but Brother Kevin's faithful companion, a spirited budgerigar. 'Nigel can be such a *naughty* boy you know,' he exclaimed. 'I'm trying to get him to recite the Hail Mary with me but he won't have any of it. Now let me take you to your room.' We wandered along past endless doors on a gloomy corridor. 'Those three doors are all bathrooms,' said Brother Kevin pointing, 'except only one's working.' It looked like the room which I had been allocated was on what the friars called 'Regent Street', a busy thoroughfare above the main ground floor cloister. Two of the three bathroom doors had makeshift notices on them covered in a black marker pen. '*Out Of Use Until Further Notice.*' I was puzzled. 'Have you got major plumbing problems then?' I asked Brother Kevin. 'I mean, that's one loo for about nine people on this corridor.' Before he could answer, we were distracted by the sight of a man with thick, tousled grey hair making his way towards us. He looked like he was sporting a huge silver cauliflower on his head. A very large, too large, white arran woollen sweater with holes in it covered his torso and shoulders and multiple knee patches adorned his ragged-looking jeans. He was my very own shambolic hippy grandfather. 'He'll tell you why we only have one bathroom working,' said Kevin. 'Herbert, this is one of your new novices.'

This was the famous and eminent theologian, Father Herbert McCabe OP, one of the world's greatest experts on St Thomas Aquinas, mediaeval master theologian and the most famous figure in the Dominican gallery. For my first year, Herbert was to be responsible for my formation as a new Dominican. Rumour had it that he hadn't been exactly keen on taking on this new role. He stared at me quizzically and said nothing. 'Are you going to show one of your new novices what you're up to in the bathrooms?' asked Brother Kevin in his sing-song voice. Father Herbert looked slightly nonplussed and then beckoned me step forward to follow him. I followed him in to the centre bathroom. He stepped to one side and gestured towards the bathtub. It was a metre high in golden peaches. Beyond it lay what must have been twenty or thirty tins with the recognisable *Del Monte* red logo on an emerald green background emblazoned on them. 'Peach wine.' These were my novice master's very first words to me. 'Last year was a good vintage ... but rather spoiled by a stray pubic hair which caused a bit of alarm to one of the brethren.'

I was dumbstruck. 'Go and unpack,' he said. 'I suppose we need to have a talk at some point.'

I went to my room. It was bigger than all the three bedrooms in our Salford council house combined. But even on a bright September Oxford afternoon, it was horribly gloomy owing to a small low-set window that looked out onto the inner courtyard being the only source of natural light. I switched on a naked overhead lightbulb and two further standard lamps and began to unpack my very basic supply of clothes. Two minutes later a knock at the door. In stepped Brother Richard Conrad, a tall, bearded man in his thirties with 1960s black spectacles. In his distinctly monotone voice, he welcomed me to the community and then produced a small black notebook. 'When-is-your-birthday-and-what-cake-would-you-like?' His delivery was linear and affectionately staccato. It was Brother Richard's tradition to honour all the brethren's birthdays (all thirty six) and bake for them. I explained my birthday was the twenty first of December, the shortest and darkest day of the year. I plumped for 'death by chocolate,' which was duly inserted into his little black book and I agreed to follow him down to the kitchen/scullery area for a cup of tea.

We passed numerous friars on the main cloister and as we approached the kitchen door what can only be described as a pained wailing sound grew in intensity with every step. 'Ah. We might have to be careful here,' said Brother Richard looking a tad awkward. 'Let me go first.' He pushed open the large wooden door. With no warning at all, an enormous casserole pan was spinning through the air at an alarming rate, pursuing a tubby old friar with silvery grey hair and a beard. A high-pitched canary-style voice pierced the air. 'Get out of here you beastly man.' The huge pan missed its target by a foot and clattered into a set of shelves to our right leaving poor Father Julian to exit the kitchen and scuttle off up the stairs to his quarters.

'Giles,' said Richard. 'This is one of our new novices, Mark.' Giles immediately had the wind taken from his sails. He stepped forward a pace or two and took a long inquisitive look. 'Well,' he said. '*Hello!*' A huge beam stretched across his face. I clocked his ears. Metal rings in both of them. '*Put it this way, you'll not be the only one.*'

In a flash, I knew this was going to be OK.

Even by the English Dominicans' considerable reputation for eccentricity, Father Giles Hibbert OP was something else. He was an ex-military officer, son of an army general and an inspirational electrical engineer ('they called me 'Buster' you know.') He stopped at nothing to lay his considerable practical acumen at the service of the brethren and, as an engineer, he saw the Blackfriars priory building as something of an experimental playground.

'Now come with me. I've something to show you. I've got it all sorted. You're going to be three shorts and a long.' Whatever was he on about? Guiding me by the arm down the cloister, he took me to a large wooden display at the front of the priory. It resembled a sort of electronic cricket scoreboard with all the names of the friars listed in order. And there was my name under Father Fergus Kerr OP.

'So. This is how it works,' he explained. 'You flick this light right when you go out and left when you are in the house, so we know what's what.' Then he showed me inside a small telephone booth. On the wall was a series of numbers next to the name of every member of the community. Mine said '58'. 'So, we only have one telephone line. If someone calls for you, I simply dial your number, like this ... and magic.' He dialled the digits '5' and '8' and, out of nothing, a hooter sounded a crisp morse code signal: three shorts and a long. In the weeks and months ahead I saw how it worked. Every friar knew their very own morse identifer. Speakers were stationed around the house and on hearing their personal code, they would abandon their investigations into Wittgenstein or a precise exegesis of Old Testament Hebrew and come hurrying out of their rooms.

Giles was an extraordinary sight physically. He was all of six feet four, with a huge pair of shoulders, waspish chaotic hair and a reedy, feminine voice that belonged to an entirely different body. I'd spotted a selection of large tattoos on his arm that first day, most of them butterflies. On a later occasion in his room, sipping a glass of cold dry jerez in the company of Verdi's Requiem, I made a huge faux pas. I asked him how many he had altogether. It was exactly the cue he had been waiting for. Before I could stop him, most of his clothes were peeled off to reveal a plethora of ants, insects, spiders webs and God knows what else. St Dominic's very own ugly bug ball. 'From the waist upwards,' he declared, 'winged creatures in prayerful ascent to their maker, and from the waist downwards … slugs and creepy crawlies. My body is a meeting of Dante's vision of heaven and hell!' On other occasions he claimed it was all based on Aristotelian anthropology. An old friend had bequeathed him a hundred pounds in her will a decade ago and stipulated that the sum should be spent 'on himself', a condition which Giles took out to the last literal degree. He had fantasised for years about adorning his body. Once the hundred pounds ran out, a good deal of his paltry income as a friar had financed further regular trips to the tattoo parlour until such point that practically his whole body was covered. The legacy had been his decorative *coup de grâce*.

So this whirlwind of eccentricity had been my welcome to religious life. And what a counterblast to those siren voices of gloom that had warned me that the church was going to be 'dull and boring'. My life for the next few months was a looping, contrasting figure of eight. There were practical duties and serious study, mixed in with daily vespers and evening mass. A typical day? Up for morning prayers (matins and lauds at 7.30am, it would have been 4am if I had joined the Benedictines), plan to cook a casserole for thirty five friars, Latin lessons studying St Thomas Aquinas' gigantic *Summa Theologica*, and fulfilling duties as deputy infirmarian by spending time with the elderly friars who had everything from Parkinson's to chronic haemorrhoids.

I was generally conscientious but on occasions my standards slipped. And when they slipped, it tended to border on the spectacular. Cue Brother Richard's elderflower wine (a fine alternative to the peach variety proffered by my novice master). One evening, I joined him in his quarters. Over the next two to three hours, I lost count of how many times he topped up my glass. It was sweet. Delicious. More like a jolly fruit cordial but probably about three times the alcohol content of your classic Jacob's Creek. God knows how I slalomed back to my room and found my bed, but at 6.50am when the alarm went off, my head felt as though it was clamped in an industrial vice. You have no idea what feats of physical dexterity it requires to co-ordinate tunic, cappa and scapular, the constituent parts of the religious habit, when you can barely focus on what is two feet in front of you.

The bells sounded in the cloister bidding us to prayer. My head groaned in pain with every step I took.

As I staggered towards the wooden choir stalls in the church, horror of horrors. There were about twenty brethren in attendance but no one was sitting in the cantor's seat to intone the various psalms and hymns. My novice master fixed his eyes on me and gestured me to take up the vacant seat. I had done this before and had generally taken well to it, but on this occasion even Lazarus in the tomb would have had more life about him. It was the seat of doom. Never had the opening words of morning prayer seemed more apposite:

'*Oh God come to our aid*

O Lord make haste to help us.'

I got through the opening hymn and the antiphonal psalms, but during the readings from scripture, I tried to focus on the crucifix at the far end of the church which increasingly resembled a nightmarish Catherine Wheel. There were beads of sweat falling onto the printed music below me. Seconds later, sounds of ringing in my ears. A most unwelcome bout of elderflower wine-induced tinnitus. I had to get outside to some fresh air. Fast.

We all stood up and my legs almost went from under me. I intoned the Our Father and then to everyone's astonishment, I made a beeline along the front row of the choir stalls past all the startled friars for the sacristy. I pushed open a door which led to an outside space between the church and cloister and as I heard the friars singing, '*and lead us not into temptation, but deliver us from evil*,' I chucked up all over the pavement and slumped with my back arched up against the priory wall. Three minutes later, morning prayer finished and all the friars emerged.

'Feeling a little plain are we?,' asked Brother Bill. 'Come on, let's get all this mopped up and you into some new clothes.' Father Herbert, my superior, took a long look at me, shook his head, and walked off to get his breakfast. I got the distinct impression this had not been a unique occurrence. I skipped breakfast. And lunch. And had two Ryvita biscuits without butter for my evening meal.

I didn't touch a drop of alcohol for six weeks.

Naturally not a word of this was shared with my mother and father during our weekly telephone chats. With the exception of spending my first ever Christmas away from the parental home, my entry into religious life appeared to change very little with them. In reality, it was not much different than my prolonged stints away at university. My elder brother, Christopher, had now married, had set up home and was training to be a chartered accountant. My younger brother, Antony, 'the Ginger Kid' as my parents dubbed him, had already decided he would study medicine. A satisfied mother once told me over the phone: 'I've hit the jackpot haven't I? As I say to the neighbours: 'One to look after my money, one to look after my body and one to take care of my soul.'

But I couldn't help wondering whether the appointed caretaker of her soul hadn't conveniently got his folks off the hook with his embrace of the Order of Preachers. They would not be the first, nor the last, Catholic parents to deflect unwelcome questions of marriage and children about their gay sons with the standard formula... 'of course he'd have made a wonderful husband and father, but he has given his life to God.' This is a dynamic that applies specifically to the calling of the would-be celibate Catholic priest since Anglican trainees have that oh-so-tiresome marriage option, and no vocational 'get back into the closet free card'. More than once I have wondered whether the vigorous opposition to married priests inside my church among some of the clergy is explained, at least in part, by a conscious or unconscious desire to keep this convenient arrangement intact.

My new family were a pot pourri of colourful eccentricity, at times maddening individualism but above all, superb intellectualism. If my doubts about God as a young university student had been the troubled platform from which I had made the leap into religious life, then in choosing the Dominican Order, He had guided me gently into the most promising of pastures. As I had begun to question the bedrock of my faith at university, I had got dangerously close to accepting a crass formula: that somehow belief in God was inversely proportional to one's intellectual abilities. If you had done an average IQ survey at Blackfriars, the result would have been in the top two percentile range. If it wasn't Father Brian Davies taking you through binary truth tables and logical propositions about God and the existence of Evil, it was Father Paul Parvis helping you examine the rich writings of the early Christian fathers in Greek and Latin. Your theology not contemporary enough for you? Why not engage with Father Fergus Kerr and his musings on how Wittgenstein's study of language games in his *Philosophical Investigations* help us make more accurate sense of what we can and cannot say about God? All this I devoured. This fayre had never been remotely served up anywhere in my entire Catholic life. It is no exaggeration to say that the Dominicans helped me save my faith.

And lest you think these inspirational men were a bunch of ivory tower dwelling navel-gazing hermits with a hatred of the real world, many of them had a huge commitment to issues of justice and peace that put them at the radical end of the spectrum. This made me even prouder to be associated with them. I had studied politics and the last thing I wanted was a faith divorced from the nitty-gritty of life's most pressing issues. Father Timothy Radcliffe, who was made prior in the Oxford House and who later went on to became the first ever English Master General of the whole international order, was one of a number of friars who became especially caught up in CND (Campaign for Nuclear Disarmament.) In the early winter months of 1982, we were at the height of a new Cold War. US-manufactured Pershing and Cruise Missiles planned for western Europe threatened to obliterate eastern European cities, just as Soviet SS-20 intermediate range weapons could reduce a city like Oxford to a smouldering rubble within minutes. Greenham Common near the US base at Aldermaston was less than an hour's drive down the road. A group of friars, dressed in our black and white habits, joined a group of locals and set off for Upper Heyford, site of the American military base, that housed a squadron of F-111 bomber planes whose mission was to drop their nuclear loads on targets behind the so-called Iron Curtain such as Leipzig, Budapest and Prague.

The strategic aim of our coterie of thirty or so anti-nuclear protestors was to block access to the main airbase by lying on the tarmac at the main entrance and refusing to move. I don't know what St Dominic had to say, if anything, about civil disobedience, but here were his followers doing their bit to lay bare the evils of nuclear deterrence and MAD ... the threat of 'mutually assured destruction'. We pitched up at the crack of dawn on a pitifully cold January morning. An army of woolly hat-wearing activists laid out a tarpaulin on the road in front of the gated main entrance, took out the flasks of tea, flapjacks and began the inevitable round of 'We Shall Overcome'. I thought we'd be scooped up and arrested within a few minutes, but after half an hour we'd seen no sign of air base personnel. After an hour, several of my fellow Catholic revolutionaries were trembling with cold, but with five layers of my woollen habit over thermal vest and trousers and an olive green woolly hat, my body was well insulated against the piercing proto-Siberian wind. Still no sign of the military. It was beginning to look as though they had got wind of our impressive anti-nuclear tactics and were staying away. Another half an hour passed. Noses were turning cherry red and lips a strange blue as, out of nothing, a cry went up: 'Look. Trucks.' Four large military vehicles appeared on the horizon. They grew progressively larger as the seconds passed by. We were at the moment of truth. Our group formed a tight line and locked arms with an impeccable precision borne of at least ten minutes of carefully planned drills. The huge carrier trucks were almost upon us. Would they draw right up to our faces and blare their horns? Would American soldiers step out and attempt to forcibly evict us? Were there to be ugly scenes with condemnatory pictures on the front page of the *Oxford Mail* (somewhat unlikely as nobody among us had actually told the press what we were doing.) None of that. They passed straight by. 'Where are they going?' shouted one of our group. They drove on another hundred metres and then, horror of horrors, we spotted another gate. Four army personnel stepped out to slip back the locks and then the trucks glided in unopposed. Amidst our band of merry anti-nuclear warriors a sub-zero silence filled the air. The twentieth century had been witness to some extraordinary feats of imaginative non-violent resistance but RAF Upper Heyford January 1982 was not one of its more glorious moments.

Resistance soon folded as the pangs of humiliating defeat took hold. A small number were seriously annoyed by the whole thing, but most of us simply turned the whole event into an exercise of Monty Python-esque self-deprecation. It was worthy of a scene from *Life of Brian*: the People's

Revolutionary Front of CND Oxford. On our journey back
to Oxford, I especially enjoyed the chat with an intriguingly
gentle man called Michael. He had been with the Dominicans
in the 1970s and was said to be close to taking his final vows
before he had left to teach law at the city Polytechnic (now
Oxford Brookes University). Michael had kept on good
terms with many of the friars. He was a regular squash
partner with the prior of the house and I also knew he was
attending seminars on Wittgenstein with Father Fergus Kerr.
He described himself to me as 'post-Catholic' and a curiosity
set in. Why he had left Blackfriars after investing so much
time and energy in study? How can you decide to become,
'post-Catholic'? I mean, surely 'once a Catholic and all that?'
'You can't answer that in five minutes,' he had quipped in
the car on our return back to Oxford. 'Best over a pint, or
two?' Now offers of pints to young, cash-strapped friars are
rarely, if ever turned down. It's true, our monthly income had
recently just enjoyed a huge fifty per cent rise, climbing from
ten to fifteen pounds a month. This pocket money, known
by the Latin epithet, *ad honesta* (for honest things) had been
stubbornly fixed at a tenner since the early 1970s, but no one
in the community meeting was going to stand in the way of a
bit of inflation-adjustment. Just because you're a friar doesn't
mean you are hermetically sealed against the evil influences
of the fluctuating retail price index. Nearly all my money
went on one thing: Mahler concerts. Once a month, if there
was a suitable event on, I asked my novice master for special
permission to travel to London to the Royal Festival Hall.
(Thank goodness I hadn't plumped for an enclosed order
like the Carthusians.) The symphonies of Gustav Mahler had
erupted into my life late on Christmas Day 1977. Paul had
given me a boxed set of the composer's longest work, the Third,
conducted by Sir George Solti with the London Symphony
Orchestra on the Decca label. The huge piece spanned two
separate vinyl discs. 'I figured with your birthday coming
four days before Christmas, you could have one for each,' was
his smart rationale. At just before midnight on 25 December,

long after all the memories of Elton John and Penelope Keith on the Morecambe and Wise Show had faded and the family were in bed, I plugged the headphones into my Dad's new amplifier and placed the first movement of Mahler's epic masterpiece on to his Pioneer turntable. I switched all the lights off to magnify the sensory impact. Although I had been into classical music since I was twelve years old, I had heard *nothing* like this ever before in my life. It can't have done any harm that the young man who had given it me was someone who had set my soul on fire, but the music of Mahler with its uncanny double-edged dialectic of elation and melancholy, took me to a very special place. It still does.

But a young friar's fifteen pounds a month simply evaporated once bus fare to London and concert ticket were factored in. I'd noticed that the more experienced community members appeared to supplement their meagre income with either financial help from outside the house from family and/ or well-placed contacts outside the priory. Michael's offer of beer was, therefore, welcome. It gave me a much-needed counterpoint outside a potentially claustrophobic community of men, and a chance to carry on 'God-talk' with a serious adult ten years my senior. He had years of Dominican experience to share. Moreover, he was from a working class northern family like myself (Liverpool, but an Everton fan, so easily forgiven). In essence, he was a precious new liaison. He was also seriously into music. Oxford University had a prestigious choir called the *Schola Cantorum Oxoniensis*. Michael possessed a lyrical high tenor voice which most good choirmasters would die for. As the weeks and months passed, I found myself inside splendid venues such as Magdalen and New College Chapels listening to quite wonderful Bach motets and masses by William Byrd. His choir would tour, often to exotic international destinations and a succession of postcards began to appear in my pigeon hole at 64 St Giles. I assumed it all to be innocent platonic fun, but one or two of the other friars thought otherwise. And said as much. But I dismissed them as being over-protective.

There was much to be done. Within a couple of months I would be at the end of my novitiate year. The trial period of induction would be over and, presuming I was serious about life in the order, the community would meet to decide if I was worthy of taking my vows and committing myself for three years more. These were so-called 'simple vows'. The 'solemn' pledges came further up the line. All very sensible. No rush. Plenty of time to discern one's vocation, or for my brothers to decide I was not suited to the call of Dominican life. So it was a time to be vigilant.

And it has to be conceded, in addition to 'Elderflowergate' there had been other rough patches. Following the Easter Vigil service which had ended at 1.15am the community invited the congregation in for cocoa to the huge refectory, before hitting the harder stuff upstairs at 2.30am in the common room. When you are celebrating the fact that God has, through his only Son, conquered the snares of death and reconciled the world to himself, your serious Catholic does not see this as an excuse to merely break open a few bottles of Tree Top fruit cordial. In fact I once heard a senior theologian assert that Gordon's Gin ought to be cited as a serious argument for the existence of God, invoking a variant of St Anselm's argument from design. There were plenty of bottles of liquid proof on offer, and no sooner had I appeared among the brethren than a large glass was thrust into my hand. I'd had a 'G and T' only once before. And it had been nothing like as strong as this one.

Two hours later, the gin was talking and I was now its melancholic, attention-seeking microphone. Every time I heard a casual conversational reference to God, or theology, I sauntered over, glass in hand, and raised my voice: 'It's all bollocks. And you know it. It's just a load of made-up junk meant to keep us all from fretting about the fact that life is *meaningless.*' Eyebrows were raised to the ceiling. Those Mahler symphonies were clearly not doing me an awful lot of good. Instead of the 'tedious drunk on the bus', we now had 'pissed novice in a habit.' An especially camp and cheery Aussie community member, Bill Phillips, summed it up thus:

'Oh dear. Another tired and angry possum.' He came over and placed his arm round me to shut me up. Then he led me off to my room, put me to bed and within five hours was knocking at my door. Before I could say a word, he sped in with a tea-towel folded expertly over his head, a la Florence Nightingale. 'Morning you little groggy eyed wombat. Sore head?' he chirped. He rested a metal tray on the side of my bed which contained an expertly freshly-cut grapefruit, black coffee and three paracetamol tablets. And I was meant to be the infirmarian.

Such blips were not deemed serious by my seniors, but all part of the process of enquiry. Those Eastertide questions were real and heartfelt and had their roots in those taunting probes at university about the essentials of my belief. But what happened over those months was the emergence of a kind of faith by proxy. In addition to all my studies, I looked around at two to three dozen people who were the brainiest people I had ever encountered. They had read their Nietzsche and their Sartre long before Richard Dawkins later popped up with his rather crude fundamentalist atheism. If it was good enough for them, did I really have a case that was superior to theirs? Moreover, I had joined the Order of Preachers and there was every nascent sign that I was measuring up for the part. In the summer of 1982, Father Herbert took his three novices over to County Kerry in south west Ireland (we went by train and boat – he donned his leathers and took his motor bike.) The McCabe theology summer school took place in a remote pub in a tiny village called Glencar, and many of Herbert's dedicated disciples came from all corners of the UK and Ireland to hear him. Think Dominican Glastonbury with Guinness and Jamieson's whiskey. On one especially beautiful day, we had mass in a local field. Mooing cows and the sound of wild birds provided the soundtrack. About fifty of us squatted on the grass as Herbert put on the most rudimentary vestments over his short-sleeved shirt and jeans. 'By the way,' he said looking over in my direction, 'You'll be doing the preaching.' What? I hadn't even studied the gospel of the day, or the readings from scripture. So it was all done on the hoof. You read about country parsons agonising all day Saturday about the content of their homilies and I was being thrown in at the deep end. When the gospel came, Matthew Chapter 18: 2–4, 'Truly I say unto you, unless you become like little children, you shall not enter the Kingdom of God,' I had but a minute or two to compose some thoughts and share them with Herbert's entourage, a dozen admiring cows and the odd magpie or two. I listed the annoying habits of needy, whining children and dismissed them. But if God did not want that, what was the gospel asking of us? Essentially, I preached a lesson to myself. A child when presented with a need to make a response is instinctive and can say an affirmative, 'Yes', in a way that an over-intellectualising, dithering adult is incapable of. 'God wants us to say a "Yes", and act on it, in spite of the doubts and reservations,' I said. 'A child does not know the corrosive gnawing disease of cynicism where every human action in the world is interpreted through the basest possible motive. Of course we cannot turn back the biological clock. But let us cast off that aspect of our adult life that constantly finds fault with others and clothe ourselves once more, in our best child-like natures. Let us say a resounding "Yes" to life and to God.' When I stopped there was a near silence only punctuated by the sound of a distant babbling brook. A cormorant flew overhead and dipped towards us, before arching back up towards the direction of the coast. When mass ended, I overheard Herbert's sister, Eileen, in conversation with my superior. 'Well what can I say?' she said. 'You've found another one. He's a natural.' I fell foul of the sin of pride. And enjoyed it. Bring on my permanent berth on *Thought for the Day*.

Back in Oxford, as summer was coming to an end, we were preparing for a wedding. The city of dreaming spires, it appeared to all intents and purposes, was littered with ex-Dominicans. John Rayneau had also tried his vocation with the Order of Preachers. John had lasted four years. Then an abrupt dramatic existential realisation that the religious life was not for him ended with him packing a case and fleeing without explanation. His brothers were in consternation. His room was bare. Where had he gone? It later transpired he had turned up and sought refuge and covert protection at the house of yet another ex-Dominican, the post-Catholic tenor supremo, Michael. John had fallen in love with a vivacious young teenage Oxford girl, Donna Butler, and John was 'coming home' to declare his commitment to her in the very location where he had played his fiddle, and studied the dogmas of the Church. He had decided that he agreed with God in Genesis Chapter 2 verse 18, 'it is not good that man should be alone' and so, just as the nuns turned out for Maria as she took the arm of Captain Von Trapp, so the friars were lending their brotherly support.

The wedding service was amazing. John was plugged into a formidable network of local musicians who played with zest and passion. Donna was a picture of captivating charm and innocence. At the reception afterwards, the ale and wine flowed. I found myself quizzing Michael about his role in offering lodgings to John in his own home and once again, our conversation turned to his struggles with the Catholic faith. 'There's a book I think you ought to read,' I said, perhaps a trifle patronisingly. 'It's upstairs.' Had I intended to go and fetch it, or was this an invitation for him to follow me? Five minutes later in my room we were deeply locked in conversation about post-modernism, the difficulty of using human language to talk about theological propositions and the like. Then, it just happened. We kissed. Tenderly. Ever so gently. That stream of faithfully despatched postcards, all those chats in the pub, suddenly it all made sense. And the last thing I wanted to do was push him back. Music from the wedding party down below blasted up through parquet floor and as the sound of Irish reels gathered momentum, I locked my door. We nestled down onto a rug with our arms around one another and made love energetically, knowing full well that the backdrop of noise from the party offered an acoustic cocoon of protection.

The following day I was crestfallen. I had 'failed'. The pledges of poverty, chastity and obedience. The Holy Trinity of vows. When you fall short in the first and last, it might be something as simple as feeling resentful over a task you have been asked to do by the prior, such as doing an emergency evening meal for the brethren. It gets brushed aside and quickly forgotten. But when chastity goes out the window, the results are rather more spectacular. The problem was that here was a delightful, intelligent and ever so gentle man who had fallen in love with me (he confessed he had been taken the first time he saw me reading the Epistle in church some eight months ago on one of his rare visits to Sunday mass.) Suddenly, without the prospect of Michael at my side, I felt exposed, lonely. The closeness. The intimacy. That sense of 'being known,' and not being judged. Was all this a test of my vocation which I had to triumph over through prayer and self-discipline, or rather a providential sign that I had to bite the bullet and add to the swelling ranks of Oxford ex-Dominicans? I couldn't duck it. I was due to make my simple profession in just under two months' time. What to do?

Never underestimate the link in the mind, especially the Catholic mind, between prohibition and desire. Why did our Biblical ancestors in the Garden of Eden just have to plump for the only tree that was out of bounds? There were so many others on show. Take a child into a sweet shop and conduct an experiment. 'You can have anything you see here darling, but not the chocolate bonbons in the top left hand corner.' Pause. '*I want the chocolate bonbons mummy. NOW!*'

What followed for the next month was a helter-skelter state of affairs that must have driven poor Michael round the twist in which I was anything but consistent. He was always patient and never sought to exert pressure. One minute I'd go all cold on him and have no contact for days on end. He was an agent of the devil, right? The epitome of distraction and who was I kidding that this kind of test and hurdle was not going to present itself sooner or later. If I could control and master this, I could do anything. A strategy that worked for about seventy two hours after which the Manichean pendulum swung completely the other way. I caved in, pining for precious human acceptance and affection. I'd be on my bike up to his tutor's flat at the polytechnic. Later that night we would set the alarm clock so I could get up at sunrise to race down Headington Hill on my bicycle next morning. (Thankfully there was a handy side entrance on St Giles. Once inside, I only had to negotiate a flight of stairs and my room was three doors on the right.) Once inside my quarters I'd perform a 'Superman' style telephone kiosk costume change into my habit and then join my fellow friars for morning prayer. But when does 'holding things in creative tension' become a cosy rationalisation for having your cake and eating it? It was both exhilarating and corrosive. I was both a cherished lover and a hypocrite. With those vows edging nearer and nearer, I had no option: I had to go and talk to the prior.

Father Timothy Radcliffe had been a chaplain at the University of London in the 1970s. Born into a family of aristocrats from Yorkshire, his choice of priestly ministry with the Dominicans over a career in the City as a stockbroker had taken his relatives somewhat by surprise. In the house he was the Blackfriars scripture tutor and had been elected superior by his Dominican brothers earlier in 1982. Being prior is a bit of a poisoned chalice, especially in an English Dominican setting. Many in the order would have been aghast had their name emerged after rounds of voting. As prior, one had an ambassadorial role outside of the house with plenty of jolly invites to college dinners, passing the port and such like. But managing a tribe of supremely individualistic, authority-wary friars was another kettle of fish. One of Timothy's predecessors famously stuck the following abrupt note on the cloister noticeboard. '*Banana skins do not flush down lavatories. F.*'

I got on well with Timothy. He was approachable, warm-hearted and easily teased. So I booked a Sunday afternoon slot to see him and put my cards on the table about the emotional and sexual tumult that was engulfing me. When you consider that this was the early 1980s and attitudes towards gay issues were still in the Ice Age in the church, his non-judgemental stance I still find remarkable. The essence of his advice was that any decent religious was always prone to falling in love because the spirit of openness and vulnerability needed to be a genuine Christian demanded that one be exposed. One had to have a certain spirit of self-surrender or one was nothing. And I knew lots of clerical types whose sexuality and affectivity had been so boxed in, so repressed, that they had been transformed into cold, robotic characters reminiscent of the Beatles infamous 'Father McKenzie' in Eleanor Rigby, '*Look at him working, darning his socks in the night when there's nobody there, what does he care?*' Timothy knew Michael from his time in the order. They had maintained a healthy and respectful friendship. I sensed also that he had a soft spot for the young novice who had accompanied him on anti-nuclear demonstrations and given him tips on how to handle intrusive questions from Swedish radio reporters. 'This is not a time for drastic decisions,' he said. 'You have to discern what is right for you. At the moment it's not clear, but it won't stay like this. You will know in due course. Are you praying about it?'

The problem was that in just a few weeks, I would have to prostrate myself on the floor in front of him in the church in front of several hundred people as part of the traditional ceremony of making vows. And there is no way I could do that if I was in the middle of an intimate relationship. I would have felt a complete fraud. So, a few days after my heart to heart with the prior, I took another long walk in the University Parks with Michael and told him I was going ahead with my public promises of commitment to the Order and that it would be better if things between us underwent a change. He remained quiet throughout. Perhaps he had expected what was coming. I knew he had taken vows himself and was hardly a stranger to what I was planning to do. At the end of the walk we embraced awkwardly just outside the gates. I could see the heavy redbrick façade of Keble College chapel just over his shoulder. I muttered something about 'remaining good friends,' which appeared to convince neither of us. He turned and walked slowly away. I felt incredibly sad. And I felt even sadder that I had hurt a man whose only error had been to show me gentleness, patience and share his own struggles with Catholicism with vulnerability.

Some three weeks later, along with my fellow novices, Nick and Selwyn (who later on in life was to undertake the brave path of transition and become 'Sally'!), I made my vows in a packed church at the 6.15pm Sunday evening mass. My proud parents came down from Manchester, as did many close school and university friends.

'*I, brother Mark Dowd, make profession, and I promise obedience to God, to blessed Mary, to blessed Dominic, and to you, brother Timothy Radcliffe nominated by Vincent De Couesnongle, Master of the Order of Friars Preachers and to his successors.*'

As I looked round at the sea of faces in the Priory of the Holy Spirit, I noted a kaleidoscope of all the people closest to me, my very own band of nearest and dearest. All save one. He could not bear to be there. An understanding friend, the mother of Donna Butler, at whose wedding Michael and I had become romantically involved earlier that summer, took him under her wing for the evening and plied him with several glasses of wine as he reflected on events that were going on just a few hundred metres down the road.

That was early November 1982. I was now a 'simply professed' member of the Dominican Order, the nearest thing you get I suppose to getting engaged. And with it came presents, most of them theology books, commentaries on church councils and, of course, the odd Mahler vinyl album. For a few weeks in the run-up to Christmas, there was next to no contact with Michael. We had made those usual unconvincing pledges about 'staying good friends' but neither of us really believed it would be possible. The business of vows had forced my hand. How very strange it must have been for him to think of someone else with whom he was passionately involved, proceeding down the very same path he himself had once trodden. To lose the man you loved to a mission and a set of beliefs you could no longer subscribe to.

Advent came and preparations began for Christmas. On one especially cold and grey Sunday morning in mid-December, I recall singing *In the Bleak Mid-Winter* at the 9.30am family mass at Blackfriars. Inexplicably, half way through the hauntingly beautiful carol, I found tears streaming down my cheeks. I used my habit to wipe them away but they came forth with ever greater gusto. When I went up for communion, my novice master, Herbert, registered my upset with a prolonged stare as he gave me the body of Christ in my hand. I retired to my room and looked at the snowflakes falling outside my window from the leaden skies onto the small courtyard below. A huge wave of melancholy descended on me. I had never been bereaved, but I imagined this is what it must feel like. An acute, gnawing chasm of pain inside. A dawning sense that if life were to go on like this it would be unbearable. Then the tears turned to sobs. I went to lock my door lest anyone should come and discover me.

What had I done?

That all this should happen so close to Christmas was not a coincidence. A year ago, it had all been a novelty to be with the brethren and Michael had been, at best, a distant shadow. But if Christmas is all about being with those who you love and make your life worthwhile, I just knew I was now in the wrong place. I was twenty two years old. In years to come, I'd be hearing confessions and counselling couples on relationship problems and what wisdom would I have to impart to them? Was I to pass through the rest of my life without the sustained love of another person whose arms enfold you and whose very embrace tells you, when the chips are down, 'I am here for you. You are what gives my life meaning. It's OK'? I manufactured in my mind tortuous images of ending the Sunday evening mass in my solitary inner city parish with nothing for company but a crappy TV set, a mangy dog and a whisky bottle. 'It is not good that man should be alone,' says

God in Genesis, Chapter One. I thought of John Rayneau and Donna Butler. Their wedding. Subsequent events in my room. It took some painful and humiliating honesty to concede the fact that, in spite of being in the company of some of the most talented and engaging people I had ever met, I felt distinctly alone. Not for the first, or the last time in my life, my tears pointed a way forward. An hour later I telephoned Michael and said I needed to talk. Half an hour after that we were in his apartment in a rapturous embrace that lasted for hours. Timothy, my prior, had told me that all would become clear. He was right. Later that afternoon, the leaden sky finally relinquished its stubborn hold over the Oxford skyline. Michael and I took a walk down Headington Hill through South Parks and into one of East Oxford's many streets wedged between the Cowley and Iffley Roads. He took me to number thirty nine and, out of his pocket, produced an A4 size single sheet of paper. It contained an estate agent's details for a two bedroom terrace house whose asking price was £24,500. This place, he explained, if I was willing, would be my new home when he moved in, in just over five weeks' time. I looked closer at the property blurb and noticed the shadowy figure of an elderly woman in the house adjacent whose curtain twitching had been caught on camera by the estate agent's photographer.

Christmas came and went. I spent more and more time in Michael's company on long walks in the piercing winter sunshine. I told him I would try to secure a postgraduate place at Oxford University to study International Relations. But there remained the distinctly tricky business of sharing all this with my Dominican brothers, and even worse, my parents.

So in mid-January I made the trip north to Salford and over several mugs of tea and a mountain of Battenberg cake and Soreen malt loaf, I broke the news to Mum and Dad that, 'I had met someone' and could not consider myself as a serious candidate for priestly life. Silence. They exchanged looks. *'Someone to look after my soul...'*

The silence was broken by my mother. 'This hasn't exactly come at the best time love.' My father put his hand on her arm as she continued with the voice quivering with emotion. 'Your big brother was up at the weekend.' She struggled to continue, so my father took up the reins.

'He's getting a divorce. It's all over with Mandy.'

I really wish I had got my news in first. In the tribal Catholic world, a week ago my parents had a happily married and professionally successful eldest son who was looking forward to starting a family and a bright middle child who was destined to say mass and write books with one of the most prestigious orders in the church. Divorce was *unheard of* in our Catholic world. If it didn't work out you simply gritted your teeth and offered it up for the holy souls in purgatory. Now, in the space of four days, they had a divorcee in the offing and a queer son who had ironically found reciprocal love inside the very bosom of a church that preached that any physical expression of that love was 'objectively disordered'.

'What a to do,' said my mother. 'Never mind. Life goes on doesn't it?' and tucked into more malt loaf. She reminded me that ever since the age of five, when I had been asked by visitors, 'What do you want to be when you grow up?' I had answered 'A teacher or a priest.' But I could tell there was now one thing uppermost in their minds. How are we going to tell the neighbours? What do we say to the rest of the family?

As I headed back south, thankfully that particular task was not uppermost in my mind. I set about a series of very selective tête à têtes with the friars I knew best, including the prior. When I revealed my intentions he did not bat an eyelid. 'It's been rather noticeable the last couple of times I have seen Michael that he has had a rather large smile on his face,' he said. There was not a word of condemnation, or recrimination. 'We will miss you. You've been really good for this community in the short period of time you've been here. I hope in the years to come, you'll look back on this period as a positive time for you in your journey to deepen your faith.' When one thinks in the last twenty or so years how a whole series of Christian churches have tied themselves up in knots over civil partnerships and gay marriage and the bitter recriminations over the emergence of the LGBT identity, the low-key, humane, wise words of those who followed in the steps of St Dominic are nothing short of staggering.

But there were other friars I knew less well who I couldn't face and so I took the easy way out. When Michael and I hatched the plan for my exit, we chose the last Sunday of January. I would 'elope' during the 6.15pm evening mass with all my books, records and a suitcase of clothes. When the night came, Michael borrowed a white van from the very same friend who had held his hand on the night of my simple vows. All the friars were inside at prayer. We ran up and down the stairs carrying several large boxes until my room was divested of the very last hint of my existence at Blackfriars. The final object I gathered up was the brass metal crucifix on my bedside table that my parents had given me in 1967 when I had made my first Holy Communion. As we headed towards the van, whose engine had been left running, a latecomer for mass stopped me just outside the front door. The melodic strains of evening vespers plainchant wafted out through the main door to the church. She looked at the pile of boxes in the van. 'Are you off somewhere?' she enquired. 'Yes,' was my monosyllabic answer.

We sped off into the cold January night to our new home, a mere ten minutes away over Magdalen Bridge. That first evening of our exciting new 'togetherness', we ate Chinese takeaway out of polystyrene cartons huddling around three bars of an old electric fire. The living room boasted flaking orange paint, peeling yellow and brown wallpaper and any tug at the decrepit carpet provoked a mass of scurrying from an army of silverfish. But so what?

I was happy. He was happy.

Oxford now had its first semi-official ex-Dominican gay couple.

And the world was now our oyster.

5

Michael

The first morning of domestic bliss in our new East Oxford love nest had us both caught between chronic lumbago and hypothermia. It was several degrees below zero outside and the condensation on our rickety bedroom windows metamorphosed into crystalline icicles. The completely hopeless mattress resembled more a banana-shaped hammock, with Michael and I either clinging onto the outside with our fingernails, or rolling helplessly in towards the middle. Both of us had back pain. It was some time before we had enough money between us to get the council to send a van and offload the offending item. And number thirty nine was freezing. Before purchase completion, it had been uninhabited for more than six months. The modest terrace house had rising damp and no central heating. Our nostrils were, for several days, plagued with the smell of old person's incontinence. Yet none of this deterred us. We were in the early throes of giddy romance and caught up in that ever so gay hobby – gentrification. If we could get the money together, the place would be gutted and totally overhauled in a matter of months. Well, that was the plan.

In those heady first weeks of bliss and excitement, a constant procession of visitors came round: ostensibly to check out the new dwelling, but mostly they were friends of Michael's, curious to meet this very 'significant other'. The only people I knew in Oxford were really the brethren back in the priory. It took a while, but a number of them also came round for evenings of humble shepherd's pie and a bottle of cheap wine. A number of them spoke of the delight of getting out of the house for a few hours and putting their feet up. Jesus chilled out with Martha and Mary at Bethany, while some of the friars, it seems, had Michael and Mark in East Oxford. Before too long, the slightly sensitive issue of hosting our respective sets of parents was on the agenda, a development that brought with it some very particular challenges.

Michael's mother and father, Jim and Margaret, were well into their seventies. In contrast to what I had told my own parents, Michael had never really had the full and frank conversation with them both about being gay. Although he had come out to his father some ten years earlier, they had agreed not to disabuse his mother who certainly had no reason to view me as anything more than Michael's lodger. They were traditional Catholics from Merseyside and very conservative, with a small 'c', not ones to question church teaching (unlike my own folks who wasted little time telling anyone who wanted to hear that they disagreed with Rome on birth control and had had no issue at all in going with their own conscience on matters of family planning.) So on their one and only visit, in scenes that thousands of lesbian and gay couples will have played out down the decades, we wrote the script for our very own Brian Rix farce. We re-made the downstairs front room as if it were my bedroom. My books and clothes were brought in. We even went out and bought a rent book from the corner newsagents lest the other props failed to convince. A visit lasting a week in which the only physical contact we permitted ourselves was a sneaky good night kiss before I slid the door shut on my temporary abode. We creased up giggling at the near necessary absurdity of it all and wondered if upstairs, they had heard us whispering.

The young 'lodger' cooked Jim and Margaret casseroles laced with diced carrots and pearl barley. Nothing too hot or spicy or unfamiliar, mind. There were trips out to the tea shop at Dorchester Abbey in our canary yellow VW Beetle which left Michael fretting lest his dad could find nothing on the menu he liked. Meanwhile his lovely mum, 'I don't want to be too much trouble', just did her best to make no demands.

A week came and went before they returned to Old Swan at the end of the East Lancs Road. Michael and I re-occupied the double bed – with the risk of more lumbago a small price worth paying.

My own parents' first visit was rather a different matter. Considerably younger than Michael's elderly parents, there was no need for the Ayckbournesque antics, but how would they react to their first ever in-your-face gay couple? They'd met Michael once or twice over tea and Mr Kipling's Viennese Whirls in Salford, but that had been only an hour or so of exposure. This was altogether different. Now they'd be meeting the older man who had deprived them of a priest in the family (well that was the way my paranoid mind had framed it). In the summer of 1983, we beckoned over to them on the tarmac of the Oxford bus station as they descended from their Yelloways coach after their five and half hour journey via Cheltenham. They wobbled across towards us with two *huge* leather suitcases. Good Lord. How long did they think they were coming for? When we got them back home, it all became so much clearer.

'Well we knew you'd be short of sheets,' said my mother. 'So we had a root round in the attic and brought you these.' Out dropped sheets. Blue and yellow sheets. *Double sheets.* Sheets made of *nylon.* I never told them, but rather than risk burning the house down with sparks emanating from the material, we later cut them up and used them as dusters. But *double* sheets. How about that? Ten years ago Mam was frogmarching me off to the docs for anti-queer antibiotics. Now she was trying to get me and Michael lined up as pin-up boys for Brentford Nylons. Dad didn't look quite as keen at this sudden display. But he had not stood in the way. That little thoughtful gesture, I knew, had been a major advance. The fact that they had not been swish Egyptian cotton from John Lewis was neither here nor there.

And the gentrification gathered pace. New dusters were nothing compared to the radiators and new boiler, the overhaul of the compact rear town garden and redecoration of our modest terraced home, from top to bottom. A new bed finally arrived which meant our postures improved overnight. And in a well-intentioned, but fatefully misplaced attempt to avoid boring pastel shades (I had a visceral loathing for the Dulux Rose-White, Barley-White, Apple-White range), I insisted the new décor would not be 'tasteful and bland'. So I coated all the new radiators candy pink. Our main bedroom was given a black wall with a white recess arched alcove – just about acceptable until you added the battleship grey wallpaper with, what seems now, hideous stark, nausea-inducing red white and black zig-zags, and a carpet to match. Ever keen to avoid accusations of timidity, the bathroom became a mad mixture of mustard yellow and pine green – but still had also to incorporate the obligatory candy pink radiator. I called it 'retro'. I suspected tight-lipped diplomatic visitors had other words for it. Michael indulged my descent into interior décor eccentricity, partly because I think he thought it would be too much trouble to mount a fight, but also because it gave me a sense of purpose and stake in the house. And herein lay one of the challenges we did not always succeed in overcoming – the considerable disparity in income and power that simmered below and occasionally erupted.

As a polytechnic law lecturer, Michael was hardly rich, and he also had the burden of a mortgage. But it all added up to much more than I had. A combination of income support, teaching English and odds jobs had got me through the first months until I secured a place at St Antony's College to do a two years masters in International Relations. But the grant (remember those antiquated novelties from the distant past?) limited my spending power to forty quid a week. Twenty of that went in the food kitty (which often ran out before the week was up.) Money was tight. I recall one awful visit to Shropshire to stay with one of Michael's academic friends in which it was suggested we all go out for Sunday lunch to the glossy Tudor venue of Churches Mansion in Nantwich. There were eight of us. I was by far the youngest on show. All very gay. All very jolly. Until the bill came round. 'Right, if we split it all that's roughly forty quid each,' said our host. Blow to the solar plexus. That was my weekly allowance down the swannee. I briefly thought about slamming my National Union of Students card down on the table, before digging into my wallet and emptying it of its contents. I waited for a voice to pipe up with a Marxist mantra, 'From each according to his ability...' - but no. On the return journey to Oxford I was boiling with rage and our journey passed in near silence. Michael was in a classic Catch-22: had he offered to cover my share, I'd have accused him of patronising me and having me in his pocket. My anger was directed more at the others, but it pointed to a fault line in our domestic set-up that never really went away until I started work as a newspaper journalist some years later.

Fault lines. Hairline cracks that can, before you know it, threaten to take on the appearance of Cheddar Gorge. And it's nobody's 'fault' as such, just the painful business of sharing space with a roof over your head. If truth be told, the cloak and dagger intrigue of romance while I was still a friar, furtively sneaking out to grab a couple of hours here and there, had now given way to a new reality: how to share a whole life, 24/7 with a man I loved. It required a maturity and sensitivity to the other's space – a maturity I frequently lacked. And those small, irritating, maddening tics of behaviour, innocent and harmless in themselves, now took on whole new symbolic lives of their own.

About eighteen months into our new life of shared living, Michael, not one known for his love of confrontation, uncharacteristically announced that there was an item that we needed to discuss that could be postponed no longer. He asked me to draw up a chair and took a deep breath. Goodness, what was round the corner. Had he had it with the candy pink radiators? Did I have terrible B.O.? Was he having an affair and thinking of leaving me?

'There are some things I am finding it quite hard to cope with,' he said. 'I know this will sound daft, and petty and ...' I fixed my eyes on him and tried to look as open-faced and encouraging as possible. He was finding this so difficult.

'I really hate the way you leave crumbs on the breadboard.'
Crumbs.

This was a bit of an anti-climax.

'Is that all?' I said. 'Crumbs on the breadboard?'

'Well no. There's a whole host of things. For instance, shaving.'

'Shaving? You want me to grow a beard again?' (I had grown a beard briefly at Blackfriars and it had come out in a multi-coloured patchwork mess, more in keeping with Joseph's coat in Genesis 37:11 than some specimen of hirsute wonder.)

'No. It's the shaving foam. You leave it on the side of the washbasin and don't clean up. It gets all over my trousers.'

Crumbs and foam (and quite a bit else) had been going on for a year and half, but Michael had kept it all under wraps. In later years it all made perfect sense as I came to discover that in his family background, the voicing of strong opinions and objections had been deeply frowned on by his father. Any potential conflict in the family had been distinctly put on the backburner in the interests of preserving peace and quiet. After 'crumbsgate', I suggested that, in future, we could keep a small notebook that we could both write in when annoying habits were threatening to undermine us, but it never transpired. It says a lot for us that, forty years on, on the frequent occasions Michael and I spend time together, there are constant references to 'crumbs on the breadboard' as shorthand for others' relationship problems. His initiative had helped clear the air. I did not get defensive and lash out with my own shopping list of changes from him that I wanted (in truth, I couldn't really think of any – maybe if he could stop being so damned flawless?) But his speaking up like this was rare, a fact that pointed to another area of our emerging difficulties.

I defy anyone on earth to point to a kinder, gentler man than Michael. I thought that then and I think it now. Walking around a compact city like Oxford with him was, and still is, like being on an election campaign. People crossed the street to shake him by the hand. He didn't kiss many babies, but it wasn't far short of it. He was an amazing listener. As one friend has said of him, 'He's the guy everyone wants to take on holiday.' In our time of living together, the friends I introduced him to would leave after dinner and tell me I was incredibly lucky to have him. And I was. He had engaging blue-green Irish eyes and an undermining kind smile that would have seduced the Devil. Women friends especially would marvel, saying, 'He makes you feel like a million dollars,' And he did, largely because in this madly egocentric, busy world, so rare was it to find a human being who was utterly present and there for you, who defied that all too familiar 'Anyway that's enough about me, how do YOU think I am?'

He possessed an acute observational wit. Frequently a man of few words, but every one counted. Moreover, he was intensely loyal. How many gay men would take a phone call at one in the morning and rush out, all because a best friend was in labour and her hubby was out of the country dealing with the Honduras forestry commission? From gay partner to birthing partner at the John Radcliffe Hospital; all in a matter of minutes.

Friend, I guess is one thing, partner another. The needs and demands are totally different agendas. So one thing I struggled with was his intensely private nature. Why did I want him to be an open book? If you love someone, isn't it all about taking the person as they are and not moulding them into some selfish pre-conceived model that fits your own life? Easy to say this now, but as the younger man, and more 'heart on your sleeve,' I felt terrible rushes of insecurity. I prided myself on a self-image of autonomy which was a distorting lie. While my head told myself and the world that I was a gregarious, self-contained independent soul, my heart knew that his every mood swing, his every word and look had the potential to unseat me, unsettle me. I was no longer (if I had ever been) in control of my own destiny. I started to play mind games. And these games weren't unconscious, below the radar affairs. I knew exactly what I was doing. I'd go all quiet and withdrawn for days on end, hoping it would provoke a response. If none was forthcoming, the withdrawal was stepped up. There was little physical contact between us, just a simmering mood, a backdrop of initially low-key humming, that built and built and then after a week or two just exploded in shouting and rage from both us. These quarrels often harked back to totally misunderstood words, or incidents such as agreeing to go out with another person to the pub and not checking with the other person if it was OK. Michael's wider-based social universe in the city (he had been there since 1971 after all), often meant that he was out night after night and I played the abandoned victim, trapped at home trying to write a Masters thesis on 'Afghanistan: the Demise of a Buffer State'. The explosions were occasionally volcanic. Inevitably they resulted in tearful, energised part-ecstatic, part-desperate sexual exchanges. This would buy us days of relaxed calm. And then, the cycle would start all over again. A chaotic dance of love – and destruction, and more love and …

I often wondered if our hard-of-hearing elderly neighbour heard any of this. Mrs Redgrave was a rather cantankerous type who I felt I'd met before we'd even moved in. When Michael had first shown me the estate agent's details of number thirty nine, he'd giggled as he pointed to the photo of the mid-terraced house. The camera had also captured the façade of number forty next door. There, on sentry duty at her listening post, perched up by the net curtains looking straight down the lens was our neighbour to be. The image bore out a truth that occasionally crossed our path. In October 1985, 'Vanessa' as we dubbed her, caught me over the fence, hanging out the washing. 'Which of you twos does the cooking then?' she probed. 'Take it in turns,' I replied. 'Like we do the washing.' She thought long and hard about this before her next starter for ten. 'When's that friend of yours getting married then?' she wanted to know. I stared back at her face, and that uneven mouth half full of crooked brown teeth. 'Not sure he's the marrying type,' I quipped. She gave a long hard look up at the sky and then returned her gaze on me.

'I bet that Rock Hudson wishes he'd got married.' And off she strutted, to brew up.

The *Sun* had reported that morning that the legendary Hollywood actor and hearthrob, Rock Hudson, had died of AIDS.

Charming.

What the tabloids and vindictive religious zealots called 'the gay plague' cast a huge shadow over the mid 1980s. Michael and I joined a group of a hundred gay men at the John Radcliffe hospital for a two year study programme in which they took blood samples, carried out skin injections and quizzed you confidentially on sexual lifestyles. No stone was left unturned. The indefatigable Sue Trotter and Barbara Morgan would sit opposite you and go through a list of every possible sexual activity under the sun. With one or two of the terms I had to ask for more precise clarification. I mean, 'felching' sounded more like something to do more with preparations for crop rotation than a carnal pastime. And when I was bluntly asked if I had engaged in any 'fisting' since the last appointment, a cry of primordial disgust within had me blurting out, 'Certainly not!' Mary Whitehouse herself could not have been more defiant.

Thus Michael and I found ourselves, from time to time, sitting on plastic chairs in the waiting room, biding our time before we went in to bare all with these well-intentioned intruders, all in the hope of furthering the chances of a scientific breakthrough. For the first few interviews, this was fine. But then that was before Dez appeared on the scene.

In those early days of romantic attraction, the thorny discussions around monogamy and 'open and closed' relationships had never surfaced, even remotely, between us. I think there was an implicit assumption that ours was to be an exclusive encounter. However, bit by bit, alternative voices began to prey on one's mind. 'Wasn't all this monogamy a legacy of a system in which religious and cultural values endeavoured to control people's freedom of expression?

The boy meets girl, marriage and kids nuclear model, still dominating Hollywood movies and our advertising narratives, had enslaved hundreds of people whose 'natural' sexual identities did not fit this one size fits all model, had it not? I had struggled through coming out and facing up to all this with my family, a message of personal liberation, only to opt for what was ostensibly a very familiar way of living. Was there anything queer, anything really radical about setting up home and living happily ever after in a monogamous union? These were all abstract, but nonetheless interesting questions, until the landscape gardener turned up on the scene. And, with no small amount of willing help on my own part, turned our lives upside down.

I met Dez through the University Gay Society. He was not himself a student, but used to help out with the DJ-ing at various social events. He worked freelance on garden development, was a keen giver of organ recitals and had a devoted partner in Andy just a few minutes' walk away from us in St Mary's Road. Two East Oxford gay couples with everything under the moon to talk about from Thatcherism and the Miners' Strike, the John Radcliffe AIDS survey (both were guinea pigs like us) and our fascination with a rather tacky but talented duo called George Michael (talented) and Andrew Ridgeley (tacky) who together constituted the new group Wham! Dez and Andy had been together for years – moving up from Streatham in South London, to the more refined, quieter life of alternative East Oxford. But that quietness was soon challenged by what can only be called an explosion of animal lust.

It exploded between Dez and myself. I will not dress it up with feelings of sentiment. I was never remotely in love with him. There were no odes and incantations. It was just a juggernaut of unstoppable physical desire. When it started between us, these were hardly new pastures for Andy, who had slowly resigned himself over the years to accepting companionship and very little, if any, action between the sheets. But for Michael and myself, this was a bombshell that threatened to redraw all the rules and, who knows, blow the whole project at number thirty nine wide apart.

I didn't pull the wool over his eyes. There was no sneaking off for 'a bit on the side'. I just stated factually that this was happening and I had no intention of pursuing matters beyond the purely physical. No plans to leave, no plans to be Dez's partner (shudder the thought, his scattiness and disorganisation drove me mad most of the time). But there was this electric physical chemistry that seemed so powerful that it would be crazy to thwart it. There was a lean, sinewy muscularity to him which just hit various hormone buttons. Our dealings followed a typical pattern. We'd agree to meet one evening and while Andy and Michael often met up in the pub for a consolatory pint or two, Dez and I would be in the back of his steamed up landscape gardening van in the middle of an Oxfordshire field. I recall one occasion in which we were disturbed by an angry farmer. Typically, I cringed and tried to duck for cover, averting my face. The non-Catholic Dez, simply thrust half of his naked body out of the vehicle and dared the farmer to jump in and join in. At this, the beleaguered landowner simply freaked out and scarpered off across the fields towards the setting sun.

None of this needed necessarily to be a zero sum game for Michael and me, but in our case it was. Trust and ease between us were the victims. It led to tension and tears. This all now seemed a very long way from the exhilaration of escaping the priory and running off into the sunset holding hands. And it was to get worse. Much worse. Several months into all this, Dez called me at home one morning. I was deep into chapter three of my thesis on Afghan tribal politics and I did not especially welcome the distraction. His voice, usually perky and rather Peter Pan-like, betrayed a near funereal tone. 'Come round,' he said. 'Come round. *Now*.' This was not an invitation but a woeful plea. What on earth had happened?

Five minutes later, I was with him at 9 St Mary's Road.

'The AIDS survey. The questionnaire and blood tests,' he said. His eyes welled up and tears began streaming down his face. No, I thought. No. Not him. Not now. Not me. Not Michael. Where might this all end?

As I embraced him and as he sobbed, the cursed word 'HIV' forced its way out of his lips. I felt gripped by a maddening mixture of total pity and mind-numbing anxiety rooted in a total threat to my own physical existence. Yes, we'd 'taken precautions' and as far as I could recall, not gone beyond the line. But there were grey areas. Cases had been reported in the press of people getting AIDS after a handful of cases of oral sex. How to make yourself present one hundred per cent to someone like this, when the voice in your head says, 'it's possibly you next my friend?'

Dez told Andy that evening and I had insisted to him that I must tell Michael as soon as possible. As I trudged back home, all I could think of was a terrible scenario of injustice playing out – that it would be the faithful and utterly loyal Michael who might have become infected by the deathly virus. If we'd both stayed in the Dominican Order we'd now be both writing books, who knows, preaching at the Sorbonne and wrapped in cotton wool away from danger. We were twenty years away from HIV retrovirals and effective medication. This was a mortal sentence. Dez knew it. I knew it. And Michael had to be told. How was I going to find words for this one?

I needn't have worried. As I agonised for the next twenty four hours about how and when and what words to break the news to him, I arrived home early next evening from a long stint in the Bodleian library. Michael had heard me chaining the bike up outside and was waiting inside with our usual tipple (Tesco Fino sherry at £1.69 a bottle was the best our budget would stretch to.) As I sipped away, he looked at me sternly.

'Dez was round an hour ago.'

What the…? I knew by the look on his face that he had spilled his guts and blurted it all out. He'd stolen my lines but I could hardly find the energy to blame him. He'd been seized with guilt and full of remorse. And Michael, being Michael, did not make a big deal of it. He could have done, but chose not to. Perhaps in some small, unconscious way, he now knew that the affair would be over. He was right. It was never the same again.

Dez died at the age of forty three. On the last few occasions I saw him, he had succumbed to attacks of mental instability, delusions and paranoia. His funeral took place at All Saints, a convent of Anglican nuns on the other side of the road in Oxford from where he had lived. It was a fitting location to say our farewells as he had spent hundreds of hours inside the grounds, landscaping the gardens, planting dozens of new shrubs, and nurturing a new rockery. About sixty people turned up, eighty per cent of them gay men, including the well-known singer Tom Robinson, he of the iconic 'Glad to Be Gay' hit from the late 1970s, a long time friend of Dez and Andy's. The Mother Superior of the community had taken it upon herself to perform a eulogy and after the scripture readings, she set about her task.

'As we gather here today to remember Dez, I think we can all agree on one word that describes him down to the core. It is a word that you will all agree on I am sure.'

I could think of a few, especially as my mind dwelt rather bizarrely on events that had gone on in the back of that white van of his.

'That word, ladies and gentlemen is … infectious.'

Tom Robinson, in the pew in front of me, turned and looked. Michael also turned to look at me. We all exchanged looks of 'She doesn't know does she?'

Mother Superior was now in full flow.

'Dez infected everyone he came into contact with. Yes, that's right. Everyone. Without exception.'

Could no one pull the plug?

'His infectiousness came through his love of nature, his immense talents as an organist, his joyous, boundless love of life …' And so it carried on. Later in the after service gathering to feast on salmon spread finger rolls and dinky pork pies, Tom Robinson and I began exchanging stories. I discovered that for Dez's fortieth birthday, several of his older London friends from the S and M scene had clubbed together for a special kind of fund: he'd been granted lashes by a coterie of leather men: one for every year of his fast fading life. No doubt he 'infected' all of them with his inexhaustible desire for pain. I thought it best not to share this with the nuns over the black forest gateau. Michael and I left the gathering and strolled back to number thirty nine in near silence. If I had been him, I would have been sorely tempted into unworthy thoughts about staying the distance and having the final word after all those years. But not a shred of bitterness. Just a sombre, respectful silence. With Dez no more, I reflected on a simple truth: not once during that crazy liaison had Michael tried to force my hand, making me choose or using his understandable upset to curtail my behaviour. Love can indeed be humbling. Maybe this impressive *sang froid* was all down to a gently unfolding new outlook on the world?

Michael's post-Catholic ventures had led him to become a keen attender of the Oxford Friends' meeting house. While I continued to attend mass, mostly at Blackfriars, with the Dominicans, he had tentatively embraced the Quakers. Throughout all the highs and lows, the exhilaration of intimacy and the poisonous threat of jealousies and insecurity, we were sustained throughout with a healthy respect for the big questions. And that usually meant him coming, once or twice a year, to the Church's big feasts of Christmas and Easter and staying up well into the wee small hours, among friends, pondering the outrageous, but yet consoling claims of the gospel's resurrection narrative. Rome's 1986 document, 'On the Pastoral Care of Homosexual Persons,' written and signed off by Cardinal Joseph Ratzinger, landed on us like some unexploded bomb during this period. *Homosexualitatis Problema*, to give it its full Latin name, informed me that I was 'objectively disordered' on account of my same sex attraction and that my living with Michael amounted to grave sin. It was a teaching so utterly at odds with the grace and gift of this man's life to me that I took all of ten seconds to dwell on it and place it to one side. I knew in my heart that the core of my faith was the Incarnation of God as human. Jesus had said not a single word about people like me in all his teaching ministry. His non-judgemental outlook and siding with outsiders like the Samaritans, the hated tax collectors and the like spoke a hundred times more to me than *Homosexualitatis Problema*. Michael, of course, could casually quip that the Quakers had no such thing as a teaching Magisterium. It's just that for me (and yes, I did attend quite a few of those meetings with him), all that silence and a string of 'Thoughts for the day' type contributions from middle class Oxfordians did not quite cut the mustard, even if as human beings the Quakers were infinitely more engaging as practioners of good works compared to my own Roman tribe.

Post Dez, we embarked on a calmer phase. In time-honoured fashion, the childless couple adopted their 'children', two black and white moggies: Derek and Pushtu (the latter's name emerging from my academic work on Afghanistan, the name of the language of the Pathan tribe of the North West Frontier Province). We discovered hiking and bought our first serious walking boots. After a modest start, over a spell of three or four years, an impressive array of ordnance survey maps and walking books was amassed which, more often than not lured us to Shropshire and the Welsh borders for idyllic sojourns in Housman country. That Afghan connection, by pure serendipity, landed me my first proper full time job. *The Times*, in the guise of the then Deputy Editor (now Sir) Peter Stothard, had placed an ad for a trainee journalist, in the University of Oxford Careers Service. He took a room at the Randolph Hotel on the corner of Beaumont Street and on a late Friday afternoon I was the last of sixteen candidates to be interviewed. 'Come in, come in…' he beckoned. 'I've been at this for two whole days. I think we need a drink, don't you?' Within ten minutes we were sipping some fizz, talking about monasticism, the Dominicans and Thatcherism. 'The boss knows all about Afghanistan. You need to come up to London and meet him.' The boss was Charles Douglas-Home, a successful editor who had doubled the paper's circulation, but, aged only forty eight, was now battling with cancer and was in the final months of his life. When I met him a week later, I didn't even have a suit and had to borrow a rather ill-fitting black stripy affair from a mate. But by now, those earlier late 1970s nerves at St Peter's College had dissipated. I got the job. Within weeks, I found myself being asked to write editorials on foreign affairs for *The Thunderer*. On an old fashioned typewriter. Share prices in Tippex went through the roof. Then within six months, the Murdoch group made a dramatic announcement. They were ceasing production of all their papers at Grays Inn Road in central London and relocating to Wapping at a new plant with state of the art new technology. Many of the traditional printers' jobs would be lost. News International had spent nearly two years with Brenda Dean's SOGAT union trying to agree redundancy terms. There was little public sympathy for the printers on account of decades of their corrupt Spanish practices, so when Murdoch lost his patience and announced his fait accompli, what was I to do? I'd been paying my monthly subs to the National Union of Journalists and the NUJ line was decidedly boycotting the move to Wapping. On a Friday evening in late January 1986, I asked a union rep where the NUJ chapel meeting was to be held.

'Er … you can't attend pal.'

'Why ever not?'

'You never did your two years of training in the provinces. A lot of the members opposed your membership.'

'But you've been cashing my cheques every month.'

'Er, sorry about that. Look on it this way, if you go to work at Wapping, you won't be a scab.'

So off to Wapping I went. I lost a number of friends, many of whom joined in the Saturday night picket on Pennington Street London E1, to try and stop the News International newspaper lorries leaving. The Thatcher government's defeat of the miners was still fresh in the mind and Wapping was seen as the next chapter in the battle. (I never saw the disputes having much in common, but that is another matter.) Three years ago I'd been in a secluded Catholic priory contemplating Aquinas. Now I was being bussed through a war zone in armour-plated vehicles. The pick-up point for these metal-grilled chariots changed from day to day and we all had a top secret number to call every night to check on next day's rendezvous point. On one terrible morning, just as one of the buses was approaching Tower Hill, a group of five heavies (presumably printers from SOGAT, or their allies?), grabbed me as I tried to climb onto the bus. I was kicked and punched repeatedly...

'You bleedin' scab. You nicked our fucking job.'

I'm sorry? How precisely had I stolen their job? I'd like to have seen them write editorials on the Strategic Arms Limitation Talks (SALT I and II), or President Reagan's SDI, Strategic Defence Initiative (or 'Star Wars' as it was more commonly called). Be that as it may, they made a mess of my face, cutting my eyebrows, bruising my mouth and upper lip and taking a large chunk out of my upper right incisor. Charles Wilson, the new tough Glaswegian editor nicknamed 'Gorbalschev', who had replaced his cancer-ridden predecessor, wanted to put my mug shot on the front page of the next day's *Times*. It would have been a huge PR coup for News International in the context of the ferocious industrial clash:

'Union thugs beat up young ex-friar reporter'

But mindful of my mother's potential reaction, much to Wilson's annoyance, I declined to co-operate. Mr Murdoch's finance department picked up the dental bill for four sessions of root canal treatment. Within two years, nearly all the papers, many of whom had slated Murdoch's introduction of the new technology, had also left Fleet Street and had installed the new modes of production. As one commentator remarked: 'Murdoch forced his way, with scars and wounds, through the barbed hedge and the rest of Fleet Street followed him through the gap he forged.'

Commuting from Oxford to Wapping, regularly a 6am to 9pm engagement, was leading to the old batteries being run down. Michael suggested I put down a deposit on a small one-bed *pied-a-terre* to reduce the daily drudgery, so a charmingly modest top floor pad was acquired off Peckham Rye Common in East Dulwich London SE22 on my £14,500 salary for the bargain basement sum of £37,500. To avoid us becoming a 'weekend relationship', he'd make the trip to London at least once a week. When I left newspapers for TV, first with London Weekend TV's *Weekend World* and then BBC2's *Newsnight*, the impact on our time together became even more pronounced. On one occasion, following the Tiananmen Square massacre in Beijing, Michael returned to our East Oxford home to find a curt post-it note on the kitchen counter.

'Won't be back tonight … gone to Hong Kong.'

All this to-ing and fro-ing was just accepted as part of how it had to be. And as we know, if over exposure is the Achilles heel of a long term relationship, who's to say that these periods apart were necessary detrimental? And protracted time spent together was usually relaxed and increasingly took in far flung horizons. By 1990 we'd graduated as far as house exchanges, with an especially unforgettable five week trip to California with university friends Ruth and Jeremy who announced, on arrival in San Francisco, that they had made a pledge to marry each other on holiday, seven thousand miles away from their families. Marriage vows were made in front of a Nevada Sheriff named Judge Doug Struthers and the epic journey continued down to Death Valley, playing bowling at 2am in Las Vegas and hiking in the Grand Canyon. On the return, through the two hundred and twenty nine square miles of the Zion National Park in Utah, with its steep red cliffs, waterfalls and hanging gardens, something happened which proved to be rather portentous.

On one especially steep ascent of one of the red cliffs, walkers were invited to complete the journey across a very narrow ledge. To provide support, there were chains secured on posts on the side of the path. It was fairly hairy going, but I had Ruth and Jeremy ahead and so I just followed suit. But behind me Michael had began to struggle. It was partly vertigo, but also partly he was saying 'No way am I walking across that tightrope.' Crassly and insensitively, I castigated him for it, just as I had done when he had declined to descend the horrendous loose scree of the Fox's Path on Cadair Idris in Snowdonia National Park three years before (where several fatalities had occurred over the years). It was almost back to schoolboy name-calling on my part – and I cringe now when I recall it. He made his way back to the start alone. After Ruth, Jeremy and I stormed the summit, we rejoined him, but that night, there was one of those awful atmospheres again, where every word, every look and gesture was magnified, open to misinterpretation. It touched a nerve underneath – even though neither of us could quite nail down precisely what it was.

Summer the following year and another house exchange. But this time it came with 'fatal' consequences.

I had sold up in South East London and opted for a larger two bedroom flat in Cricklewood, North West London, which was hugely more convenient for me at my new producer's job with the BBC in Shepherd's Bush. The chosen summer vacation location was Bologna. Our exchangees, Alberto and Emilia, came over from Italy the night before. They had broken English, and I had cobbled a few adapted phrases together from a hastily purchased Berlitz phrase book. It's amazing how you can explain how the boiler works with a few well-appointed visual cues. Derek and Pushtu's electronic cat flap and their specially procured collar magnets were items of particular fascination for *I Bolognesi.* Our bags were already packed for our early departure, but over dinner, a few words from Alberto filled both Michael and I with a certain apprehension.

'But your flat … I mean it is so large and spacious … and so peaceful. So quiet.'

Emilia now joined in.

'Yes, I mean you have beautiful garden. We feel so bad. Our flat is not … is not, er … the same.'

This was dismissed with English politeness. On retiring to

bed, we anxiously looked, once more, at the photos they had sent us through the Intervac agency. The place looked modest. But it was about a mile and half, two miles from the centre and – hey – it was for two and half weeks only. And goodness, the previous year the boot had been on the other foot. Our lovely Californian couple, Larry and Judith, had bequeathed us an enormous four bedroom Victorian townhouse with landscaped terraced garden in San Francisco's Noe Valley in exchange for our humble Oxford terrace. You win some you lose some.

The following afternoon, nine hundred miles from home, we were now able to understand fully the Italians' unease. It was nearly forty degrees when we pitched up off the bus. The drab multistorey building which housed their apartment was located about five metres from the slip road to the motorway. Once we gained access to our new home, we saw that the lounge and bedroom windows were perched over Italy's M1 motorway. The place was like an oven, but the moment you opened the windows to allow a little air in, it felt like an army of deafening HGVs were about to pour in through the windows and mow you down.

'At least there was a promise of air conditioning,' said Michael, eager to rescue the situation. The 'air conditioning' turned out to be two huge black blocks, like loudspeakers, erected on stands. The moment you flicked the switch, they roared into action with an eardrum splitting intensity that was twice the decibel level of the traffic. Two and a half weeks. I pined for our garden – and the pussy flap.

Typically, I became all mopey and quiet. But Michael got the map out. 'Look, we chose Bolgona because of its rail access. You can get everywhere from here.' And he was right. It was just over an hour down to Florence, with Siena a short distance beyond. Ravenna was just up the road to the north east, and further afield, even Verona and Venice were well within our grasp. Anything that meant getting out of that cauldron of an apartment.

And so, several days later, to Venice. Gondolas, Dirk

Bogarde as Von Aschenbach and the adagietto of Mahler's fifth symphony, Titian, Giotto and St Mark's and … well I had seen it all on television but would it deliver in real life? And the Bridge of Sighs, *Il Ponte Dei Sospiri*, where legend has it that lovers will be granted eternal happiness together if they kiss on a gondola underneath it at sunset. Venice did NOT disappoint, especially in the evenings. It is only then when the crowds dispersed. You got off the beaten track and your spirit was caressed by the sounds of lapping water and radiant amber sunlight on church windows.

On our final evening in Venice we were both in especially high spirits. We'd had the good fortune to happen upon an eccentric English tour guide on day one at St Mark's who had been worth his weight in gold. Over a post tour coffee he'd started to rave about an island called, 'Torcello'. 'The Last Judgement mosaic there is better than anything in Venice,' he said, so, on our final day, his two new disciples had joined him on the one hour boat trip to the seventh century Basilica of Santa Maria Assunta. Neither of us had ever seen anything like it. Hell divided into six compartments of eternal separation, but suspended above them, the souls of the saved in Abraham's bosom, cast as children. The Good Thief from the Crucifixion, who indeed had found paradise as he had been promised and the Archangel Michael, fighting off demons whose elastic arms were trying to tip the judgement scales and send souls down below. Wild beasts and sea monsters, on the Day of Resurrection, spat out their victims. All pain and injustice was being countered in one almighty suffocatingly stupendous tableau.

On our final evening, we were still raving about the imagery as we sauntered together through the Venetian streets, in search of an after dinner drink in a bar called, 'Paradiso Perduto' … Paradise Lost. I'd seen the place listed in a travel magazine and it had been described as 'bohemian'. We found it tucked away on the Fondamenta Misericordia. It was now just after eleven pm and as soon as we entered, I scanned the place and it was full of 'alternative types' … few, if any tourists, not an obviously queer place, but a few looks cast in our direction suggested we weren't the only gays who had strayed from paradise. I went to the bar and ordered two large glasses of Amaretto, thinking to myself, 'this place looks good for a few hours. A few more drinks, talk to some of the people, maybe a bit of silly late night dancing … what the hell.'

I took the drink over to Michael. After a short silence he said. 'Better not take too long over that, there's a sort of curfew at the hotel and I think they close the doors around half midnight.' These words entered my ears. My brain processed them and it was as though a huge hammer then shattered a large pane of glass. I thought, 'We're so different. How could I be thinking 4 or 5am and Michael is thinking that?' It wasn't a crude sense of 'I'm right and he's wrong,' just a simple formula of words that had opened up a space. A disturbingly large space. I said nothing. Years ago, I'd have argued the case for the all-nighter, but I simply mumbled, 'No, you're right.' We walked back across the semi-abandoned piazza in near silence just after midnight.

That night I didn't sleep a wink. Three double espressos taken between 4pm and 10pm may have had something to do with it. But I can now still see the room. Michael was dozing to my right. Through the bedroom window, a piercing street light caught the outline shapes of some folded cotton sheets that were perched on top of a wooden wardrobe. Their creased outlines appeared to change shape at regular intervals throughout the night – like a menacing kaleidoscope of haunting faces looking down menacingly from on high. I looked at Michael sleeping angelically next to me and a torrent of tears began to flow. This man who had never betrayed me with anyone. Who through all the Dez business had never once threatened to call it off, or make me choose – who had borne it all with such grace and restraint at no small personal cost to his own sanity and that terrible 'green eyed monster' of sexual jealousy which carves out your guts. Whose very life I might have put at risk with HIV. And what was I thinking now? That there was an unassailable chasm between us in our attitudes to risk, to uncertainty. And all because of a difference of opinion in Paradise Lost over a late night drink. Maybe it was the eleven year gap between us that explained a growing gulf in energy levels? Or perhaps I was still harbouring a religious impulse for total transcendence and was guilty of a crass idolatry, expecting that this merely mortal man could single-handedly solve all my soul's ills? As the night moved on and dawn broke, I knew that this wasn't some passing nocturnal horror show. I knew I had reached a point of no return. In a very deep, but unthought-out way, I felt that I was being held back, stifled. I had no real sense of where I wanted to go from here, but that my wings were being clipped.

We returned to Bologna the following morning and I tried my best to mask what had happened. That evening, in another bar, *Il Circolo Pickwick*, ironically situated on the Via San Felice, I spilled my guts. Michael looked at me incredulously. Neither of us had seen this coming, but at least to me, it did all now make some kind of sense. It wasn't long before we were both engulfed in tears. We must have looked a very strange sight together on that Sunday evening late in August 1991.

How we got through the last days in that hellish apartment without a joint nervous breakdown I will never know. When we returned to London, we were mercifully spared the separate beds dilemma. Many weeks previous, Michael's brother, Peter, had hatched a plan to come down from Liverpool and visit with his wife Ann and their three young children. In a two bedroom apartment, this meant Michael on the sofa-bed in the lounge and me? … I found myself in a hastily-erected tent at the bottom of the hundred foot garden, under an enormous pear tree. I communed for a week with an army of pesky grey squirrels.

Within a month I had moved out. During our final year together, Michael had moved to London to take up a temporary post as director of a charity, Disability Alliance. His misgivings about a non-disabled person heading up a disability campaign proved to be well founded and so he would eventually return to Oxford and embark on a disability research project at the ancient university, before returning to the Law Department at what had, by then, become Oxford Brookes University. But that would be some way down the road. In the immediate aftermath of our separation, there was no way that I could have asked him to leave that London flat. He had been put through the mill enough as it was. Car, cats and our north west London neighbours offered a scarce crumb of continuity.

In the aftermath of one of the most painful periods of upheaval in my life, I have often asked myself this question: 'would I have done all this if we had been civilly partnered or married? Or even more, if, in a church, I had earlier publicly vowed to stay with this man through thick and thin?' Did I, in the end, call it right, or, lacking a wider context of support and restraining voices, did I pull the trigger too quickly and end up leaving us both scarred? Perhaps one truth lies in a conversation I recall having with Michael many years into our bold adventure. 'What would you have done if marriage had been an option for us?' he had asked me. My response was perhaps telling, 'Well maybe all this lack of equality has a silver lining.'

'What do you mean?', he remarked, looking puzzled.

'I'm so glad it's not an option. In that way, I don't have to face up to it.'

The words, perhaps, of a commitment-phobe?

Twenty six years since 'Paradise Lost', Michael and I talk at least once a week.

His is the first name and address in my passport 'contact details' section.

We holiday together still, from time to time.

I avoid leaving crumbs on the breadboard – at all costs.

And he is, still, the person who knows me better than anyone.

6

When my father helped me bury my father

People often do strange things after major relationship break-ups. And the 're-bound' syndrome can take on a variety of manifestations. Some embark on a wildly promiscuous campaign in which they sleep with everyone and get to know no one. Others withdraw into a private world, trusting nothing and no one, their sole purpose in the world it seems is to line the therapist's coffers. But there's a third type who just go for sublimation into the world of work. Post-Michael, that was very much my way of being in the world and for months on end, BBC news and current affairs was the recipient of all this diverted emotional energy. Of course, you're trying to bravely look forward from your scary vantage point of being single once more in the world. But then the past leaps out to grab you and plunge you into what can only be described as pure black comedy.

BBC *Panorama* editing suite, late October 1992. I've been in Arkansas for what seems an eternity, making a documentary about Bill Clinton's bid for the US Presidency. We've called the film, 'The Comeback Kid'. It's been a Herculean labour of love, but once it's safely on air at 9.35pm, I slumped into a chair in the office and watched the finished product going out 'live' on TV. The opening sequence featured a paddlesteamer on the Mississippi River and a country and western guitarist pitching his musical satire at the incumbent president, George Herbert Walker Bush.

'No the trickle down didn't, and the well is running dry, and the man at the top don't even know why.
I guess the joke's on us, I guess he was only kiddin'. 'Cos the rich got richer and the trickle down didn't.'

At this juncture our newly discovered artist from Little Rock, looked straight into the camera and delivered, with perfect timing.

'Read my lips.'

This is the mantra that Bush senior had used for nearly every day of his 1988 election campaign to assure the voters that, under no stretch of the imagination would he put up taxes. On gaining office he – surprise, surprise – put up taxes.

I'd seen the sequence about forty times, but I still managed a fatigued smile, before a member of the production team appeared from out of the blue and drew up a chair. She had a most serious expression on her face. What now? Had I gone over my allocated programme budget?

'Are you feeling strong?' was the question. I'd hardly slept for three days. A simple shrug of the shoulders was all I could muster. She then resumed, 'because we've had a phone call from one of your relatives.' Hello?

'I'm afraid your Dad's passed away. I've never had to do this kind of thing before. It feels a little crass, but I can't think of any other way to tell you. Mark, I'm so sorry.'

What the …? I'd spoken to him before the United game at the weekend and he'd seemed as right as rain. This is the pre-mobile era of course, and all the family had known I was up against the clock at *Panorama,* hence an expected radio silence. I sensed a litany of faces in the office staring at me. A glass of whisky for me now appeared from nowhere. My head felt as though it was on one of those Hitchcockian merry-go-rounds. When it slowed up, I pulled the phone on my desk closer and rang... It was now 10pm.

'Hello, Swinton 8199.'

A voice beyond the grave. It was my father. I said nothing. My mouth was in a vice.

'Hello … hello, who's that? Wrong number is it?'

'Dad, dad, it's me …' I heard him cover the mouthpiece and then my mother's voice perked up, 'Tell him he's spoiling the programme. Tell him we're still watching it.' I was flattered they were even tuning in. It was, after all, way beyond their bedtime.

So I called back in fifteen minutes, once I'd got over the second 'Comeback' of the night. And this time, I'd got my story ready.

'Just rang to see what you made of the goalless draw at Blackburn on Saturday.' I never, *ever,* called as late as 10.15pm. I sensed Dad thought it all a bit odd. 'Are you in trouble?' he asked finally after an uncomfortably awkward silence. I shrugged off his question and our rather forced chat came to an abrupt end. Immediately I made a beeline for the production team member who'd imparted the earlier news of my father's, now it seems, not so untimely death.

'He said he was your uncle, your uncle Ronnie,' came the reply. I retorted straight away that I had no such relative of the said name. 'This is weird,' said Amanda. Hang on, the name's on a piece of paper.' The slip was duly handed over. *Ronnie Craddock.* Next to it was written a number with a recognisable Stockport STD dialling code.

Craddock. Craddock. Hang on a moment.

Oh hell.

Bob Craddock was a welder who'd worked for Schreiber Furniture in Manchester's enormous Trafford Park industrial estate. I'd met him in the most bizarre of circumstances. In my final year at grammar school in 1977, I'd been gently popping my head above the parapet on the city's nascent gay scene. Once a week there was a disco at Manchester Polytechnic and there, dancing to the sound of Baccara and Boney M, I'd come across a tall handsome chap called Andrew who'd asked me out on a date. We'd met three times, before he made it very clear that sexual contact was a key part of his core needs. I was now 17 and, bearing in mind all the historic heartaches with Paul, I figured it was about time I acquired some real experience. On Maundy Thursday evening, after the mass of the Lord's supper with the air thick still with tales of Judas's betrayal, I made my excuses to my parents. I told them I was staying overnight at Paul's house at Astley near Leigh (he had been supportive and agreed to cover for me). At 9.30pm I pitched up at Slingsby's, the newest of Manchester's gay venues. I looked round the club for Andrew but he was nowhere to be seen. 10pm came. 10.15pm. Still no sign of him. The bloody Judas – I had not even been betrayed with a kiss. Then I felt a hand on my shoulder. I turned round to find a very thick set, squat man in his late thirties. He looked like the kind of hard bloke you saw in prison movies – a touch of Shawshank in Salford. His distinctive square jaw provided the baseline for a mischievous smile. He winked at me. I blushed instantly and thanked the Lord for the very low-level moody lighting.

'He's not coming,' he said.

'What do you mean?' I answered back.

'Andrew. He's got back with his ex, André. He sent me here to tell you. Fancy a drink then, buggerlugs?' He winked again and I looked around anywhere but into his eyes. Why is somebody fancying you always so embarrassing? Bob knew I was in a pickle. Footloose and fancy free on the town with nowhere to go. 'Fancy a ride up to Dundee?' he quipped. 'What, *now*?' I asked. It transpired he'd promised an overnight lift in his work van to three singers, music students at the Royal Northern College of Music. Bob certainly had an eye for the younger man – *Death in Venice*'s fated hero was now recast as a welder. He'd seen me with Andrew in one or two of Manchester's bars such as the Rembrandt and the New Union in recent weeks and had clearly been biding his time.

Why did I begin a tempestuous two year affair with a manual worker from a factory that made some of the UK's best value bedside cabinets? He was no oil painting, for sure, but he was your classic 'man's man'. Fond of the drink, he was known on the gay scene as 'Bacardi Bob,' a man whose bouts with the booze often ended in some fairly savage fights. Bob was frequently barred from pubs and clubs only to re-emerge from the 'sin bin' to start all over again. Within weeks of this first Maundy Thursday meeting, he was unambiguously besotted with me. Given the context of the ongoing tensions with my father, here was an older man throwing himself at me unconditionally. It made me feel good about myself, perhaps, for about the first real time in my life.

Thus it was that Bob and I became an unlikely double act at Schreiber Furniture later that summer. He got me a temporary job as a 'fitter's mate' just two months before I was due to head off to University. The hours were gruelling, but paying no tax and 'stoppages' as a student, it meant I was lining my pockets and building up a nest egg to supplement my future student grant.

Now combining forbidden same-sex love and a working environment of overalled manual workers was no easy task. Many a time Bob's sudden hormonal lunchtime urgings led us to some of the darker recesses of the factory's hidden nooks and crannies and, on at least two occasions, we were within seconds of being discovered. If desire is indeed linked to prohibition, here is a textbook case of the ideal laboratory conditions for the cultivation of human sexual attraction. For what greater forbidden fruit can there be than same sex love in the late 1970s, in a factory full of manual workers, a stone's throw from Manchester United's Old Trafford football ground?

So, what on earth has Bob Craddock, 1977, got to do with the news of my 'father's death?' It all boils down to a most bizarre set of events which took place not far from the factory gates at Schreiber in the summer of that year. Bob was getting increasingly pushy about impromptu sex at work, to such an extent that he was in serious danger of blowing our cover. In truth, I was also beginning to get more and more unnerved by the extent of his doting on me. In clubs and bars he'd clock anyone who was looking at me and start up fights on the smallest pretext. Jealousy and possessiveness were coming more and more to the fore. On one especially savage night he'd glassed a bloke who'd winked at me from across the bar. Worst of all, he'd taken a simple passport photo from my wallet that he particularly liked, and sent it off to a portrait artist friend of his. One evening after work, I walked into his flat to see an enormous five by three feet framed picture of myself staring across the lounge at me. It was hideous. On seeing it I instantly felt trapped. I had become a trophy, a commodity. I moved to take it down and a scrap ensued – which ended in tears and the inevitable but temporary healing sex. But surely safer here at 56 Wood Road, Whalley Range, than in that factory?

However, as arguments became more and more frequent on work duty, the more I feared our factory workers would spot our increasingly frequent niggles erupting into shouting matches and landing us in the soup. Early one Thursday afternoon, after another ding-dong in the boiler room, I completely lost it. 'You can stuff the job. It's all over – the whole damn thing. I'm off.' I flung my overalls down in front of him and sped off at the rate of knots past the factory gates.

I could hear him shouting behind me, but with impeccable timing, a 651 bus was approaching. I hailed it, climbed swiftly on board with about a dozen other factory staff who had just finished the early shift and we departed, sans Bob, towards Eccles and the eventual destination of Clifton Junction. Some three or four minutes must have passed before I felt a tap on my shoulder. As I turned round, I recognised one of the canteen ladies. Normally she'd be dishing us up the 1200 calorie cardiac arrest fry-up at 9.30am. This time she simply said, 'Sorry love. Didn't want to disturb and all that. It's just that ...' She gestured towards the side window of the bus. 'There's a man out there and ... well, I could be wrong, but I think he's trying to get your attention.' I craned my neck over to spot a familiar looking metallic blue ford Cortina slowly making up ground. My first reaction was to look away, but gradually its driver was seizing the attention of the passengers. Our bus came to a halt at the next bus stop, not far from the Kellogg's Cereals factory, just short of Dumplington Circle near Barton Bridge and the Manchester Ship Canal. With another dozen shift workers set to board the bus, this gave ample time for the Cortina and its doggedly persistent driver to amble up alongside our vehicle, in full view of everyone on board. The problem was that the said 1973 metallic blue car had now strayed onto the opposing side of the road blocking the advance of an approaching double decker bus which was blazing its horn. The same was true of half a dozen other drivers caught behind it. At this point, Bob leant over and his contorted red face appeared out of the window.

'I love you. Honest. Don't let it end like this. Here, I'll give you a pay rise. Just, please, get off the *fucking* bus.'

My face went the colour of a Guernsey Tom. Baffled and bemused fellow passengers searched the bus in vain for the Swedish blonde bombshell – for only she surely could be the object of such a passionate outburst? But when they saw me hiding behind my copy of the *Guardian*, that was all they needed.

'It's *him*. Bloody hell. It's the young 'un! *Bum chums!*'

Holding my newspaper aloft in front of my glowing face, I stumbled down the central aisle in desperate search of the front door. Almost all of the people now stamping the floor and barracking me were Schreiber employees. I squeezed past those who were still boarding, almost falling out of the bus, and then ran round to the stationary Cortina. On clambering in to the passenger seat, a self-satisfied Bob smiled at me. 'Well. That worked didn't it?'

'You idiot,' I screamed. 'Ninety per cent of the people on that bus work at Schreiber's. What are we gonna tell them if we have to go in tomorrow? Or is that it? Have you given up your job?' I said. A furrowed expression seized the Craddock forehead. 'No fear,' he said. 'I'll think of summat.'

And think he did. The following morning, I dragged my feet along Tenax Road at 7.30am and saw the factory gates looming ahead. It was like first day nerves at school times ten. A cluster of people were hovering. As they came more sharply into focus, I could make out they were pointing at me. Within metres of the gatekeeper's lodge, they stepped forward to greet me. I had been expecting mockery and name-calling. But instead, there were looks of concern. Even a smack of the odd contrite face.

'Eh, lad ... you should have said,' said Jimmy, one of the foremen.

'Said what?' I retorted.

'About you ... and yer Dad.'

What? Dad?

'I mean we knew he was divorced and all that. And that he had a lad. But we hadn't put two and two together.'

The canteen woman who'd alerted me to Bob's marauding presence the day before, now chipped in.

'You look alike. Spitting image. We should all have guessed, but we're too daft. He got in earlier to let us all know.' Some twenty metres away, I could make out Bob, already in his welder's overalls, smiling like the Cheshire Cat.

'I mean, all that commotion,' said Jimmy. '"I love you" and all that. When we all heard him doing his pieces, we thought you were a couple of ... yer know, fudge packers.' At this point, the woman from the canteen winced. 'But Dads and sons fall out don't they? I mean, no one's perfect. Folk have to get on.'

As the truth of Bob's canny, deft cover story began to sink in, I took a few steps away from the pack and moved towards him. He'd lit up a Senior Service and was puffing away contentedly.

'So. *Dad*. Is this another one of your Walter Mitty numbers?'

But it wasn't. He took me to one side and explained how he'd got married in the early 1960s to the daughter of a local prominent businessman near Bury. She and Bob had both been young, at it like ferrets and the next thing, Bob's at the altar barely having turned twenty. The marriage lasts a mere two years, or a little more, before they part. Mother leaves with their only child. His name, Bob tells me, uncannily – was Mark.

Fifteen years separated that bizarre darkly comical scene on the bus in Trafford Park from the phone call to the *Panorama* office. After I went to University and then became a Dominican friar, I had seen less and less of Bob as I found his jealousy and insecurity at times unbearable. But this phone call from 'Uncle Ronnie Craddock' meant one thing only: Bob had gone to his grave at the tender age of fifty five or so. What's more, he'd given my name out to his family as his long lost son, repeating to them the carbon copy of the tale which had got us both off the hook in the presence of the factory workers in 1977. Only this time, he wasn't around to pick up the pieces. If I followed through the logic, it appeared I was being asked to go and bury my ex-lover, but his remaining family all thought he was my father. I was, by this account, 'bereaved' and I would now be invited to a long delayed family reunion.

Hell.

Clutching the piece of paper with that phone number on it, I make contact with 'Uncle Ronnie'. When I introduce myself, there's an audible relief in his voice, 'Thank goodness we traced you. Your Dad said you worked at the Beeb. He was very proud you know. Taped all your programmes, cut out all your press articles. We recovered them all from a pile of boxes in his flat.' Bob, it emerged, had collapsed at work with chest pains. He was rushed to Wythenshawe Hospital, but he'd suffered a massive cardiac arrest and was pronounced dead, well before the ambulance even made it into the hospital precinct. What was I to do? It's clear Bob had stayed well and firmly in his family closet. No doubt Ronnie and his wife had gone round to the flat to recover his things. *That enlarged photo portrait on the wall over his fireplace.* Had it stayed intact? Who knows?

'Look, Ronnie, I need to spell something out,' I said, 'about Bob and me. I mean, the thing is, we were very close, er, as friends, but ... well he wasn't my Dad. My Dad lives in north Manchester. And he was never a welder. He worked on the buses.'

A very long silence ensues. I can hear Ronnie weighing up what I am telling him. 'But you must be,' he said. 'I mean he never stopped talking about you. All the holiday snaps we've seen, all your TV and media business ... all the tales of how he taught you at work.'

What I try and persuade him of is that we enjoyed a friendship akin to father and son in as much as he taught me to drive, and I listened attentively to him. I'd talked long hours to him about religious faith which resulted in him returning to church attendance after twenty years' absence, a fact that his family noted with approval. Bob, it was noted after the marriage break-up, was a lost soul who'd needed some stability in his life, an anchor. But in the end, it was just 'good friends', an older man taking a younger man under his wing. As for the 'real' son – God knows where he had ended up, but that was of no interest to Ronnie.

'So you'll be coming to the funeral then?' he said. Grammatically speaking this reads as a question but its pragmatic purpose served the function of a no-nonsense command. 'Well, really I'm not sure that's wise,' I began. 'Because the thing is,' he interrupted, 'Bob talked a lot about you to the rest of the family. And after an absence of thirty years or so, you can understand that they're dying to see you.' Ronnie, it seems, had been planning his own little Death and Resurrection narrative. And he'd wasted no time. A notice had gone in the *Manchester Evening News*, alerting some of the more outrageous members of the local gay community to start polishing their shoes, booking appointments at the hair salon and stocking up on the foundation and mascara. The Schreiber welders would no doubt eagerly embrace any chance of a day off work, so-called 'respect leave', to go and give their mate an alcohol-drenched send-off. And here was Ronnie, in quite a quandary. If Bob *had* repeated all his tales about me being his son to all and sundry, my not turning up, or denying my status as the fruit of his loins ran the risk of exposing him as an out and out liar. Ronnie wanted me to play along. A day, not even a day, just a couple of hours of innocent role-playing – a short sweet service at Gorton Cemetery followed by some quick grub and a pint of beer and then we could all go our separate ways. No corpses, no bloodletting. No one loses face. This was the compromise solution that was put to me over the phone. It seemed to me the best of a lot of very unsavoury choices.

As the ensuing week unfolded, I saw the notice in the *Evening News*, but had no idea that the whole of Bob's kaleidoscopic life was going to be sucked into the vortex that was his looming funeral. The day before the service, I pitched up at the (real) parental home.

'What's the special occasion?' asked my Dad as I wandered into the front room. Mother was sitting there doing some dress alterations on her ancient Singer sewing machine for her clients. She said nothing, but I could sense she was listening acutely.

'Er, bit sad really. Funeral.' I muttered.

'Funeral?' said my father. 'Well, whose? You said nothing 'bout it t'other night on that phone call.'

'You won't remember him,' I answered. 'That bloke who got me that summer job at Schreiber's all those years ago.'

'Before he went to university,' chipped in my mother. She took the foot off her Singer sewing pedal and looked up. 'Taught him to drive. Metallic blue Cortina.' I could see that the light was beginning to dawn on my dad's face. 'That's right. Cortina. M reg.' My father had never learnt to drive and I always felt that my mother's decision to take to the steering wheel aged fifty six and pass her test (on the fifth attempt – she never quite clocked those unmarked junctions a hundred metres from the Driving Test Centre) was a gentle undermining of his northern masculinity. Where I came from, fathers frequently took their sons out for driving practice on Sundays (often, coincidentally on the deserted weekend roads of the Trafford Park Industrial Estate.) When my mother had traditionally asked how my driving practice was going all those years ago, I noted the frequency with which my father either fell totally silent or used it as an opportunity to head off and put the kettle on and take refuge in the Tetley tea bags.

'Well he can't have been that old. In his fifties? What was his name now … Bert. Billy … no, *Bob* …'

'What did he die of?' asked my mother looking all concerned. *Did she know?* She had that look on her face. Her X-ray machine gaze. Her, 'I know but I'm not letting on in case your father finds out' face. 'Heart attack at work,' I said. 'He was fifty five.'

'Blimey,' said my father.

'So are you doing a reading then?' Ever since the grammar school debating team had needed a chairman, my father had been proud of his son's confident public speaking. 'That's right,' I said, 'A nice bible reading. Not sure if there'll be a eulogy.'

After a silence hovering somewhere in the no man's land between comfortable and awkward, my father piped up.

'Tomorrow you say. Where?'

'Gorton Cemetery. Midday.'

The words that followed next will be indelibly etched into my left temporal lobe where speech and language are housed, for the rest of my life.

'*Well I'm not up to much tomorrow. I'll come with you.*'

On hearing this I noticed my mother look away. Totally involuntarily, as though they were a stream of stomach induced verbal reflux, I blurted out the words: 'You can't.'

'What do you mean I can't?' he responded. 'It's not a wedding is it? It's not invitation only. And that Bob did good by you. I mean the driving, the handy money at that factory before you got your student grant and all else besides' (what did that mean?) He looked down momentarily at the floor and then, raising his head slowly fixed his eyes on mine. 'A man has to pay his respects. No, I'll be there. What time do we need to set off? Can't be too sure with the traffic. Centre of town's a mess – road works. Got to leave plenty of time.'

That last phrase was becoming his signature tune. Mum and Dad had recently discovered package holidays and timeshares. For a 6.30am flight to Lanzarote from Manchester's Ringway airport, he had ordered the cab for one in the morning and had been slightly surprised, after having arrived at the check in desk at 1.25am, that it had remained firmly shut and unattended until 4.15am. I sensed my mother's eyes on me. I flashed her a look, but she remained unperturbed. Many years later after my father's death, I discovered from her she knew *exactly* what predicament her husband was walking into and had, indeed, tried willingly, gallantly, to dissuade him from attending. But he was having none of it.

Late that November afternoon, as the grey clouds moved in to mask out any remaining sunlight, I mused on the potential carnage that awaited the following day. If my real relationship to Bob came out, my father would be horrified. Mores and legal norms in 1977 were not quite what they are now, some forty or more years on. In 1977, Bob could have gone to prison for corrupting an under-aged young man in an act of gross indecency. In 2017, I would now be safely over the age of consent and any question of prosecution would be dismissed out of hand. The scenarios of things that could backfire multiplied in my mind like some crazy logarithm on speed. Forget about this convenient fiction that I was Bob's son, how was I going to introduce my father? Could I keep him separate in the church and tell him I was sitting apart because I was doing a reading? But then again, he wouldn't know a soul and would be left standing around like a lemon. If I ignored him he'd be hurt. Rightly so. There was nothing left for it – I had to hatch a Plan B.

Prudhoe is a small town west of Newcastle off the A69 on the road to Hexham. This is where my younger brother, Antony, lived with his wife Charlotte. They'd met at Manchester University while both studying medicine and now he'd been posted as a junior doctor to the Freeman Hospital. He was undertaking a spell of medical research. Was there any way he could, at this late hour, get time off and be Dad's minder? That was the challenge I presented him with on the phone as I explained, layer by layer, the total cataclysmic mess that was shaping up to be Bob Craddock's funeral. There was no bullshitting with him. 'Ginger' had known I was gay for years. In his university years, after Bob and I had broken up and ceased to have contact, Bob had sought him out as an occasional drinking partner in the central Manchester pubs such as the 'Briton's Protection', the 'City Arms' and the notorious 'Ducie' in Hulme, on the edge of gangland Moss Side. This was a watering hole that Bob had once told me was 'as rough as a badger's arse'. (It was one of the few places I had even seen people being 'glassed'.) My mother, now alarmed at the news that Bob had extended his family interest to an even younger and potentially more vulnerable member, had one night called my younger brother to one side in the family home. Way out of earshot of my father, she said quite purposefully, 'Be careful with that Bob. He's a homosexual you know.' It was a Wildean flourish – I mean to have lost a second son would indeed have been sheer carelessness.

Ginger had initially found the stage by stage revelations of the potential *dramatis personae* at Friday's Gorton service the source of huge merriment. But as our chat continued he did see that I was in desperate need of support. He was my only lifeline. A quick check on his rota ensued and he called me back within a few minutes to say he'd be able to make it. He was going to set off and make the drive down, cross-country through Alston and Penrith to Manchester.

'What's he taking the day off for?' asked my Father when I'm told him. 'I didn't even realise he knew him.' 'He's like you Dad,' I said. 'Just paying his respects.'

So the day of the dreaded funeral arrived. I parted the curtains in my bedroom. No surprise there – a typically November Mancunian leaden sky with a persistent drizzle. A passing teenager with his bag full of newspapers was coming out of a house opposite. He saw me staring at him. To think, less than twenty years ago, that had been me.

I'd stayed up late the night before and agreed a strategy with Ginger. We'd discussed the various stages of the day ahead and finalised our plan on one enormous priority. *Under no circumstances must Dad be allowed to set foot in the post funeral reception.*The church service at the cemetery chapel would be a relatively tightly-scripted and taut affair with scant possibilities for social intercourse. The minefield littered with explosives was most definitely going to be the pub reception where, amidst the gallery of miniature pork pies, vol-au-vents and cubed pineapple and cheddar cheese on cocktail sticks, one false phrase out of turn had the potential to ignite the whole powder keg. If anyone asked who my Dad was, I was just going to introduce him as 'Ted, who knew Bob some years ago' … the fact that I had never in my life referred to my father as anything else but 'Dad' was a major impediment that I could do nothing to change at this critical juncture.

Our first port of call was to go and meet 'Uncle' Ronnie who had asked me to gather at the Heaton Chapel Co-Op funeral parlour half an hour before the service. We arrived rather late, leaving little time for anything other than cursory introductions. The first awkward moment came when we arrived at Gorton cemetery, fifteen minutes later and headed into the chapel, where a series of prominent seats near the front had been specially left reserved, presumably for 'next of kin'. Now if there's one universal law that binds Catholics in their liturgical habits, it's the desire, instilled in us from raw infancy, to sit near the back of the church. Dad, therefore, was most uncomfortable about our box office placings. 'What we doing 'ere? We're not the family,' he stated, *sotto voce*. I turned round from my vantage point at the front to take a good look at the assembled gathering of respectful well-wishers. At least half a dozen were men I had not seen since the late 1970s – 'scene queens'. Blusher and foundation were much in evidence, a little rouge here and there, and lots of lip gloss. It looked like a miniature version of the wedding chapel episode towards the end of *La Cage Aux Folles*. I held my gaze too long. First, Dad turned round in his seat to see who I was looking at. Then, a number of them began to wave, aided by some of the limpest wrists this side of the Pennines. 'That's Frank Lammar,' said my Dad. 'What's he … she doing here?' Frank 'Foo Foo' Lammar had been a 1970s and 80s legend on the Manchester entertainment scene and Bob had been a regular visitor to his night club, eager to show off his prizes (of which I was one) to some of the more elderly punters. On one evening, Foo Foo had come over to our table, perched himself adroitly on my lap and started to make clucking noises – this was 'chicken', a not so subtle code word for teenage talent. 'Have a feel of these,' he'd said, pointing to his emerald earrings. 'You know something? On a clear night, you can see these glistening in Morecambe.'

So here he was, fifteen years later, to see off 'Bacardi Bob'. To answer my Father's question I muttered something to my Dad about Bob being a 'man about town' and something of a 'local celebrity'. This seemed to work, until about a dozen welders all arrived en masse. Many of them were still in their navy blue overalls and had clearly been on an early shift at Schreiber's. Their noisy entrance led to a marked flutter a few rows back. 'Will you check *that* out' said a guy in a dark suit and pink shirt next to Foo Foo. 'Talk about *butch*. You don't get that kind of talent on a Saturday night at Napoleons.' I threw my wallet on the floor next to my Dad's seat to serve as a distraction and prayed for the minister to start the service and silence the ad libbing.

I stared at the coffin some ten or twelve feet away. Inside that wooden box was the remains of a man whose bed I had shared on dozens of occasions. A man who'd driven me insane with his zaniness, his suffocating obsession. But he had also been a man who had given me his all – he'd made me feel good about myself. And the necessary subterfuge and intrigue to keep what we had a secret had only added to the thrill of it. Those weekends in my first year at university when I had made those five hour trips by train back from Exeter just to see him – weekends when, if we went into town, we ran the gauntlet of being spotted by family members who'd be straight on the phone to my parents if they spotted me. '*I've just seen your Mark outside Pauldens on Market Street – you didn't say he was coming up from Uni.*' The tenderness. The ecstasy. Bacardi-induced sex on the rug in front of that awful 1950s fire which leaked gas fumes through its cracked tiles. The violent fights when he was so convinced I was being unfaithful that he'd picked me up by my ears and torn the skin inside my earlobes. The drunken night when he'd foolishly believed he was still capable of driving, overturned the Ford Cortina in a ditch at six in the morning, set the damn thing on fire and yet still shown up furtively at our meeting spot on the patch of land behind the Golden Lion pub, with the crimson red carpet above the chassis still smouldering away. All that and more, much more, was in that box. Five foot seven of human, turbulent, mendacious madness. How was I supposed to grieve, to feel loss with this Brian Rix farce about to implode around me?

The minister came out and our service began with an appropriate hymn: 'Lord of all hopefulness, Lord of all joy'. He said a few words about Bob being taken early from this life, how it was a shock for all his family (real and pretend). As we moved on to the responsorial psalm, the congregation were required to recite the words: 'The Lord is My Light and My Help'. But as soon as we managed our first rendition of this, there was a power cut in an already gloomy funeral chapel and the place was plunged into darkness. Cigarette lighters came out to illuminate the service sheets, while some of the welders had pocket torches. The minister bravely soldiered on. I knew why. Such is the rush of daily mortality that managing cemetery chapel and burial/cremation slots was akin to the task of meticulously prepared airport traffic controllers. One stray service and the whole set of people in the schedule after you would be placed on some awful death-related holding pattern. The show had to go on. And it did. We got to the end. No calamities so far. Now for stage two. I looked at Ginger. It was time to launch 'Operation get Ted home and out of the way as soon as possible.'

Bob's coffin disappeared into the sodden earth in the steady drizzle at the Roman Catholic section of Gorton cemetery. He was buried next to his parents, John and Margaret. The black umbrellas then all moved off in harmony, like some morbid ballroom formation dancing entourage, back to where all the cars were parked at the imposing iron gates at the entrance to the cemetery. I walked over to Ronnie, with Ginger and 'Ted' close in attendance. 'Very nice service,' I said. 'I was a bit surprised to see the light blue of City discretely on the coffin though,' I said to Ronnie. I half wondered if this tribal indiscretion had also been spotted by my father. Ronnie's brow furrowed. 'Surprised. Why? He was City. He was always City.' What? Bob had always told me he was a Red. He knew

I worshipped at the Theatre of Dreams and that I had been to every home game in that fateful 1973–74 season after that turncoat Denis Law's treacherous backheel at Old Trafford had won the game for City and condemned us to the Second Division. Bob had been to games with me. (I'm sure he cheered. Had it all been for effect?) This revelation made one thing abundantly clear: he'd been living for years inside his very own football closet.

'So you're coming back for a bite to eat then?' said Ronnie. I wasn't going to let this get out of hand. 'Well the thing is this, Antony here's a busy man. Hospital shift back in Newcastle. And he's driving … *Ted* … he's driving Ted home, so best say your farewells and that's that.' A puzzled expression came over my father's face. That was the third time I had 'Tedded' him in the space of an hour or so. ''Ere hang on. Not so fast,' he remarked anxiously. 'I've not had any lunch.' 'Late lunch at home,' I retorted with a rapier thrust. Ted now stepped forward and delivered a question that was totally left field and that floored us all.

'Will there be sherry trifle?'

Silence. Baffled looks all round. What a strangely specific thing to say. The question hovered, unanswered in the air, until one of Bob's elderly relatives who had overheard the inquiry, now stepped forward.

'We've done the catering. Of course there's trifle. And there's plenty for all.'

A look of delight now dawned on my father's face.

'Come on then, let's move.' He looked at Ronnie. 'Can we follow you in the car?'

Ginger looked at me and shrugged his shoulders. I should have seen this coming. There's a real ritual to the northern, post funeral spread, with all the trappings of the paper plates, the dinky pies and pints of Boddingtons. My Dad would have done this dozens of times in his life for workmates, neighbours in the street and members of his local Catholic parish. On the catering front there'd be no surprises. The grub was always the same and its familiarity was part of its comforting appeal. My paranoid self was telling me he was doing this just to be awkward and 'not fitting in with the plan'. But he was oblivious to any plan. He was digging in deep to an almost primordial and unconscious script: if you go to pay your respects and people have the decency to put on a spread, then the least you should do is not make your weak excuses and scuttle off. Besides – there was all that sherry trifle. And possibly seconds, if his luck was in.

All we needed now was for the outlandish gays to start importuning the startlingly attractive 'bits of rough' in the form of the welding community and we were looking at a full on meltdown. Thankfully, when we all arrived at the post-funeral venue, they had separated into quite distinct groups. I stressed to Ginger the importance of keeping Dad on a tight rein and forbidding any kind of interaction with Bob's family. And, generally speaking, that all came off – well at least for half an hour. 'Ted' was always a fairly retiring type. He'd always wait for people to come to him rather than thrust himself forward. He was not exactly shy, but socially rather lazy and passive: a quality that, at this point in time, suited me down to the ground. But I was a fool if I assumed it could last.

It was all the fault of that bloody sherry trifle. The catering team of relatives (were they elderly aunts?), spotting Dad going over to the trestle tables to top up his dish, came bundling over to engage him in chat. 'That's going down well? Seconds is it?' Dad looked a little bashful, as though he'd been caught raiding the penny tray in the local sweet shop. 'Er, is that all right? It's belting this is. Always been partial to a spot of trifle.'

I inserted myself between them. 'Lovely spread ladies. Such a fabulous effort. You've all done Bob proud,' I said, and gave them each a delicate kiss. They were flushed with pride. Then they eyed each other and began to giggle. What now?

'Shall we tell him?,' said one of them. My dad looked on perplexed. 'The thing is, we were talking after the funeral service. That reading you did from the Bible.'

'What about it?' I asked them.

'Well it was only then that we really noticed. That you really do have your dad's eyes.'

Ted looked on and then broke out into a huge smile.

'That's the nicest thing I've heard for a long time,' he quipped. 'Thank you very much.'

The two ladies stared at him as though he was a sandwich short of a picnic. Why was he taking the credit? I mean, who was this interloper anyhow, this trifle-guzzling eccentric? Ginger, spotting that Dad's pint glass was only a third full, instantly hoiked him away towards the bar, leaving me alone with the bewildered ladies.

'Who is that exactly?' said one of them. 'Because Ronnie told us the lad with the red hair was your step-brother. Your mam remarried, didn't she, and you took her maiden name … for professional purposes.' Did I? Blimey 'Uncle' Ronnie, that was quick thinking! 'We understand,' said the taller of the two women. 'Being in telly and all that. But you could have stayed with 'Craddock'. And that man. Why did he say, "Thank you"? I mean, he's not one of us is he?'

'We're filming,' I said rapidly, saying the first thing that came into my head. 'You know I'm on that *Panorama* programme,' I said. 'And he's … he's … one of the case studies. The thing is, we had to cancel the filming because of the funeral and I've brought him along.'

The two of them exchanged looks. Then a knowing smile erupted. 'I've got it,' said the one in the smart dark grey crimplene suit. 'Mental illness. I saw it – that preview in the *Radio Times*. They're doing a big in-depth feature on that … what's it called, "Care in the Community", It's all these schizos isn't it, being left out on the streets? Is he one of them?'

I remained anchored to the spot. For once, words would not come.

'I ask because … well earlier I had a word with him when you were at the gents. And he introduced himself using your family name. I thought, that's odd. Then I thought to myself, he's not quite all there is he? The poor love. Explains it. If I was like that, I'd be looking for life's compensations. I mean, he loves his trifle doesn't he?'

A preposterous theory, but one in the circumstances I was happy to embrace as a way of getting off the hook. I made my excuses and went back over to the bar. This horrendously close call was all I needed. I asked Ginger to make it snappy and say something to my Dad about medical needs in the North East, hospital rotas – anything. The thought occurred to me that dad was now so well entrenched that he might wave Ginger off and tell everyone he'd bag a lift with someone else, or get a cab. But dad was never a 'cab' kind of person. He'd been on Lancashire United Transport too long to turn down free public transport and fork out an unnecessary tenner for a taxi. He'd had his pleasant fill of sherry trifle and was now happy to leave with his youngest.

The drizzle had now turned to full-on Mancunian downpour. I said my farewells to them, making some excuse about having to talk to Ronnie about the gravestone and mingling a bit more with my old Schreiber colleagues who I had barely acknowledged all day. As we stepped outside, I held up my brolly to protect my dad from the rain. He clambered through the passenger door of my brother's pristine white Toyota Corolla and off they sped into the Mancunian monsoon in the fading afternoon light.

Relief.

In the days afterwards, reflecting at distance on the whole near miss, I tried to fathom why this day had been so potentially undermining. Beneath the possibilities for black comedy and farce, a much darker subset of issues was lurking which made me dread my father's discovery of Bob's lie, his cover story. It was not as if my real father didn't know I was gay. There had been ample evidence of this by now and, even if he was a 'tolerator' rather than an 'accepter', the fact remains that the potential unfolding of my backstory with Bob wasn't an issue of having my closet status exposed. No. We were well beyond that by 1992. The deeper and more menacing element was the terrible hurt my father may have felt, to realise another man had usurped his position. Not only that, but with an added sexual aspect to the whole relationship. Even more, what would it have done to us, if he felt that I had colluded all along, if I had adopted Bob as a *de facto* father? That half-expressed resentment at the driving lessons was veering extraordinarily close to an abyss I did not want to peer over.

How well do we know ourselves? Is not our capacity for self-deception almost infinite? I can't stare from some external vantage point into my own heart and soul, but I do remain convinced of one thing after all these years: that had my own father embraced me more positively and unconditionally in my teenage years once my gayness began to unfold, then the liaison with Bob would have been much less enticing. That is not to blame him. You play the cards you are given. We are talking about the 1970s, not post gay marriage Britain. We are talking about near certain shame in the pub, and nods and winks in the smoke-filled bookies where my father spent a lot of his leisure time. My father was not some touchy-feely Hampstead therapist: he was like that wonderful Dad in *Billy Elliot*, torn between devotion to his son and yet with his mooring ropes anchored firmly in a world that was not sympathetic to his son's ambitions. (It's uncanny the number of people who, having seen this film, talk about the father's problems with Billy 'being gay'. He's a dancer. That's it. Billy's sexuality doesn't really come into it.) All this and more was why my father went to his grave none the wiser about Bob and his preposterous face saving antics.

Graves.

It was twenty four years before I next returned to pay Bob a visit in Gorton Cemetery. After twenty years or more in the over-populated south east, in 2014 I upped sticks, and returned north to my roots. Even after all that time, I summoned an odd discrete tear or two and as I walked back along to the main gates, at the exact point where my father's trifling urges had got himself invited to the slap up reception,

I became obsessed with a question. Was there, in Bob's life, really a son? If so where was he? What did he know of his father after his parents broke up in the early 1960s?

An archivist friend had been doing work on my family tree and so I enquired if he'd be up for any more investigative work. So as a coda to this most bizarre of tales, here are the salient facts that several weeks of meticulous detective work established:

Bob did indeed, as he said that day at the factory gates, have a son.

He was a gynaecologist in Greater London.

His name was Mark.

He was born six weeks after my birthday in early 1960.

And to cap it all – he was gay.

You really couldn't make it up.

7

Queer and Catholic

Mercifully, no further funeral escapades intervened. As the 1990s unfolded, my life now was work, work and ... more work. Where did I *not* go with the TV cameras? A rapid *Panorama* on Timothy McVeigh, the Oklahoma bomber; the civil war in Sierra Leone; primary school teaching methods in Taiwan; and nearer to home, no fewer than six in-depth films on Northern Ireland and the fall-out from the IRA ceasefire of 31 August 1994. We even managed to get to Gaza to record Yasser Arafat's homecoming after decades of exile following the peace-accords signed between the Palestinians and Yitzhak Rabin's Israeli government. My unreliability and unavailability became something of a barbed joke among friends. On one occasion, making a programme on celibacy with the racy title, *Sex and the Priesthood*, I'd travelled to Cratéus in a remote part of northern Brazil, to interview a Bishop about his outright hostility to the Vatican's opposition to married priests. At three in the afternoon, the phone rang in my hotel room on a distinctly dodgy line from London.

'Where are you this time? I told your office it was urgent. We're all here waiting to start. You were meant to be supplying the dessert.'

Eleven years of service at the BBC and I was ripe for change. No regrets, but the grey carpet and endless editorial meetings at White City, the layers of bureaucracy – all of these corporate trappings meant I was beginning to feel more and more like Reggie Perrin pitching up outside the offices of Sunshine Desserts. Then I got my break. A good friend, Marion Milne, had helped set up an independent TV company, 3BMTV, on Soho's Beak Street. Through them, I pitched the idea for *Queer and Catholic*, an examination of the reality of the Catholic priesthood as a 'gay profession'. It was typical Channel Four fare: personal, quirky and, the in-word at the time, 'edgy'. My old BBC boss, Tim Gardam, a devout Anglican, was now head of programmes at Four and had lamented the absence of intelligent religious programming at his new seat of power in Horseferry Road. 'Great idea, but you'll never get anyone to talk. It's a huge taboo.' Tell me about it. I reassured him that, by hook or by crook, we would get him a lengthy documentary for broadcast in the spring of 2001. My aim was not to 'out' people and crassly unmask frightened individuals. It was more to pose my Church a question: how can you use the antiquated language of 'disorder' about a perfectly naturally occurring minority phenomenon such as same sex attraction when you rely on such people to represent Jesus in the daily acts of administering the sacraments? By the year 2000, it wasn't just inquisitive journalists like myself who were using the term 'gay profession'. A very experienced seminary rector in Cleveland, Ohio named Father Donald Cozzens had just published a book, *The Changing Face of the Priesthood*, in which he had specifically devoted chapter seven to 'Considering Orientation'. In theory, the church law of celibacy made equals of all priests, heterosexual, bisexual or gay. But it was not quite so simple. As he went on to tell us in the film, 'if Father has a male friend and they both play golf together or take a holiday together, the reaction is typically: "Isn't that nice that Father has company." But if another priest is seen out having dinner with a woman more than once, tongues begin to wag.' I have personally known such women becoming the butt of scorn from other possessive and jealous female parishioners. Moreover, wrote Cozzens, the Church had a 'one size fits all' approach to celibate living, but in reality, in matters of chastity, it is ten times harder for a young gay man surrounded by other (largely gay) males, than for a straight man. No one had really raised this question in such a high profile manner before. I contacted him and we spoke for what seemed like hours on the phone. When I asked him directly about some of the figures he quoted about the percentage of priests who were gay (roughly anywhere between 40 per cent to 60 per cent), he'd conceded that this could never be an exact science, as there were no surveys to go on. Moreover, even if there were, there had to be doubt about reliability in such a delicate area as one assumes that many people would never speak honestly if they felt a sense of shame and unease. The seminary rector was understandably nervous. A discrete book where you have total control is one thing, but granting an interview to a high profile international documentary was quite another. So in February 2001, off we flew to St Mary's seminary in sleepy Wickliffe, a suburb of Cleveland and prepared to start filming.

On the eve of our seminary visit, there was an incident which was typical of the whole filming process: Father Cozzens and I had agreed that we start the day at mass and film what the Americans called, 'some B roll' … establishing footage of Donald in the seminary with his fellow priests and students. I have always liked, where possible, starting the day with celebration of mass, so it seemed a fitting way to begin. As I checked in to my hotel room, and unpacked, I noticed a flashing red message light on my phone. It was from the seminary over the road.

'Mark, this is Donald. (sigh) Er … I've just had some seminarians come to see me – quite anxious about the filming. I want to honour their concerns, so I'm asking you not to film the mass tomorrow.'

A large number of them, perfectly aware of Cozzens' book and his raising of the gay issue, were so terrified that people might ask questions about their own orientation, that they'd asked to have the cameras banned. The following morning, after we conducted an excellent interview with the rector, we'd asked if we could film some shots of me walking around the long, sunny corridors. For those thirty minutes I didn't see a soul. All the seminarians were effectively hiding in their rooms. Many of them may have been straight guys, just anxious that if they had been featured however fleetingly in our footage, then questions may have been posed: 'Are you or aren't you?'

Back in the UK, I was wondering whether any of the apprehensive closeted clergy I knew might possibly take the leap and use the programme to declare themselves. A very useful conduit for this enquiry was Fr Bernárd Lynch, an Irish priest with the Society of African Missions. In the mid 1970s, Bernárd had been posted to New York and became a thorn in the flesh of the Catholic hierarchy there as he accused those in the senior echelons of silence and cowardice on the issue of AIDS. He was working with dozens of young men and their families as thousands of lives were ravaged by the merciless HIV virus. His refusal to curb his charges of homophobia against bishops and cardinals resulted in scandal when a young student, John Schaefer, totally out of the blue, came forward and alleged sexual abuse by Fr Lynch when he had been a 14-year-old student at Mount Saint Michael's Academy in New York. Knowing how Cardinal John O'Connor and senior officials had viewed his work and prophetic ministry, Lynch immediately smelt a rat and hired legal counsel to defend himself. When the case came to trial, Schaefer took the stand and conceded that he had been put up to fabricating the accusations by the FBI. The trial collapsed and the Judge, the Honourable Burton Roberts, took the exceptional step of exonerating the Irish priest and declaring him not guilty of all charges.

Channel Four had made a programme about the whole grubby affair, *Priest on Trial*, which had aired in 1990 and which had made a huge impact on me, so hearing that he co-ordinated a group for gay clergy called 'Search', I got in touch with him and spoke to several of their members on a totally off the record basis. For some weeks, it seemed that one of them might come out on our Channel Four broadcast, but as the weeks ran by, I think he, totally understandably, lost his nerve. Bernárd knew all too well about the pressures. He had been asked outright in the 1980s by RTE presenter, Gay

Byrne on *The Late Late Show*, if he was gay and had answered in the negative. We've all done it. We've all had our 'cock crowing three times' denial scenes which lead to later self-accusation and resentment. In the eventual eighty minute broadcast, he was one of only three ordained members of the clergy who appeared in front of our cameras who was openly gay. In matters 'Queer and Catholic', Bernárd has been and still remains to this day, a colossus. In January 2017, courtesy of a resounding Irish referendum result in favour of same sex marriage, he married his partner of more than twenty years' standing, Billy Desmond, in his native County Clare. I was one of nearly two hundred people who witnessed their marriage vows.

The other ordained minister in the documentary was Chris Higgins, a former seminarian from the venerable English College in Rome, who agreed to appear with his partner Dennis Caulfield. Chris and Dennis had fallen in love while training for the priesthood in the 1990s, a development which presented them with huge dilemmas given the requirement of celibacy. For a while they broke up. Dennis departed from Rome and Chris continued on to ordination. But when faced with the pain of being apart, they simply could not cope. They reunited and Chris was left to renounce his ministry after barely a year. Their interviews provided a fascinating insight into the pressure cooker of seminary life. I asked Chris to comment on the anxieties contained in one circular I had come across in which a rector from an English seminary had warned against unacceptable camp behaviour in the form of overtly sexual humour and offensive language which might upset and alienate non-gay students. 'I would be especially worried,' said the superior, 'If I came across men calling each other by girls' names.' Had this happened when Chris was in Rome, I wondered?

'We had one who was called Shirley, "Big Shirl." Then there was a "Daisy", a "Phyllis" and a "Mavis", he told me. 'I recall in one spiritual conference, our superiors told us we shouldn't use words about one another which were bovine, canine, feline or feminine.' Knuckles were rapped and the campery ceased. For about a week. And then it started up all over again.

If desire is, at least in part, founded on the unintended bedrock of prohibition, then an institution that recruits huge numbers of gay men into a confined physical space, and informs them that all sex is off limits is heading for trouble, unless God has bestowed on these hordes of young men that rare and oft-times elusive gift of celibacy. Chris and Dennis recalled one Trinity Sunday when they spotted two students playing footsie under the table. The wine was flowing, inhibitions were put on hold, and the pair had retired to one of their bedrooms to take the footsie business on just a few more notches. A hapless neighbour, trying his best to concentrate on his late Sunday afternoon spiritual reading, was finding it impossible to concentrate due to the incessant grunts and ecstatic acoustic offerings penetrating the adjoining wall. He had fallen back on a handy solution. Some music, at full volume, to drown out the decibels of carnal desire. A little Palestrina perhaps? Or maybe the rousing Gloria from the Bach B minor mass? Our man opted for a Take That album. The problem was it was played so loud that the noise attracted the attention of all and sundry who made a beeline for his room and pulled the plug on Robbie Williams and Gary Barlow's 'Back For Good', only to leave the unmistakeable waves of man-on-man action throbbing through the door and walls for all to hear.

So far, so funny. The inevitable foibles of human nature you might conjecture, but no corpses. However, Dennis drew my attention to an altogether more serious issue. He told me that, in moments of boredom and frustration, he had occasionally wandered up to a park, a mere twenty minutes' walk from the college, which was a well-known cruising ground – the aptly named, Campidoglio. Dennis said he had, from time to time, spotted fellow English College students there, engaging in acts of casual sex. 'The people in college who were the most anti-homosexuality were often the most gay students,' he said.

'That's not to say that they were all practising. That was only a small minority, but often the most vociferous defenders of church teaching were people I knew to be gay.' This did raise a fascinating and potentially disturbing question. The official line from the 1986 Vatican document was that, 'although the particular inclination of the homosexual person is not a sin, it is a more or less strong tendency ordered toward an intrinsic moral evil; and thus the inclination itself must be seen as an objective disorder.' But what if the Church was full of repressed, psychologically unhealthy gay men who were distinctly uncomfortable in their own skin? When they berated you for the 'sin of Sodom' and the like, how much of this was genuinely upholding a perfectly well reasoned-out orthodoxy and how much was a statement of utter self-hatred and contempt?

This was an area of enquiry I pursued with Elizabeth Stuart, an openly lesbian Catholic academic, who has published many books in this particular domain, among them, *Daring to Speak Love's Name* and *Religion Is a Queer Thing*. She adopted a Desmond Morris, 'Naked Ape' type approach to examining much of the anthropology of clerical behaviour and had some especially interesting things to say about those priests who were renowned for their near obsessive compulsive disorder in matters of church rituals. 'Priests who fail to reconcile their spirituality and their sexuality often take refuge or somehow seem to redeem themselves through almost obsessive attention to detail,' she commented. 'It's a bit of a cliché to talk about people being 'liturgy queens', but if you're a Catholic you're aware of priests who are obsessed with the length of the altar cloth or their own appearance in the liturgy. Or other clergy who are absolutely hard in their attitude towards other peoples' moral struggles and peccadillos,' she told me. 'And I often feel that these are people who are dealing with their own demons concerning sexuality.'

Liz shared with me a particularly riveting anecdote. In 1994, she'd gone to a screening of the film, *Priest*, written by the Liverpool-based screenwriter, Jimmy McGovern. The ground-breaking narrative featured a young, judgemental curate, 'Father Greg', who'd been sent up to Merseyside to get some experience of life on the ground in a tough parish. He was a posh-talking southerner with a fondness for *The Times* and preaching Thatcherite sermons about personal responsibility and individualism. Next to nothing in common with the parish priest, a *Guardian*-reading lefty with a nice little thing going on with the housekeeper (female). Father Greg had not taken kindly to this flagrant flouting of the celibacy requirement, but then on a night when loneliness overwhelms him, he dons his leather jacket and pops down to the gay club and meets a man he falls in love with. The film is an outstanding work, rooted in humanity, brokenness and forgiveness – one of McGovern's finest in an outstanding output spanning thirty years. On the weekend it had opened, Liz recalled going along to an Arts cinema in Wales and being captured by the unfolding human drama. 'I sat down and looked around,' she said. 'And if you're a cradle Catholic like I am, you quickly learn to spot priests in "mufti" (slang for civilian attire). The cinema was full of Roman Catholic priests trying not to look like priests. I found that tremendously moving because here was a film that was addressing the issues of their lives.'

Priest's writer, Jimmy McGovern, came to have first hand experience of the Catholic Church's supreme nervousness about its gay clergy. In the run up to filming, McGovern had combed Merseyside looking for suitable locations for the shoot and thought he had secured the permissions for several key parts of the drama. It was a week before the cameras were due to roll, and director Antonia Bird and all the actors were in place. Returning from an arduous day, running a writer's workshop in a prison, the screenwriter came back to find his answering machine stacked up with urgent messages. Word had got round about the storyline. The local church hierarchy had plunged itself into a collective panic.

'They say that God rules the world in mysterious ways,' McGovern told me in his study in Woolton, in south Liverpool, 'but the Catholic Church uses a fax.'

To use the word 'mafia' in the context of Liverpudlian Catholicism is not to assert financial corruption, but rather an extraordinary nexus or web of closely knit relationships. As the writer explained to me, once the Archbishop's office had got wind of the gay plot line, it took less than two hours for the word to get round. Electricians and transport companies, among others, took the view that if they stayed loyal to *Priest* they might run the risk of losing out on future contracts. One by one, the production company lost location permissions and key support staff.

The worst thing of all was where to film all the church interiors. The Jesuit-educated McGovern had hoped to shoot in St Francis Xavier's, the scene of his own baptism in 1949, but like many of the other venues, that was now off limits. Busy actors were booked and could not be re-scheduled. In haste, they discovered an Anglo-Catholic church, St Mary of Eton in Hackney Wick in London's East End. The female minister there had no such qualms about opening up her doors, and so dozens of extras and actors were bussed down from Merseyside. 'We ended up transporting thirty young girls in communion dresses down to London in the middle of winter,' he told me. The shoot went ahead on schedule. Fittingly, that was the church that we also used for the filming of *Queer and Catholic*.

The institutional panic induced by Archbishop Derek Warlock and his staff merits closer inspection. Why is it that mention of this topic is like waving garlic in front of a vampire? In one scene in our film, I attempted some 'vox pops' in St Peter's Square using, as a prop, a copy of *Il Confessione*, a book by Marco Politi, a seasoned so-called Vaticanista with the Italian daily, *La Repubblica*. The tale, based on one of the author's numerous clerical contacts, was about an Italian priest: a man of saintly good works by day, and by night, a man forced to seek sexual and emotional intimacy in some of Rome's darker places. Everyone, and I mean *everyone* was talking about the publication when we filmed in Rome. A typical pattern emerged when we descended with the cameras. Most people seemed happy to engage – that is until they saw the book in my right hand. Then they'd do an extremely good impersonation of a car going from third gear into reverse. Often they used their lack of English as an excuse to duck out, but with the help of my delightful production team member, Annalisa D'Innella, I'd stocked up on the key Italian phrases, so they couldn't wriggle away on grounds of linguistic incomprehension. French and Spanish were OK, though one Franciscan Friar from Belgrade jabbering away in Serbo-Croat proved well beyond my grasp. He did seem to recognise the book though and hastily fled off through the masses of pilgrims. But why all the fear?

The thought had never occurred to me, but the more I dwelt on it, somewhat surprisingly the subject of contraception came to take on a bigger and bigger significance. As the church teaches that all sexual acts have to be open to the possibility of procreation, same sex acts are, essentially not dissimilar from heterosexual married couples who use artificial contraception. In 1968, amidst huge controversy in the encyclical *Humanae Vitae*, Pope Paul VI had upheld the traditional Vatican line that condoms, the pill and any other form of birth control other than the 'natural' rhythm method was off limits (ask many Catholic couples who have attempted to regulate their sex lives and appetites surrounded by thermometers, calendars and weird looking graphs and you might hear dissent on the use of that word 'natural'). So, though the connection was not at first sight obvious, homosexuality and birth control were connected in this carefully constructed house of cards. Touch one part and change it and you open up Pandora's Box. And this was about something no less than the teaching authority of Rome. Many in the Church claimed that the ban on artificial birth control, since that had been taught consistently, could not be changed without a damaging admission of historical error. A veritable domino effect could come into play and then where would we be? – cast onto the stormy high seas of modern relativism where individual subjectivity and opinion rule completely.

To which my response was simple and clear: I have no problem with seeing procreation as a central core element in humanity's sexual make up (indeed I wouldn't be here writing this book without it!) But creation contained a naturally occurring minority variant of same sex attraction – not only in the human species, but in the wider animal kingdom. Sexual affective love between humans was a gift that could reach moments of transcendence, taking us, fleetingly outside and beyond ourselves. Why did all this have to be sacrificed on the altar of Rome's Magisterium and *Humanae Vitae?* How odd to think that what some gay men did with certain parts of their anatomy might lead, by a process of doctrinal logic, to the very collapse of the Church of Rome's teaching authority!

None of this merited scrutiny before the late 1960s. Gay priests lived in their so-called, 'lavender rectories' and no one asked any questions. It was all very much a case of 'wink wink nudge nudge'. But the Stonewall riots in New York in June 1969 put paid to all that. When police stormed a Manhattan gay bar, the LGBT community, having tolerated years of brutish behaviour by the cops, had had enough. The ensuing fight back made international news and catapulted gay liberation onto the agenda. Advances in employment rights, equality legislation, civil partnerships and same sex marriage can all be traced back to the scenes on 28 June 1969 in Manhattan's Greenwich Village. No aspect of modern life was left untouched and that certainly included the Church. The safe space of the clerical closet was no more. And revolution brought in counter-revolution in the form of groups like Roman Catholic Faithful (RCF), a no-nonsense outfit which based itself in the United States. In an interview with its president, Stephen Brady, the organisation unashamedly conceded that they used considerable sums of their donors' money to pay for private detectives at two hundred dollars an hour to go and spy on suspected gay clergy. I had not told RCF that I was gay when I approached them about our programme, nor had I given them a working title for our documentary (in truth, 'Queer and Catholic' was decided upon very late in the day, just before the *Radio Times* went to press so we could not justly be accused of withholding information.) I think Mr Brady and his staff assumed that because I was a Roman Catholic, I would automatically defend whatever steps they took to uphold what he took to be 'orthodoxy'. When they saw the eventual programme, I received a vicious homophobic email from their offices in which the concluding paragraph from the author stated that he would be praying to the Virgin Mary in the hope that I died of cancer of the rectum. By your fruits shall ye know them, indeed.

Contrast that with the story of 32 year old Eric Cole and 47 year old Roman Catholic, Joe McMurray, which ended our broadcast. Joe had lost two previous partners to AIDS and had subsequently suffered from depression and isolation. The two met, by chance, in a church-sponsored San Francisco soup kitchen dishing out food to the poor and needy. When our cameras pitched up, it was their wedding day in a branch of the Metropolitan Community Church. Emblazoned on a pillar at the entry to the building was a quote from the Talmud which greeted the wedding guests: 'The Union of Two Souls Unites the Universe'. The minister's voice trembled with emotion as she shared her thoughts on what these two men were about to do: 'as all the debates rage in the church over the subject of same sex love, all I can say is that I know of few people, if any, who are better Christians than the two of you. You met here at "Simply Supper" and you have both consistently placed the poor and social justice at the very heart of your lives.' If those words brought out the handkerchiefs, it was nothing compared to the ceremony of commitment in which the pair, totally without a script and off the cuff, made their pledges. Eric turned to Joe. He held his gaze and the pair locked hands together.

'I say these promises, these vows from my heart to your heart. My heart is where the basis of my spirituality is and it is the place where God lives in me. So, from my heart, I promise to listen to you when you need it, not only with open ears, but more importantly with an open heart.'

And from Joe to Eric, 'Sweet Eric. Whenever I show your picture to someone who has not met you I am always compelled to tell them this truth. You are every bit and more, as beautiful on the inside as you are on the outside.'

At this point, I caught Eric's father, a burly bearded hulk of a man from Kansas, wiping tears from his eyes.

On returning to England I challenged the Rt Rev Peter Smith, the then Bishop of East Anglia, now Archbishop of Southwark, to relate to me what the Roman Catholic faith made of such an event and such a commitment. Who was he to say that physical sexual love expressed between two such committed people could not be a place where God dwelt?

'One of the terrible consequences of original sin is that we can often delude ourselves and go in the wrong direction,' he told me. 'Those two men, however sincere their intentions, basically objectively speaking, according to church teaching, will probably not achieve what they think they will.'

Three years after that interview, on 14 February 2004, Joe and Eric became one of the first same sex couples in the USA to marry in full recognition of the law. California's Supreme Court subsequently did a *volte face* on theirs and nearly four thousand other marriage licences, so it was not until 2011 that finally, in New York, the two were irrevocably joined under full legal statute. This time there was no about turn. Sixteen years later they are still firmly together and now live in Salina, Kansas, Eric's home town. Joe spent many years working with people with learning disabilities before recently accepting the post of chaplain to St Francis Community Services in Salina, Kansas. This charity dedicates itself to protecting and nurturing children through supporting foster carers and adults who seek to adopt vulnerable children. Eric serves as the executive assistant to the Dean at Kansas State Polytechnic in Salina, a satellite institution of Kansas State University in Manhattan.

'Both will probably not achieve what they think they will.'

Sixteen years on, I wonder if the Archbishop might want to revise his comments?

When our *Queer and Catholic* programme aired on Channel Four in May 2001, it hardly broke ratings records, securing an audience of under a million viewers. But it was one of those broadcasts that punched well above its weight. In the weeks that followed there was some notable fallout. One or two senior bishops had gone to the press at the time of airing and condemned the content of *Queer and Catholic* as ostensibly an attack on the institution of the Church. However, these very same individuals, when I met them in Catholic social functions such as the annual jamboree for Catholic media, confessed they had been rather impressed, but felt under pressure to toe the line from the Holy See. In other words, playing to the Vatican gallery. And how odd that a church which denied the existence of a very large cohort of gay men in its ranks in 2001, could, only a short time later in the wake of the burgeoning paedophilia scandals in its ranks, now conveniently conflate the two issues. 'People with these inclinations just cannot be ordained,' opined Pope John Paul II's press spokesman and Opus Dei member, Dr Joaquin Navarro-Valls. 'This does not imply a final judgement on people with homosexuality. But you cannot be in this field.' This was tarring a lot of people with a very broad brush.

And what of my own family's response to my first ever appearance as a TV presenter on mainstream British TV? My father had kept rather quiet as I informed them about the nature of this delicate project. I gave them a transmission date. Weeks after the film had aired, I was back up in Salford and had a chance to catch up with them.

'We had a delegation round a few days before the programme. Concerned relatives,' my father informed me.

'There was about eight or nine of them. They said: "You don't get the *Sunday Times* do you? So you won't have seen the TV previews for next weekend's programmes." '

My parents had shaken their heads, but had had an idea where this was heading.

'Well, it's your Mark. We thought we should let you know. He's on telly. Doing a programme. Calls itself *Queer and*

Catholic. I mean, not being funny or anything, but we just wanted you to know in case you got a shock.'

Ted looked the anxious aunts and uncles in the face.

'Known about it for ages,' he said.

'What?' said one of the aunts. 'The programme … or him being … you know. Gay … like?'

'Both,' came the abrupt riposte.

One of the uncles piped up. 'Well you never said anything about it.'

To which my father answered.

'Well you never asked did you?'

Queer and Catholic did what Channel Four wanted it to do. It made a noise and put the cat among the pigeons, forcing an important issue into the open. On a personal level it meant that the channel's religious affairs department now knew that they had someone they could turn to in the years ahead to tackle such thorny issues as Islamic militancy, the rise of Fundamentalism, the sex abuse scandal in the Catholic Church and populist ventures with grabby titles such as *Hallowed Be Thy Game*, a treatise of whether football had become an all-conquering modern day religion. And as testimony to its longevity, I recall this recent scene when strolling through St Peter's Square on my way over to collect press passes from the Vatican media office on the corner of the Via Della Conciliazione. Out of the corner of my eye, a man in Archbishop's purple started to make a beeline for me. As he got near he stretched out a friendly hand. I hadn't got a foggiest clue who he was, but I carried on.

'Hello,' he says. 'We've met before haven't we?' I looked back in a state of non-commitment. Then, in a flash, his facial expression morphs from openness to mild horror. 'Oh, you're … you're the man from that programme aren't you? That … er … programme.'

A swift turn and off he scuttled in the direction of Borge Pio.

Some will say, of course, that it's all now different under Pope Francis. His now famous comments a few months after he took office, 'If a person is gay and seeks out the Lord and is willing, who am I to judge that person?' were seen at the time as a watershed. But only the mood music has changed. The official language of disorder continues. Moreover, to huge disappointment in December 2016, the Argentine Pontiff approved *The Gift of Priestly Vocation*. This document on admission to and formation of would-be priests in seminary upheld a previous 2005 text that sought to ban candidates with 'deep homosexual tendencies'. Francis appears to give with one hand and take away with the other. The result is to indirectly cast aspersions on thousands of serving gay clergy and effectively to encourage gay candidates with genuine vocations to cover up the truth about who they are. This is fundamentally unjust and unhealthy.

Meanwhile since the airing of our film in 2001, at the level of the laity, more and more horror stories abound, none more so than the case of twenty three year old Connor Hakes from Bloomington, Indiana who was forbidden from singing at his grandmother's funeral by the local priest, on account of his 'gay lifestyle'. This amounted to no more than appearing in photos of a Gay Pride march some years previously. His case is one of hundreds of injustices. In the Catholic tradition, at the Easter Vigil and on other special occasions, we sing something called the Litany of the Saints: a roll call of Holy women and men down the ages whose exemplary lives inspire us to ask their intercession before God. Since 2007, the New Ways Ministry in the USA has been keeping its own litany ... of LGBT employment casualties. These are the hundreds of teachers, musicians, priests and church workers who have been shown the door and dispensed from their services. The full list can be seen here: https://newwaysministryblog.wordpress.com/employment/

Their typical offence? To declare their love publicly for another human being and confirm this by a civil law of union.

I ask you.

What on earth would Jesus think?

8

Pablo

Quito, Ecuador. At nearly 10,000 feet above sea level, the second highest capital city on the planet. It is ten o' clock at night and very chilly indeed on the exceedingly dimly lit *Calle Baquedano.* My Lonely Planet guide says there's meant to be a gay discotheque at number 188 called, rather unpromisingly, *El Hueco,* 'The Hole'. I was expecting neon signs and rainbow flags fluttering outside, but nothing. Zilch.

I am about to give up, when I see two silhouetted characters about a hundred metres ahead of me. They halt at a building and ring a bell. As the door opens, the sound of Cher's 'Believe' penetrates the night air:

> *Do you believe in life after love?*
> *I can feel something inside me say*
> *I really don't think you're strong enough.*

This has to be it, I think to myself. Within two minutes I am in a subterranean vault, the only 'gringo' out of a hundred plus gay men. I spot a handsome, well-built guy at the bar. A drink is offered my way. We dance. And dance again. He asks me to buy him a packet of cigarettes and then we drink more and dance – again. Ricky Martin's 'Living La Vida Loca' seems to be on loop. The rum is now flowing and the time flies. At 3am, the club is due to close and it's now already 2.50am. I tell him I'm staying in an apartment ten minutes' walk away. 'Vámonos' he says, and takes my hand.

Upstairs, in the brightly lit reception area, I am just waiting to get my coat when I spot my new friend looking around cagily. In no more than a second, the main door I passed through five hours earlier suddenly flies open. A white hatchback now pulls up outside, driven by a young woman with flowing black hair. He darts through the entrance. In a flash she leans over to push open the passenger door. Within five seconds the tyres are screeching and the car has sped off into the night. All this has happened in about twenty seconds. I stand there, aware of lots of attentive smiling faces and dwell on the one drink he bought me, compared with the rather large bill I have now run up.

I am about to crawl out of the 'the hole', a sadder but wiser man, when I feel a tap on my shoulder. As I turn round, I fix on a small, wiry man in his late twenties with a vaguely plaintive face.

'He always does that,' he said. And shrugged his shoulders, sympathetically.

This was how I came to meet Pablo.

It all came about at the end of an exhilarating sabbatical year. By the end of the 1990s I was burnt out. I saw my female colleagues leaving the BBC's *Panorama* to start families and startled the Beeb's HR department by telling them I needed a year's unpaid 'gay maternity leave'. I packed my shiny new sixty five litre backpack and departed Blighty. Fifty-six thousand miles. A two month safari in Africa followed by six weeks in New Zealand as part-time Dad (carer, not biological) after lesbian friends Stephanie and Diane welcomed their first born, Alexander, who arrived on 21 December, coincidentally my own birthday. I wonder how many gay men have found themselves frantically driving around on 24 December trying to secure the purchase of silicone nipple shields and breast pumps before the shops close their shutters for Christmas?

But the lion's share of this amazing year was spent in South America. After the unforgettable Sambadrome at the Rio Carnival in February, I took five months to travel down to the southern tip of the continent at Ushuaia in Argentina's Tierra del Fuego, then all the way up the spine of the Andes through Chile's Torres del Paine national park, the Atacama

Desert, the Bolivian Altiplano and Peru's Machu Picchu to end my Andean marathon in Ecuador.

That bizarre introduction to Pablo heralded a huge turning point. I had never met anybody like him before in my life. He was a junior accountant with the state-owned petroleum company, Petro Producción, and he was the tenth of twelve – yes read again, *twelve* children. Pablo was only three years old, when his father, returning home drunk, fell down the stairs and fractured his skull. He died almost instantly, leaving his poor mother, Georgina to raise a dozen little quiteños.

I had only three weeks left in South America before my sabbatical year was due to finish and so initially, Pablo became, or so I thought, a classic holiday romance. We went sightseeing. My rudimentary Spanish went up a notch or two. I met a handful of his friends in the murky, undercover closeted world of the Latin America gay scene. Pablo's eyes welled up when he told me he was dumped by his last lover – a married man who'd hired hotel rooms for the night, and then always ran off to his wife and kids when the deed was over. I was, of course, kept totally off limits from his shanty town neighbourhood in *cinco esquinas* in an especially run-down southern part of the capital.

Just a few days before my intended departure, we'd paid one last nostalgic trip back to *El Hueco*. Sauntering back in the icy night air, Pablo stopped in the street and looked me square in the eye.

'There's something I need to say. I lied to you.'

About what? His age? He said he was twenty eight, eleven years younger than me.

'It's about where I live. You know I said I had my own room at home, well …'

Within seconds he was sobbing uncontrollably and I was cradling him in my arms, much to the curious bemusement of passers-by. In these last two and half weeks I had built up a detailed mental picture of his life at home. Mother cooking endless *sopa de gallina* (hen soup) for the masses. Then there was a mongrel dog called Tony which ran around the back yard in a small rickety house where at least three or four of her offspring were still at home. What I hadn't understood was that there were only two bedrooms, one of which was mother's own space. The truth was that there were often three or four to a bed – the classic scenes of topping and tailing that one associates more with poverty in Dickensian times. For reasons of pride, he'd oversold his independence to me, his own status. But once he fell apart like that in front of me, something inside me snapped. I wanted to save him. I wanted to take him away from here and give him what his parents could not give him: the chance of a new life in a first world country where gay men had a much better time of it. Latin America's macho culture often meant that openly gay living was near impossible. Quito had seen one or two nascent Gay Pride marches, attended by a few dozen folk who had frequently been jeered at and been pelted with stones. This was a country in which more than eighty per cent of the population was Catholic. The Bishops were conservative. To declare yourself openly gay was risking total social ostracism. I wanted to take him away from all this. Thus it was that I became Henry Higgins to Pablo's Eliza Doolittle. Our very own Latin American *Pygmalion*. We hatched a long term plan – he would come to the UK and live with me in my flat just a stone's throw from St Paul's Cathedral.

Five months later, I flew back to Quito to spend the last hours of 1999 and the first days of the new millennium with him. For days I waited in Miami for a flight connection as black ash from *Guagua Pichincha*, Quito's locally active volcano, filled the air and made a descent into the capital's Mariscal Sucre airport impossible. After kicking my heels for seventy two hours, I finally made it. My new Latino partner arrived sporting a surgical mask and immediately thrust one on me to protect me from the thick clods of volcanic matter that were raining down from all directions. Our taxi had the windscreen wipers on full pelt for the whole journey which took place under a suffocatingly leaden sky. Pablo told me he had not seen the sun for weeks.

Since my summer departure he had moved out of home,

helped by some UK subsidies, and got his own one bed place closer to the more selective and safer part of the city near the Alameda Park. Somewhat nervously, he planned to introduce me to the huge family clan as 'a friend who was sponsoring me to go to England and learn the language.' I was to be the first gringo ever to be honoured to set foot in the family home and, by all accounts, days were spent cleaning before I walked in at 8.30pm on New Year's Eve in what appeared to be a re-make of the Hollywood classic, *Guess Who's Coming to Dinner?* As we all tucked into the *sopa de gallina*, Pablo's mother had a direct question: why wasn't I married? 'Because,' she assured me, 'I have three single daughters here who'd all make beautiful mothers.' Pablo choked on his *gallina*.

'Señora,' I said, 'with my work, full of international travel, it would be cruel to abandon my wife and children for such long stints. Believe you me, it breaks my heart to hear my married colleagues on the phone to their loved ones being separated for such long spells. So no, marriage is not an option, regrettably.'

Approving murmuring and nodding all round, though one of the sisters looked a tad let down I thought. Abruptly, Señora Rodriguez now wanted to satisfy one particular line of enquiry. Did the Queen of England eat potatoes? 'Because,' she said, 'I had heard all about the potato famine in Ireland and know this is the food of the poorest. So, does she join in with her subjects and eat with the masses?' I assured her that, as far as I was aware, potatoes were most definitely on the menu at Buckingham Palace, Balmoral and elsewhere. We had a toast to '*comiendo papas*' (eating spuds) and then I shared the tale of how the Anglo-Saxon world, on account of having no gender article, often confuses *la papa* with *el Papa*. The potato and the Pope. Laughs all round and then it was time to see the New Year in. Hoist by my own linguistic petard of smugness, much to Pablo's eternal shame and embarrassment, I proceeded on the chimes of midnight, to go round hugging everyone and wishing them *'feliz ano nuevo.'*

Año with a wavy line, the *tilde*, over the 'n' means 'year'...

Ano, without the all critical *tilde*, however, means 'anus'.
A happy new arse to you.
And we were trying to stay inside the closet.

By June 2000, the time had come for Pablo to leave Quito for pastures new in London. He had never been out of the country in his life, nor had he even scaled the steps of an aeroplane. The task of acquiring his first ever passport and a visa to visit the UK had taken two days of queuing. When I went to meet him at Stansted airport, despite the fact that the connecting Lufthansa plane from Frankfurt had arrived on time at 1.30pm, by 3.00pm he had still not emerged from customs. Then I got a call to my mobile. It was the airport security police. He had been subjected to a one hour interrogation and a very intrusive physical inspection by a team of officials with very rudimentary Spanish. When he finally emerged he was sandwiched between two hefty officers and had a face like thunder.

'You are Mr Dowd?' said one of them. I nodded. 'So this unaccompanied male from Latin America has some cock and bull story about you meeting last year and him coming to England to learn English. You expect us to believe that?'

'Has he done anything wrong?' I asked. 'Highly suspicious' said the second of them. 'Why on earth would you, a journalist with the BBC, take in someone like him who doesn't even speak English?' My blood was boiling.

'If you'd been born into a family of twelve kids and lost your dad when you were three, you might have been grateful for the help of a stranger to enhance your life chances,' I retorted. 'Now. Any more questions or can we go?' The two heavies looked at one another and nodded. Pablo now walked forth with his enormous suitcase and we hugged, rather self-consciously. Over his shoulder I saw the two men smirking. It had not been the nicest of welcomes to the UK.

Cultural adaptation was going to be a huge challenge. This came home to me very early on, on a trip north to Nottingham to present Pablo to my younger brother Antony and his wife Charlotte, now both proud parents of three year old Tom and the recently arrived Ben. On the East Midlands train up from St Pancras the catering trolley passed through our carriage. As it pulled up alongside our table, Pablo's eyes lit up. He then behaved like a fox in a chicken coup, emptying half the trolley of its contents. Coronation Chicken, Prawn Supreme, Beef and Horseradish Surprise – you name it, it was now piled high on our table. I could hardly see his face. The attendant, looked totally shocked, as did everyone around us on the packed late afternoon train.

'You must be starving,' I said. He shrugged his shoulders and relaxed with a beam on his face. That is until he saw the calculator coming out. 'Twenty nine pounds and thirty eight pence,' I was told. The expression on Pablo's face now became a rather intense blush. 'No es como el avión entonces – hay que pagar?' (It's not like being on the plane then – you have to pay?') When I informed him that this was indeed the case, he loaded everything back on the trolley and looked around at all the people staring at us both. It took all my restraint not to quip: 'So sorry about my friend – he's from Barcelona.' (Imagine if I had had to decode that one for him.) I knew I could now take nothing for granted.

English lessons were secured for him via a language school on Oxford Street. I explained to Pablo that this student status now entitled him to register with a doctor, get health checks and effectively ask for a physical MOT. This he duly did. And when the results came in it was a total shocker – a development that most definitely had me thinking that history was cyclical and not linear. It was mid July when a call came through to my phone at the BBC in White City. A voice whimpered on the other end of the phone. He kept repeating one word over and over again before he burst into tears … '*seropositivo* … *seropositivo* …' His blood tests had revealed he was HIV positive.

Just as with Dez fifteen years before, a rush of thoughts – a veritable spaghetti junction of anxieties. From who and for how long has he had it? How advanced? Am I OK? How soon can I get tested? Then a calmer, but more menacing second wave of concerns. I knew there were now the beginnings of anti-HIV retroviral drugs to combat the virus and HIV was no longer a certain death sentence as it had been with Dez. But all that depended on where you were in the world. There was nothing like this in public health in Ecuador, so Pablo would be OK so long as he was here and studying. But he only had a one year student visa, so what would happen after that? I knew there were moves afoot to extend to the international partners of same-sex couples, the indefinite right to remain, but that meant proving to the Home Office beyond all reasonable doubt that one had been in a committed relationship for three years or more. But the worst of it was this question. *What happens if it doesn't work out between us and he has to go home?* With private anti-HIV medicine going at around eight to ten thousand dollars a year or more in many parts of Latin America, Pablo would be priced out of survival. No, he had to stay in the UK. But this now left me feeling there was a large revolver placed at the side of my temple. All this was swimming around madly in my head as I looked at my notes and attempted to fashion a *Radio Times* billing for our forthcoming *Money Programme* on the financial woes of Marks and Spencer. Once this was done I popped into the editor's office and explained why I was somewhat discombobulated. Within minutes, the BBC had ordered me a cab to go directly home to be with the poor terrified Pablo.

That evening we strolled through Lincoln's Inn Fields to the Catholic Church of St Anselm and St Cecilia at Holborn. Pablo's religious beliefs rarely required him to be at mass, but he was the kind of Latino that, as soon as life proved difficult, found supplication to the Virgin Mary incredibly easy. We lit umpteen candles and prayed at her statue. Afterwards, we sat closely together on a bench in St James's Park. He was silent for minutes on end, looking ahead at the small lake ahead of us. Finally he spoke up.

'I just can't believe it. It just doesn't seem fair,' he said. He was pointing towards a small formation on the lake.

'How is it that those ducks are going to outlive me? In a few weeks' time I'll be dead and they'll be here swimming away happily.'

As I followed up these comments, it became abundantly clear that Pablo drew no distinction between having the HIV virus and AIDS itself. So, in a stiff test for my Spanish, I had to go into detail about the erosion of *los globulos blancos* – the white T-cells in the immune system, terms like viral load, CD-4 count and how the new drugs meant he could live with HIV and, if he looked after himself, possibly might never succumb to the dreaded AIDS. By the end of our chat, he seemed convinced that he might outlive those fluffy mallards on the lake after all. The next day, we registered him at the Mortimer Market Health Centre off Tottenham Court Road and he was assigned an HIV specialist consultant. Right from the outset the standard of care and treatment there was nothing less than exemplary.

But there remained another central question. Was I also now a HIV carrier? This was the year 2000, not 2017. HIV detection tests were still in their infancy. These days you know in an instant if you have the virus or not, but back then, you were told you had to wait for up to three months for any antibodies to show up in your blood. A long and sweaty late summer lay ahead.

As events turned out, by early November, just as I was about to discover the test results, a phone call came from my father in Salford that was to put all this into the shade. His voice was hesitant and troubled. For once there was no obligatory mention of the football and Man United's latest performance in the Premiership.

'We've just had a visit from the police. It's Chris. They've found him in a hotel room in Edinburgh.'

A long silence.

'They're saying there'll have to be a post-mortem. '

My elder brother was forty six years old. Twice married, twice divorced, we all later discovered he had been seeing a series of psychiatrists for clinical depression. His then current partner informed us that he had attempted suicide five months earlier but she had discovered him in time. But none of this had been shared with us, his immediate family. He had been up in Scotland on business for a management consultancy firm and on the final evening of his life, had actually spoken with my mother on the phone just an hour or two before he took a massive overdose of whisky and sleeping pills, assuring her that they'd 'talk again soon.'

No parents expect to survive their children and this was a monumental shock to them both – a shock which, in typical style, they attempted to play down. At first they were in denial. I had spoken with the Edinburgh police and took the plane up for the unpleasant task of identifying Chris's body in the local morgue. They handed me his clothes and a laptop in a leather bag.

'And er, one more thing,' said the police constable. 'We found this under the bed.' He handed me over a plastic Tesco shopping bag. It was full of hundreds of pound coins. To this day I have no idea why he had this in his possession. A slot machine addiction? As the Edinburgh train south to Salford broke down in Preston at 10.40pm, I beckoned to a cab to complete the rest of the twenty five mile trip along the M61 and A666 to the parental home. 'Twenty seven pounds fifty,' said the cabbie as his engine purred outside their home in Clifton. I saw the drawn curtains part and there was the lonely figure of my mother looking out into the night. I started counting out thirty pounds – thirty coins from the Tesco bag. The cabbie switched his light on. I could see he was eyeing my actions up, courtesy of his driving mirror.

'Excuse me pal. Question. Are you a drug dealer? Or, maybe a pimp? Just couldn't help noticing the coins.'

There was more than four hundred and fifty pounds' worth in that ridiculously heavy bag.

'If you really knew how I came to have all this, you just wouldn't believe me,' I responded.

It was left for me to tell my parents all the details of what the police had revealed, a task that took me all of two and half days, because every time I suggested we sit down to talk to spell out what had happened, they always found a reason to get busy: to visit a garden centre (in November?), to dive into their new Toyota Corolla and get more shopping in, pop off on an impromptu visit to see friends, attend the morning mass at St Mark's. I knew what they were doing, and I could hardly blame them as the pain of rejection must have been bordering on unbearable. You bring children into the world to nurture them and protect them, not to bury them before their fiftieth birthday. I wasn't close at all to Chris, so I found myself oddly detached emotionally, rather like Camus' French Algerian, Meursault, in *L'Etranger* at his own mother's funeral. Chris and I were like chalk and cheese and the gay thing had always been, to him, a source of awkwardness and embarrassment. During all this, just about the only time I nearly cracked up with tears was when I had to share with Mum and Dad, a small detail on his farewell note which had been addressed to his current partner:

'*I'm sorry I didn't have the strength to get through this and have had to leave you ... please make sure Ginger* [my younger brother Antony] *gets the guitar.*'

Once I told them, they coped with it by going into practical mode. My father expressed a firm desire that the nature of Chris' death not be made public. This was a move which I interpreted as a desire to protect both himself and my mother, so the official line was that he'd had a heart attack (Occasionally my mother got her lines wrong on the phone and mentioned stroke in her account of his death which had my father making rapid gestures towards his chest to get her back on track.) My parents were raised in a church that had traditionally taught that suicide was a mortal sin. There have even been stories of individuals being denied burial after taking their own lives. Yet the Catechism of the Church states that for this to be grave sin, my brother would have had to be in total control of his faculties and give full consent to his actions. Given his history of mental health issues, that almost certainly was not the case. I suspect my parents also knew this. What informed my father's desire to keep this all from public view, I suspect, was a very real and yet unjustified sense of shame that they had 'failed' as parents. Not for the first time in their lives, they were being unduly hard on themselves.

I've thought long and hard about narrating this story, as it goes against my father's express wish of seventeen years ago. The fact is that neither my mother nor my father is now around to suffer this terrible loss and its consequences. Moreover, as my younger brother pointed out at the time, the decision to push all this under the carpet only adds to a situation in which the mental health agenda stays hidden from public view and discussion. The unsavoury truth is that men between forty and fifty years old are twice as likely to kill themselves as any other sector of the population. The least my brother deserves is that the pain which led to his death is recorded and acknowledged so that the real challenge of dealing with suicidal thoughts among middle-aged men is placed at the centre of our mental health policy discussions.

My brother's tragic demise now meant that Pablo faced a very tricky assignment up north with his slowly improving English. He was whisked up to Salford from London and met my parents for the first time. What a baptism of fire. He barely had any words for them, short of 'I'm so sorry', but what he lacked in prose, he made up for with endless embraces and hugs for my mother. He found our cold, undemonstrative British reserve in time of mourning totally indecipherable.

'If this were my country and someone's 46-year-old son had died, everyone would be howling and wailing in the streets and in the church,' he remarked. 'But here, you're all too quiet. Why is no one even crying?'

A good question. But it still makes my eyes well up to think of our journey from the family home, accompanying the funeral hearse. Salford's Catholics from the parish and many other locals lined the streets in their dozens and elderly men doffed their caps as the cortege passed by down Manchester Road where I had been born, turning right into Station Road at the Windmill pub. Even the oncoming traffic halted when the lights were on green. It was as though time had stood still. And there in the long seat behind me was Pablo, holding my mother's hand and stroking her.

'I'm so sorry, I'm so sorry.'

She'd got none of this tactile attention from the other men in the family and she wasn't refusing it either. To think that the woman who'd rushed me off to that doctor for a medical cure for my gayness, was now accepting her son's partner, stranger and foreigner that he was, into the fullness of her life – a life now so pained and crippled with grief. As the public speaker in the family, I had been charged to perform the eulogy – a fact that I explained to my parents could look almost hypocritical given the fact that Chris and I were known never to have seen eye-to-eye. So I went for the safe option and settled on some tales from his early years.

'He was destined to be an entrepreneur,' I told the congregation. 'Aged only seven, he bred and sold off pigeons at a decent mark-up price. Then, spotting a gap in the market, he moved up a notch into budgies. Nothing could hold him back.' A sea of smiling, approving faces.

An hour later, at the funeral wake, a tap on my shoulder from two of my many uncles. 'A word if you don't mind. Those pigeons – you got that bit all wrong.'

'But he bred pigeons,' I insisted. 'I remember that shed he kept them all in and all the bird muck. The back yard was inches thick in it.'

'But he couldn't sell 'em. That's the point. He was a rubbish entrepreneur,' said Uncle number two. 'Your Granny Reynolds. She wrang all their necks one night after he'd gone to bed. We had a whip round and gave him the money but he thought he was a dab-hand little businessman.'

Then Uncle One, with the *coup de grace*.

'We had bloody pigeon pie for weeks on end. With apple sauce. Sick of the stuff we were. So – Mr Journalist – get yer facts right.'

Challenges of delivering the eulogy apart, there lay one other rather tricky obstacle ahead inside St Mark's – the very church where I had first reported for altar boy duty in 1967, aged seven years old, opposite Dr Bhanji's practice. No one had ever seen Pablo before and there was a fair bit of elbow nudging and tongues-a-wagging as he took his place beside me with the immediate family in the front pew. As the coffin bearers began to process out, my mother and father formed a natural unit and began to follow them, leaving me a split second to decide what to do with him. I felt all eyes on us. The closet suddenly returned. I simply could not face processing out *a deux*. Catching the glinting eye of my very sympathetic cousin Helen in the pew ahead, I startled her by lunging forward, yanking her out and sandwiching her between us both. I guess she rather resembled Angela Rippon wedged between Eric and Ernie in that priceless 1976 Morecambe and Wise Christmas special.

Following the wake, Pablo and I returned south to three key milestones. First, my HIV test results came through. For the second time in my life I had got away with it – negative. Second, Pablo got his student visa extended by a further year. Then by early 2002, after dozens of visits to the clinic and blood samples, we discovered that the HIV virus had so eroded his immune system that his CD-4 count, the level of white T-cells, had fallen to about one hundred and eighty. He now needed to start the anti-retrovirals urgently. The team at the Mortimer Market Centre at University College Hospital prescribed him a cocktail of drugs which he had to take twice a day – about a dozen tablets in all. They all seemed to end in the suffix, '-ovir' and I recall one long brown one the size of a torpedo that he reacted particularly badly to, producing violent sweats and fevers for weeks on end.

We'd now been living together for two and a half years, and it was three and half since we had first met. Pablo, technically, now had access to an indefinite right to remain in the UK if we could prove to the immigration authorities we had been together for more than three years, two of which had to be co-habitation. To this end, we had been keeping every shred of evidence: postcards and Christmas cards sent to us both, dated holiday photos. I'd even backed up all my emails sent to him in Ecuador 1999–2000 and had collated them in a large lever arch file. We also now needed the testimony of about at least a dozen people who would corroborate our story. Most friends, even though they perhaps had their doubts about the long-term possibilities of this endeavour, knew about Pablo's health situation and the death warrant that lay around the corner if he'd have been forced to go back home. But would my parents offer their help? For understandable reasons, especially after the terrible shock loss of their first-born, there was no way I was going to start bleating on about Pablo and HIV. I rang them up early one evening in December 2002.

'A letter? What kind of letter?' asked my father.

'To the Home Office,' I explained. 'They need to know from reliable sources that we are a genuine partnership.'

Long pause.

'Well what do I write? I mean, I'll have to do it 'cause yer Mam hates writing letters. Maybe you should draft it and we can copy it?'

'No dad,' I replied. 'It really has to come in your own words. Whatever you want to say. Tell them when we met, when you first met and that Pablo has come up to Manchester and … yes, remember that first time he ever saw snow in Bakewell at that holiday cottage at Christmas? Put that in. I've got the photos to prove it.'

A week later, a letter arrived with a Salford postmark. I sensed it was 'the missive' and, on my way out to work, hastily put it in my pocket so I could read it on the tube. As the Central Line headed west from St Paul's, I unzipped the envelope and saw, on pristine pale blue Basildon Bond writing paper, a letter which began: 'To whom it may concern at the Home Office.' The blue ink sloped quite dramatically upwards from left to right. This was a classic hallmark of my father's writing.

'My son Mark first met Pablo in South America in 1999, the year Manchester United won the treble.' (An unnecessary detail perhaps, but Dad always associated my flying to Barcelona and back from Quito for the Champions League final to write an article for *Match of the Day* magazine with my encounter with Pablo – and anyway, it made it look authentic. As a die-hard Red, no way was I putting a line through that.)

It continued.

'We first met him in November 2000 when he was a source of great support to us following the loss of our son, Christopher. He has spent Christmas with us twice now and both my wife, Pat and I can honestly say that the two of them are I understand, what is called in modern day parlance, "*an item*".'

On reading this, I had tears streaming down my cheeks. Whereas my mother had eased up considerably over the years on the whole gay issue, my father had always held back. Tolerance is not acceptance. But this was a total game changer. Passengers on the tube were staring from the seats opposite and then looked away quickly in embarrassment when I clocked them. A very assertive and confident woman next to me who could not escape my emotions, put her hand on mine and simply asked, 'Bad News?' I explained the letter, its context and how my father had never had to commit to anything like this before publicly and then handed it to her to examine. When she saw, 'an item,' she erupted into laughter.

'Even the most heartless apparatchik at Lunar House Immigration Croydon will not be able to doubt this. It's priceless. You couldn't fake it.'

She was right. You couldn't. I sent it off to my local Tory MP, Mark Field, to also ask for his support. Within four weeks, a large registered-post brown envelope arrived, confirming that Pablo did now indeed have the right to remain indefinitely in the United Kingdom. His passport now contained a stamp with those very words. He was safe. 'The item' had made it – with no small help from friends and family. The first person I rang with the good news was my father.

'Well I reckon it was our letter that clinched it,' he said.

'You may be right there,' I answered. 'Dad. Why did you say we were "an item?" I've never heard you say anything like that before.'

'Oh, that was yer mother,' he said. 'Did you not like that bit? I said to her, I said, "are you sure?" I thought items were things. Objects like a vase, a stapler, that sort of thing.' No,

I assured him, 'item' had been just fine. Who knows, it may have been the decisive element?

The novelty of Pablo's entry into UK orbit, the drama of his precarious HIV condition, my brother's death and the drive to get his immigration status normalised; the combination of these factors had served to obscure my judgement and take a long hard look at the way that this relationship was panning out. I know this now from speaking to my friends who had remained tight lipped during this period, but there was a definite sense of cracks being papered over. Cracks which now threatened to become full blown craters.

Once Pablo had flown in from Quito and got used to the idea that he might live quite a bit longer than your average mallard thanks to the huge advances in medicine, he took to London like an enthusiastic child in a sweet shop. At first there were maddening features: his customary habit of turning up an hour late for social meetings (he had huge issues with 'Northbound' and 'Southbound' signs on the tube and more than once found himself up in Harrow and Wealdstone on the Bakerloo line when we were meeting at Waterloo.) Some nights he would come home very late in the small hours, or not at all. I remember a call at 5am in which an inebriated voice cried down the phone, 'Cuchi' (piglet) ... 'I'm on the twenty-five bus and I fell asleep. The driver keeps saying "terminus". Where is terminus?' He was in fact in Ilford, some nine and a half miles from our home at Ludgate Circus. Bad enough, but made much worse because of the fact he was due at work at the Hilton Hotel near Hyde Park Corner at 8am, to mastermind their hotel linen operation. More than once I received angry calls from bosses (to my phone number which Pablo had handed on as an emergency contact), demanding to know why he was not in work on time.

Slowly but surely, the memory of how his own father had met his fate became etched more and more in my mind. I recalled times in Quito 1999/2000 when he would leave for work on Friday morning at Petro Producción and come back Saturday afternoon absolutely bladdered after a typical in-house work beer binge. When we had friends round and the wine was flowing, I got to recognise that tell-tale sign of glazed eyes, slurred voice, insistent and boorish behaviour bordering on aggressive/violent. He went out one night with some gay Latino friends to *CXR* at 79 Charing Cross Road and returned at four o clock in the morning. I was due on location to start filming at seven and he stormed in and switched all the lights on, demanding that we have a (surely incoherent) chat. I exploded. I seized the brass crucifix that my parents had given me as a first holy communion present when I was only seven years old and hurled it at him with all the force I could muster. He ducked and it smashed into the wall, taking out a large chunk of plaster and breaking into two parts. To this day, it remains unstable and slightly skew-whiff on account of a botched repair job with the superglue. So when I see the good Lord staring at me at an odd angle, I think of torrid times with Pablo and the brokenness of fallen humanity. For someone of Pablo's Catholic sensibilities, hurling a holy object like this through the air was akin to a scene from *The Exorcist*. In his mind it could bring only the worst of outcomes.

'Cuchi, a veces eres más latino que yo' (Piglet, at times you're more Latin than I am) he would yell defiantly, referring to a recently discovered hot-headed impulsiveness. I was getting used to a certain rhythm. Pablo would provoke a crisis with his drunkenness and my suspicions of his debauchery. In response, I would throw plates and smash a few things up. He then seemed satisfied and this would buy us a few days/weeks of peace – and then it would all kick off again. In fact, it was all a turbo-charged replay of the dynamics of living with Michael. But whereas my partner in Oxford had played a brilliant hand and never risen to the bait, I was allowing myself to be wound up. I was jealous and insecure. Was I preferring the comfort of the rhythm of failure to the uncertainty of success?

Michael had been eleven years my senior – exactly the age gap between Pablo and myself. But at least Michael and I had had much more of a semblance of equality about us. In this respect, Pablo and I were always on a hiding to nothing.

When I explained to one good friend how he would stay out until three or four in the morning and I could not get to sleep worrying about him she simply asked me 'Why?' I blurted out that he was vulnerable, likely to mix with bad company, might get into trouble, but she shook her head.

'You can't get to sleep because you're out of control. You invited him here on your terms and now he's spreading his wings and you don't like it – isn't that more like it?' I protested, but she went on.

'What is there on display in your home that is his? Nothing. No photos from home, no mementos. He's effectively living in *your flat*. He's got no real stake in your place. It's not really for him a home, 'cos it's all on your terms. That's why you get mad and cannot sleep. Because he's not behaving how you want him to.'

Ouch. Just when you want your friends to resemble doormats.

Henry Higgins had spawned something he could not ultimately control. It seems, if my tough-talking friend was right, that our little Pygmalion plot was also not going according to plan. When people asked me if I really loved Pablo, I found myself using words like 'pity', 'duty', 'responsibility to help', but rarely the words of love based on equality and respect. Mark my words, when he was sober he was a charming rogue – deceptively intelligent and astute with an uncanny intuitive knowledge about others. He could detect insincerity and bluff in others within seconds. And when you were ill he was a top rate nurse, Latin America's very own Florence Nightingale. Countless times he'd find some weird Ecuadorean shop near Elephant and Castle and emerge with odd looking red tablets that just sucked the raging fever right out of you. For a while it was he that was saving me.

But the danger signs were also now abundant. I was getting less and less sleep. My mental health was taking a battering. Then one day, it was Pablo who was on the receiving end of that B-word – a moment of a truly horrible epiphany. We'd reached late 2004, more than four years of living together and such was my concern about my own reactions to his drinking, that I had rung Al-Anon, the telephone helpline for friends and families. In typical fashion I had banged on about trying to sort out his problem and the history of serious alcoholism in the family (his youngest brother was, if anything, worse). The very kind and attentive person on the phone explained that partners and relatives frequently succumb to an addiction of their own: a drive to cure the other person and get it fixed. This was a recipe for disaster if the alcoholic or addict sensed that they could consciously or unconsciously transfer the responsibility for kicking the habit onto you. It was the picture of co-dependency and one that had to be kicked into touch as soon as possible.

I attended my first Al-Anon meeting just a stone's throw from St Paul's, barely five minutes from my own front door. It was a 7.30am start as ninety per cent of the attendees were financiers in the City of London. For an hour and a half came tale after tale of people dealing with the demon drink. I was totally mesmerised and had never, until now, realised that this 'underworld' existed. My superficial view of alcoholism had been the drunken homeless on the street, or the guy in the pub who could not take his liquor. Now I was hearing about people on two hundred thousand a year who'd come in at midnight after a twelve hour day managing the bulls and bears of the stock market and then down nearly a bottle of whisky before going to bed. As a newcomer I 'shared' briefly. When the meeting ended two of the regulars stayed behind to offer some words to me.

'It's not about you fixing the other person. It's a chance for you to get support from others here when you can't cope. There's a 24/7 telephone list here – you can call anyone day or night and, maybe, you'll be happy enough to have your own name down on it at some point?' The thought of being rung at four in the morning by a distressed Al-Anon member just as Pablo was coming in drunk was not especially appealing. The other person who had been waiting to get my attention now chipped in.

'You need to get him to leave and change the locks. If I've heard this story once I have heard it a million times.' Get him to leave? But where would he go?

Some weeks after I started attending these meetings, it all came to a head. I had prepared dinner for around eight pm, but there was another no-show. And neither was there an answer from Pablo's mobile. In fact, no answer on various occasions between then and eleven fifteen. I ate alone and my inner rage grew hour by hour. Then the doorbell went. He had his keys, so who could it be at this hour? On the intercom, I heard his drunken voice muttering something about 'losing his keys' at work. Inside I was now blazing out of control. I ran down four flights of stairs and sprang open the door. He was totally wrecked and I could stand it no more. I began lashing out, pummelling him, punching him with all my might. I had never done anything like this before in my life. In the passage way of Bride Court where I lived, a handful of clients at the noodle bar opposite my front door looked on in horror as I carried on assailing him. He was too weak and under the influence to fight back. I registered a terrified child-like look on his face. Shock. Total absolute shock that I had been reduced to this. I was finally pulled off him by three or four of the onlookers. A woman waved her fist at me angrily. 'Shame on you. Treating this poor defenceless man like that.' She put her coat around him and walked off into the night in the direction of Blackfriars Bridge. I later learnt that Pablo had spent several nights on her sofa in Greenwich, during which she had attempted to satisfy some of her own pent up desires, with him cast in the role of reluctant participant.

If Paradiso Perduto had been the denouement to my time with Michael in Venice, the events of domestic violence outside the Chi Noodle Bar meant that Pablo and I had hit a point of no return. We had to separate. I was becoming a danger, not only to him but to myself. I lay awake that night thinking: why had I got into all this in the first place, turning into the father he never had, nothing but a raging, dangerous parent? Where, deep down inside me, lay that impulse to save, an impulse that had almost certainly meant Pablo had survived the horrors of HIV but which had brought us face to face with destruction? He now had the English language, the share of space in a flat off Fleet Street in one of the richest cities in the world, no mortgage or rent to pay and secure employment prospects with the Hilton Group which meant he could send money home to his cash-starved mother. He had marvelled at my parents' acceptance of him and felt oddly weird about coming to mass with me from time to time – could not this have been Pablo's very own Good News? That people like me, like us are really, deep down, OK?

After he moved out of Bride Court, Pablo fell on his feet, at least for a while. He'd met a British Airways cabin steward called Brad and within weeks they were living together in his flat south of Vauxhall. I was introduced. We all got on. I felt relief. Baton transferred. Pablo seemed more sorted, more sober. Maybe this Brad was a good thing? Their relationship was far from perfect. This I knew from several messages left during the night on my (switched off) mobile – they'd been fighting and police had been called. But once every few months, I saw him on my own, and he would tell me he had turned over a new leaf. He was a reformed man. All was looking up.

Then in February 2008, returning from a conference in South Wales on Catholicism and the challenges of climate change, a call came through to my mobile as I was standing on Newport station. It was the Metropolitan Police.

'I have some rather grave news about your friend Brad. An ambulance was called this morning but I'm afraid they couldn't resuscitate him. And the guy living with him, er Pablo... Can you get here as quickly as possible?'

Without going into all the grim details, Brad had died in a drugs accident. His grief-stricken parents flew all the way over from Adelaide to recover his body and then invited Pablo all the way over to New South Wales for his funeral. It was a terrible shock to him and one he is still coming to terms with after a number of years.

My role now? We talk on the phone intermittently. He cuts my hair from time to time. I do my best to support – but from a distance. It's the dilemma for anyone close to someone with addictive tendencies: do you pull out totally and hope to instigate the shock that promotes recovery and responsibility, or stay part of the equation with the gnawing feeling that the other person will always feel that if you're somehow 'around', you will fix them? Even though he was not legally entitled, after Brad's death I petitioned the trustees of British Airways to consider Pablo as a deserving pension beneficiary by collecting witness statements. After some deliberation, the trustees' panel agreed that he had indeed been Brad's *de facto* partner and carer which meant a life-saving sum of money every month for the rest of his life.

A friendship and relationship that began in bizarre circumstances in a Quito bar, seventeen years on, has achieved some semblance of stability as far as his life-threatening HIV is concerned, but this had not been *Shirley Valentine* by any stretch of the imagination.

I am a still a man of prayer, however hard it seems to conceive that God is somewhere in the midst of all this, and Pablo is always at the top of my list of intentions. Some time ago, in supplication one morning in a church after mass, the words of a marvellous song from *Les Misérables* came into my mind. When I invoke the Almighty, these are still the words for him that I hope make my prayer soar to heaven:

> *God on high*
> *Hear my prayer*
> *In my need*
> *You have always been there*
>
> *He is young*
> *He's afraid*
> *Let him rest*
> *Heaven blessed.*
> *Bring him home*
> *Bring him home*
> *Bring him home.*

9

Vale of tears

Whether it's the pressure of the advertising industry with its images of silhouetted (straight) couples walking off into the sunset or the accumulation of centuries of social convention, most of us carry within us a conscious or unconscious script that there is, for sure, a 'Mr' or 'Ms' Right – that elusive individual who will magically complement you, be balm to the soul and put an end to all the restlessness. Post-Pablo, I was rapidly coming to the conclusion that this way of thinking was not only flawed, but that it was bordering on idolatry. The dating industry's, Hollywood's and society's very own golden calf. I felt scarred. I felt suspicious of intimacy. So I now opted, like millions of others have down the years – for sublimation.

After the earlier television success of *Queer and Catholic,* a whole new world of work opened up. There were investigations into the enigmatic and controversial Catholic group, Opus Dei. A three part series *Children of Abraham* took me on a post 9/11 trip through the Middle East in search of common ground between the oft-warring descendants of the great biblical patriarch. And with no 'significant other' around, I often threw caution to the wind. A scene in Rafah in the Gaza strip, face to face with balaclava-wearing members of Islamic Jihad toting their AK-47s, had my mother reaching for her tranquilisers. Most of these documentary ideas came either from myself, or the commissioning editors at Channel Four, but oddly enough, perhaps the best thing I have ever produced was unwittingly down to my father.

Christmas 2004 was spent in a sweet rented cottage in Grindleford, a picturesque village in the Peak District. I'd been out for a long hike high up on Curbar Edge on a scintillatingly crisp day and returned around four in the afternoon, ready to join my parents for Boxing Day dinner. As I entered the lounge, my father was glued to the TV set looking very distressed. My mother stood in the doorway with a potato peeler in her hand.

'What's happened?' I asked.

He sat there and just shook his head. He was looking at the first pictures of the aftermath of the south Asian tsunami which would claim nearly a quarter of a million lives. Finally my father prised his eyes off the screen and turned to me.

'God could have stopped that,' he said.

My mother looked at me, then turned to return to the kitchen.

'Well hang on,' I said, 'if God is going to suspend the laws of nature on some occasions and not on others, how can we have a world which is predictable according to science? And if God intervenes every time a bullet is fired, and plucks it out of the air, what about living with the consequences of free will, or individual freedom?'

He stared back for what seemed an eternity. Then he said: 'You've always got an answer haven't you?'

Then he got up and went upstairs to his room. My mother now beckoned me into the kitchen to peel carrots, cross the sprouts and wrap up parsnips in foil. She told me he had hardly said a word since he'd first seen the coverage a couple of hours ago. We both knew this was unprecedented. He'd always been a man to question possibly the Church's precepts, rules and regulations but never the central tenet of religious faith: the goodness, nay the very existence of God. His comments had hit a major nerve, as this had always been my own Achilles heel: reconciling the existence of natural evil, earthquakes, disease, the cruelties of nature red in tooth and claw, with a loving compassionate divine Creator. When I saw the TV graphics on the news of the areas affected: Thailand, India, Sri Lanka and the West Sumatra coast off Indonesia – I had pondered how all the faith communities would react to this calamitous disaster. The catchment area was huge, taking in millions of Muslims, Buddhists, Hindus and Christians. So that very evening I rang Channel Four's head of religion, Aaqil Ahmed and told him about my father's reaction. Within twenty-four hours, we had a commission to make a marathon two hour investigation: *Tsunami: Where was God?*

Grindleford, Derbyshire, turned out to be the last place I saw my father. A few weeks after Christmas, my parents flew off to Lanzarote on a winter break. I was otherwise engaged with a Channel Four *Dispatches* with the catchy title, *Holy Offensive*, which was dealing with all the fallout and controversy over *Jerry Springer: The Opera*. Some Christian groups were up in arms about the depiction of Jesus on a fictitious film set dressed in a nappy, engaged in conversations with the Devil and the BBC was coming under pressure to pull a BBC2 Saturday night broadcast. A week before our documentary was due to air, we were working fifteen/sixteen hours a day. A message was intercepted on my phone at eleven at night.

'Hello love. It's yer Mum. Now I don't want you to worry. But yer Dad's had a bit of a turn with his heart and he's in hospital for a few tests. They think it's just a flutter.'

When I called back early next morning, she was insistent that all was in hand. Nevertheless my young brother Antony, a GP, was worried enough to book a flight out, ostensibly out of concern for my mother being out there on her own at night in their holiday timeshare. Then the day after he touched down in Arrecife, a dire worsening in my father's condition. He was suddenly getting serious internal bleeds and when I spoke to him on the phone by his bed he sounded weak. I was getting updates from my brother 'twixt all the round the clock documentary editing.

On 14 February 2005 it was not only St Valentine's Day, but also my parents' fifty second wedding anniversary. Back in London's Soho our team was under the cosh with the script for *Dispatches*. I was caught midway between sleep deprivation and intense anxiety. At ten in the morning, a call was put through to our editing suite. It was my brother. My father had had such a huge bleed that he'd needed a major transfusion. The problem was that his heart was now so weak, that the transfusion had effectively overloaded the system. The medics had had no choice, as without it he would have been in real peril. So, surreally, staring at an image of a man on a TV screen dressed in a red suit with a pitchfork conversing with the Virgin Mary, I learnt of my father's death. The production team all wanted me to stop, but I just ploughed on, anxious to keep it all at bay.

Owing to Spanish bureaucracy in matters of the repatriation of the deceased, it took us more than three weeks to get my father's body back into the UK. Even worse, the local coroner in Salford, not persuaded entirely by all the paperwork which had been carried out in the Canary Isles, now insisted on carrying out a post-mortem. The funeral directors got in touch and, in order to spare my mother, told me discreetly over the phone that they needed me to go and identify him before they could release him for scrutiny.

'Before you go in,' said the lovely Pauline from Barlow's Funeral Directors as she stood outside the chapel of rest, 'I just want you to know that the Spanish don't go to the lengths that we do. And it is three weeks.' She grimaced. 'He's not in such a great state.'

My heart thumped away and my breaths got shallower and shallower as I stepped inside. They removed the pristine white cloth and there he was – those characteristic crooked teeth (which he passed on to me). His bony face – so very jaundiced. He was not exactly at peace, but neither was he agitated – it was rather caught in a snap-shot as though you'd cut him off in mid-sentence. I nodded to the undertaker and the white sheet now covered him once more. I can see that face now, quite vividly, as I write these words. I can see it as sharply as a picture I took on my digital camera only yesterday. This was eleven years ago. But it was all OK. What I had seen was a shell, the mere remains of my father. If there was another dimension to our existence and his soul was now at rest, it was surely nothing to do with all this.

The problem was that *my* soul was far from at rest. For years my father and I had survived on the football and papered over the cracks with 'banter'. But I had always longed for a lasting, radical rapprochement with him, a moving from tolerance to acceptance – and it never came. It was never going to come from him. And if I had planned some staged ambush and manoeuvred a man-to-man chat in which my needs for approval were put starkly on the table, I can only think it would have embarrassed him. I don't think I was a coward. My reluctance was based, at least in part, on a desire not to put him on the spot and leave him floundering for his lines. But in those days before and after his funeral, when my eyes welled up, it was all a kaleidoscope of that *Persil* advert, the bullying at school, that crass poem about the Roman soldier which he exploded over. Perhaps more than anything, it was about our physical awkwardness about touching and embracing. True, there had been those small sacramental moments of acceptance, chiefly the double sheets on the visit to Oxford and that moving letter to the Home Office for Pablo. But I'd pined for something more verbal, more explicit. Maybe unrealistically.

That grieving was the nearest I'll ever come to understanding what women mean by labour contractions (without the same intense pain for sure) – hours and hours of nothing then, out of nothing, a dramatic upstart in tension. Suddenly, you are in the grip of a sobbing that takes you back to childhood; where every bone and muscle in your body seems engaged and the howls that leave your lips are propelled on rising gusts from your lungs. I did all this in private – never with others. But I know my mother often heard me in my old bedroom. One relative called by for a coffee one morning and later my mother informed me that my aunt had stopped in mid-sentence.

'What's that noise?' she asked.

'Oh, that's our Mark. He's doing his grieving,' she had replied.

Mother of course – was mother. A rock. On the night of the funeral, noticing how spent I was after giving the eulogy and being on hand all day to welcome all the relatives, she poured me out another huge glass of Merlot from Morrisons.

'Come on love,' she said. 'Let's have a toast to yer Dad.'

After we clinked glasses, she looked a trifle pensive. Then she said.

'It's better this way isn't it? That he's gone first. I've always thought it'd be better like that.'

'What?' I said. 'What do you mean?' I was somewhat taken aback to think she'd almost been plotting this out in her mind for some time.

She looked away, briefly, into the distance, and then turned her gaze back on me.

'Well,' she said, 'think of it. Who'd have got a Christmas card?'

What?

It's pure Alan Bennett – but so true to who she was. Practical, largely unsentimental, and certainly not one to play the victim card. Looking forward. Once that glass of wine was polished off, she poured us both another.

'Thing is, there's a few things I won't be able to do now. I mean your Dad always helped me get the car into the garage. Told me when to stop before I hit the freezer. Now what will I do?'

'We'll swap the Corolla for a Yaris,' I said, 'smaller and easier to park.'

She nodded. Next on the list – holidays.

'New Zealand,' she said, looking rather morose and sorry for her self for the first time all day. 'We had this plan to go. I mean we went to visit Ginger and Charlotte in Australia when they were working as doctors and they say New Zealand's even more amazing.'

'Well you can still go,' I insisted. 'I mean – maybe somebody from the parish would like a holiday? Go as your companion.'

A look of disbelief now descended.

'Oh no. Not from the parish. I mean I can't think of anybody. It's a long way and anyway, it won't be cheap. No, I suppose I'll just have to take it on the chin and realise that some things are not going to be possible without yer Dad.'

She fixed her eyes on me. I thought I detected the slightest hint of self-pity.

'Well, do you really want to go?' I asked.

'Well you've been and seen it; those friends in Wellington who had the baby – you know the, the, what do you call it...'

'Lesbians,' I said.

'That's it. Them. Anyhows, you said it was stunning scenery and like a really huge mountainous Scotland...'

A long, ever so slightly awkward silence.

'Well if you really want to go,' I said, 'I guess I could just ...'

Quick as a flash.

'I'll just go and get the brochure.'

Within five minutes we had the diary out and we were looking at glossy pictures of Milford Sound, Fox Glacier and the Abel Tasman National Park.

'Blimey. No,' she said suddenly. 'We're not paying that.'

Was I off the hook then?

'The single room supplement,' she said indignantly, 'is eight hundred and thirty pounds.'

'Well, I suppose it is six weeks,' I argued. When I heard myself actually saying it, I did begin to think I had made a serious error of judgement. I knew, I just knew what was coming next.

'No, we're not doing that. We'll share. I mean – there's nothing I haven't seen already is there?'

Thus it was that I found myself flying thirty hours on Singapore Airlines and sharing a series of hotel rooms with my bereaved mother and sixty odd largely OAPS on our 'Journeys of Distinction' organised tour. My mother managed to load up an enormous casket of Ted's ashes and pass through baggage security scanners and beagle dogs at immigration without detection. At the time I thought we were seriously contravening customs regulations but subsequent checks confirm that there is no actual restriction on taking human ashes into the country, even if we lacked the death certificate that the Kiwi authorities had recommended. Mid-way through the trip, we took this large silver object into a huge field under the shadow of Mount Cook, at 12,218ft, the country's highest peak. I then said a prayer for the repose of his soul and we each took it in turns to scatter the grey, gritty remains. Then, in a bold declaration that would have had Wittgenstein and serious scholars of linguistics reaching for their manuals, my mother smiled and proudly proclaimed:

'Now. We can truly say that your Dad has been to New Zealand.'

Dad was ever-present throughout the trip. I lost count of the times my mother called me 'Ted,' instead of my real name. This happened when I was least expecting it – such as four in the morning, when her jet lag would kick in. There would typically be a sharp shove on my shoulder.

'Ted, Ted … do us a favour love. Ring down for some fresh milk for me tea. This UHT stuff's awful.' Then she'd realise her wee verbal lapse. 'I mean Mark. I don't know why I keep saying Ted. It just comes out.'

'Mam,' I said, grumpily and sleep deprived, 'we're not in Nepal. They speak English in New Zealand you know.'

''Course I know that,' she said. 'But, well, it's just that you're very good on the phone.'

That vacation, unbearable as the lack of personal space became at times, forged us closer together than ever before. We never missed mass when there was a chance and were occasionally surprised to discover how many fellow 'left footers' there were on our coach. On one occasion, half way up the west coast of New Zealand's southern island, Pat was geeing up the driver to step on it so that we didn't miss the Saturday evening vigil service. As the bus pulled into Franz Josef Glacier, a small wooden prefab came into view just to the right of the road. This was 'Our Lady of the Alps'. Mass had just started as we entered and the local priest was startled to see his congregation of fifteen more than double in the space of seconds.

Following my father's death, there was a very deep 'death and resurrection' narrative about my mother's approach to life. Although she never said as much, because she was a tough, northern woman, blessed with fine neighbours, there must have been times when she ached with loneliness. She had been the eldest of six sisters, tragically losing her youngest sibling, seven-year-old Margaret, to scarlet fever. Pat had married at the age of twenty-three. She barely knew what it meant to be in a house alone – especially in the winter nights. Naturally, we all upped the visiting and the phone calls, but I did worry about her.

It was mainly this anxiety that prompted me to take a bit of a risk. I had recently taken on the position of chair of Quest, a Roman Catholic support group for LGBT individuals and their families which had been set up in 1973. The organisation had a membership of around three hundred people nationally and always organised a weekend summer conference – normally on a university campus. They were usually very stimulating weekends with theologians and other academics as speakers, celebration of the Eucharist and a gala dinner with plenty of wine flowing. Why not, I thought, and asked my mother if she wanted to come to Liverpool. After all it was just thirty five miles down the road.

'Will I have to pretend to be a lesbian?' she asked. 'I mean, what would your Dad think?'

I assured her that Quest was also for friends and family as well as gays and lesbians and that she'd have a good time. So when the time came, she packed her weekend suitcase and off we went. Within an hour of checking in at John Moores University, any apprehensions I had about her ability to take it all in completely disappeared. After registering and getting her unpacked in her room, we went to the bar for a pre-dinner drink. I introduced her to a few members of the committee and left to go and get her a glass of red wine. When

I returned, she was holding court like Julie Andrews on the bed surrounded by the Von Trapp children.

'I mean,' she insisted, 'it's all been going on since the Romans you know. Of course Mark's dad is sadly no longer with us, well he still thought he'd meet a nice girl and settle down.'

From that point on she felt totally at home and attended every conference she could. Often she took on the role of matriarch: sitting there sipping her wine and often talking with younger members who were having issues with their own parents. Despite being in her late seventies by now, she was more than up for a bit of bopping.

'If I want that "Dancing Queen" on again, do I have to go and ask the DJ or will you do it love?' she'd say.

My younger brother, by now a post-Catholic, post-Quaker, was slightly puzzled about why on earth I would take her to a weekend conference of LGBT Catholics. He said he'd give her a call on my mobile during the weekend just to chat and catch up. So when the call came in on the Saturday evening, she clasped the phone to her ears as she sauntered across the university campus.

'Oh hello love,' she said to Antony. 'Look, I can't really talk now. I'm just off to a champagne lesbian reception.' What would have been the odds on words such as those emanating from her lips just a few years ago?

In Quest, Pat found what she often craved and missed in the life of the Church: companionship, provocative input and reflection, decent preaching and dozens of fine individuals. At the end of that first Liverpool conference she was not slow to make an astute point.

'I mean love, the people here have had so many brickbats thrown at them by the church and others and yet they still believe, they still follow the gospel and the life of Jesus. I mean, you'd think if the bishops had any sense they'd be using this as a witness to faith instead of pretending they don't exist.'

As we returned along the M62 motorway back to Manchester, I asked her how she had found the weekend.

'Oh, what lovely people, I mean, sign me up for next year. I've never been to Norwich,' she said beaming. 'What's the organisation called again?'

'Quest' I said.

'Quest' she repeated, pondering the name. 'Quest. So much more interesting than the Union of Catholic Mothers.' To this day, I still have my regrets that we never adopted that as a slogan on our T-Shirts.

My mother would never have dared to have come along to an event like this as long as my father was alive. She'd have worried about leaving him on his own at home but also been slightly wary of his disapproval. But in the wake of his death she was sprouting new wings. When I gently pointed out that this was all in contrast to her reaction back in 1974 when she had frogmarched me off to Dr Bhanji, she looked at me with a mild contempt.

'Well no one knew anything then did they? I mean, times change.'

'Even though it's been going on since the Romans?' I retorted. She pursed her lips.

'Oh you're a cheeky monkey you are.'

Now that my mother was on her own, I had a rather different take on my journalistic travels abroad. I felt uneasy about leaving her and the country for long periods. Yet this was precisely what I had to do for *Tsunami: Where was God?*, a documentary that had been born of my father's own questioning over God's goodness. Six weeks in Thailand, Indonesia and India in which I would tour the areas devastated by the enormous waves and encounter individuals who had lost everything.

Those six weeks were physically gruelling but a period of great grace. I can still see the faces of those we met. Inspiring individuals such as Fadil in Banda Aceh who had been organising his brother's wedding celebrations when the tsunami struck. He was catapulted into the local mosque by the water and clung on for dear life by holding onto the central pillars for all his worth. When the waters receded he returned to the van he had used as a getaway for his family members when the initial warnings of the earthquake had sent them all scurrying for cover. He found his mother dead in the passenger seat. All the other bodies had been washed away. From a family of a dozen or more, he was the sole survivor. 'My faith is stronger than ever,' he told me. 'In Islam we believe that Allah will never set you a test that you cannot overcome with His support. All I have now is Allah. I cannot abandon him now in my time of need.' Yet others, such as a mother who lost her husband and three children in Nagapattinam in Tamil Nadu off the east coast of southern India told me she hated God and could not pray to him. She never stated she had ceased to believe. In time-honoured fashion, others with dubious agendas sought to make capital out of all the misery. An Islamist group in Sumatra told me that Allah had sent all the waves to kill the young Muslims who were who fornicating on the beach. The Westboro Baptist Church in Kansas, that of the infamous 'God Hates Fags' mantra, were praising God because so many Swedes had been killed while on holiday off the Thai coast – God's clear punishment, according to their twisted logic, for a country that had liberal laws on homosexuality and which prosecuted Christian pastors who spoke out against the LGBT agenda.

My own loss of my father at the age of seventy six just weeks ago now felt almost like a gentle blessing in the midst of all this carnage. Apart from all the human tales of grief, loss, extraordinary courage and faith, the aim of the programme had also been to look at the 'problem of natural evil' and God in these various traditions. We asked tough questions: of a Muslim Geologist whether God could not have fashioned a world without tectonic plates that wreak havoc and kill people. We asked Hindu and Buddhist thinkers whether their karma account of suffering (that, ostensibly, the tsunami victims had done bad things in previous lives and were reaping the just desserts for their wrong-doing), was not just crass and inhumane. We even suggested to the high priest of the new atheists, Richard Dawkins, that he might secretly gloat and enjoy the discomfort felt by believers at times like this – after all this was just a few days after Rowan Williams, the serving Archbishop of Canterbury had said he could well understand how some people could lose their faith over such catastrophes. I'd spent days in the British Library immersing myself in tomes on the subject and was comprehensively prepared on all the theory including hauntingly beautiful poems, such as this one by a Tunisian called Al Qasim Al-Shabbi.

> *Reflect, the order of life is a subtle, marvellous, unique order.*
> *For nothing but death endears life and only the fear of tombs adorns it.*
> *Were it not for the misery of painful life, people would not grasp the meaning of happiness.*
> *Whomever the scowling of the dark does not terrify, does not feel the bliss of the new morning*

Yet away from the ivory tower confines of educational institutions, I now found myself faced with completely flattened villages in Banda Aceh, staring at orphaned children sitting desolately on a handful of crumbling steps – literally all that remained of their deceased parents' dwellings. After several days on the road, my cameraman, Bruno Sorrentino, wanted to change tack.

'It's all been good so far, but it's all a bit, I don't know, scripted. I'd say this morning you should just jump of the back of the open truck. We'll drive around for a couple of hours and, off the cuff, just tell us what you see and what you feel.'

So I did. And within minutes of seeing the forlorn expression of a young boy looking for this parents amidst the rubble, my hitherto composed delivery to camera totally deserted me. I began talking to camera: '*What's extraordinary is that when my dad looked at those TV pictures and said, "What have those people done to deserve this?" I never thought I'd actually be sitting here looking at all this in such proximity, so close.*'

But at this point I began to blubber and could barely get the words out. Weeks later when we included the tear-stricken presenter in the first rough cut of the film, I cringed when I saw it on the monitor and gently suggested to my film editor, Simon Ardizzone, to snip it out. 'No way,' he said. 'It's an amazingly powerful piece of television.' The Channel Four programme editor said as much: 'it's not a TV news report that lasts two minutes which is all about facts and objectivity. This is your story. It's a hundred minutes long. Anyone would cry seeing what you were seeing. It was like Hiroshima or Nagasaki. You were crying for everyone, not just yourself.'

I think in retrospect this was right. But there was another thing that got the old tear ducts going. As I climbed to the top of our rickety hotel in Aceh and stared at the stars late one night, a thought slowly gripped me. As a man in my early twenties, I had gone into religious life, aiming to be celibate and having service to God as my full time goal. It had not worked out. But what had actually happened? I was now relentlessly single, celibate (more by accident and force of circumstance than any pious design) and spending all my time on national television 'doing God'. Moreover, as a preacher Dominican, I had been aiming to deepen the faith and understanding of others, but what was all this about God and natural evil on prime time television if it was not that? How many priests on a Sunday morning would like to be talking to a million or more people in their congregation? I had spent fifteen years or so ducking and weaving, but events had conspired to take me right back to where I had started.

I had the fortune to produce, direct and present more than a dozen documentaries on television, but *Tsunami* remains my favourite. Its central theodicy dilemma about reconciling evil and God's ways in the world has always been the Achilles' heel of my faith. The project allowed me to ask some of the finest scientific minds on the planet about how they reconciled these apparent irreconcilables. Tectonic plates, they told me, forced land above the sea and gave us land masses for human habitation. The movement of the earth's crust propagated the regeneration of soil through the churning of mineral deposits, but yes, they also produced earthquakes. Even ghastly diseases, in a radical Darwinian fashion, eliminated certain members of the species before they could pass on their genes and thus, through the survival of the fittest, human stock was in a process of refinement – all consistent with a narrative of creation. It's just that what works best for the whole system is frequently devastating to those at the cutting edge. 'Verily, verily, I say unto you,' says Jesus in St John's gospel, 'unless a grain of wheat falls into the ground and dies, it abides alone: but if it dies, it brings forth much fruit.' In the Hindu tradition, the god Shiva is both the god of creation and destruction – inseparable. If the positives in natural creation cannot be separated from all the nasty downsides, then why create us at all, knowing that suffering was inevitable? This was the question that proved to be the climax of our film. And it was answered most eloquently by Philip Clayton, an American physicist turned Christian philosopher. His reply is worth quoting in full.

> 'Anyone who sees the depth of the suffering that happens in our world and answers that question simply, doesn't get it. I would love to imagine a divine who stood and wept and somehow at the last minute felt it was better to have us than to have only the divine in eternal emptiness. You and I would probably not push the button. As Ivan argued against Alyosha in The Brothers Karamazov, we shouldn't push the button. And that God pushed that button and made creation, hints at a mystery that we don't understand. It hints at a resolution that we only hope for: God will only be God if the outcome is something so far better than what we see around us that it would make it all right. But I can only say that as a wish and a hope and not as an item of knowledge.'

But the making of that documentary, inspired by my father's initial reaction, taught me a major lesson. Any convincing answers to the big questions about God and Evil run into the buffers if one works at the level of intellect alone. In Velankanni, south of Chennai in India, I met up with Father Xavier, rector of the Basilica of Our Lady of Good Health. The church is on raised ground about a mile from the sea and on the day of the tsunami, thousands of people flocked into the building for refuge. Did lots of people, I asked him, doubt the goodness of God after the loss of so much life? 'No Mark. These questions only came from western journalists like yourself. In India, people accept that death and life are related completely. You want the world to be perfect, but you will only understand in the fullness of time, when all of God's plan will come to be known.'

There were queues of hundreds of people waiting to see him the day I visited him. Some just wanted to touch his clothes and receive a smile. This man oozed goodness. He had 'the peace that surpasseth all understanding,' a peace I craved for deep down and have rarely tasted. The tears welled up again as I spoke, off the cuff to the camera again about people like Father Xavier:

> *'There's something at the core of who they are that doesn't get communicated by the words, the things that they say. They emanate a presence which is so much more powerful than mere words. And I'm – I'm just beginning to understand that the intellect really does have its limits.'*

In essence, the life of selfless love, such as Father Xavier's, was a beacon whose language is recognised so easily by humanist atheist and committed believer alike. You can more easily *live* another person into curiosity about faith than merely talk them into it.

Armed with all this, I returned to the UK and shared a great deal with my mother who was still quietly reeling underneath from the shock of her new widowed status. She was, as ever, stoic and determined but like with so many individuals who lose a partner after decades of being together, there was, in turn, also a shock to the physical system. Within eighteen months of my father's departure she had succumbed to colon cancer and survived fairly intensive surgery for the following year or two. Then a series of minor strokes conspired to affect her vocal cords, leaving her often breathless and struggling to speak. After an especially bad incident, she was rushed into Salford Royal Hospital and was given an emergency tracheostomy to facilitate her breathing. My brother rushed up from Nottingham. I made the two hour dash from London Euston to Manchester and pelted along on my fold-up Brompton bike under darkness to make it to the intensive care unit. She was just coming out of theatre and on to the ward. I had expected long serious faces from the nursing staff, but to my amazement they were all chuckling away as they wheeled her along on the trolley. She was terribly pale and resigned, sporting a 'Well, what can you do?' sort of expression.

'Your mother is a real card isn't she?' said one of the nurses as she turned the corner onto the unit. It seemed a distinctly odd thing to say about a fragile woman with a so-called 'trachy' tube fixed to the side of her neck.

'What makes you say that exactly?' I retorted.

'Well, when she came to in theatre, she signalled for pen and paper and we gave her a clipboard.' A second nurse took up the story.

'She started writing and then handed it over to us. *'They say Hitler is dead. He's not. He's alive and kicking at St Mark's Church.'*

This was a reference to the new parish priest who she had not taken too kindly to. She subsequently used the clipboard to make her future intentions one hundred per cent crystal clear. 'If you let him bury me,' she wrote, 'I'll come back to haunt you.'

That, quite typically, was my mother. A woman who only ever had one job from the age of fifteen to when she retired in her late sixties, working in Berry's dress shop in Farnworth, near Bolton. She undercut Marks and Spencer and Debenhams with her competitive prices and, in her latter days, parading around Lancashire and Yorkshire school and church halls with a series of willing, if overweight models, she put on fashion shows while my father provided the backdrop – Mantovani on the newly purchased Garrard turntable. 'Here's a cheeky little number,' she would say as a busty woman in her early fifties struggled to keep her equilibrium along the makeshift catwalk, 'how shall I put it? Well this crimplene number, in an attractive kingfisher shade looks better on than off.' On one occasion, just outside of Halifax on an inhospitably drizzly February night, she took me to one side at the end of the evening. 'Have you seen Doris, I mean the size of her now? She almost broke the zips on two of them frocks. Remind me never to put her in hoops. It's stripes from now on.'

Pat did reach her eightieth birthday, but her final months were not good. Rarely able to communicate except via pen and paper, her deteriorating condition deprived her of the two things she loved most about life: a good natter and a decent meal. On 20 March 2010, she waved me off back to London to attend a sixtieth birthday party for one of our gay and Catholic Quest members and asked to be remembered to everyone she had met at our conferences. My brother kept vigil and she breathed her last in the small hours of the 21st.

I often wondered what would be worse. The death of the first parent, which brings home the brutal reality of mortality or the death of the second, which leaves one 'orphan' in the world with an accompanying sense of being radically alone. Without doubt, the departure of my mother hit me harder than I can ever have imagined. As I explained to the lovely Pauline at the funeral directors (now on her third Dowd family funeral in ten years. Did she offer nectar points, I wondered?), I was terrified of mucking up the eulogy on account of collapsing in an emotional mess. 'You need to have a good sob just before the service. It's set for midday isn't it, on Wednesday?'

'Yes, but how?' I enquired. 'I can't just turn it on like a tap.'

'Come in at eleven and talk to her,' she advised. 'Just sit with her and tell her anything you want.' She smiled at me. 'Trust me, that'll do the job. Now, have you decided on some clothes of hers for the funeral?'

Well no I hadn't. But back at the family home, I was soon climbing the ladder into the attic where I knew she had stashed all her years of frock accumulation, much to my father's disapproval. With the help of a solitary light bulb in the loft and a lightweight torch, I scoured around. There must have been more than a thousand outfits up there. I dithered a bit on account of the panoply of sartorial options before deciding on a simple navy blue suit. It was this that Pat was wearing when laid out in the chapel of rest an hour before the funeral on 31 March 2010. I followed the funeral director's advice and closed the door discreetly behind me. In front of her, I raised a newly dry-cleaned charcoal grey suit, collected only a quarter of an hour ago from Morrisons on Swinton shopping precinct.

'You see this?,' I said, holding up the suit on a hanger wrapped in plastic, 'I know you said I often looked like a tramp when I was on the telly, so I'm going to do you proud today. I'm gonna look my best – just for you.'

I looked self-consciously through a small gap where I had left the door ajar. Sitting on chairs near the reception, I detected one or two of the undertakers smiling and nodding in approval. I turned back to face Pat. Then I howled and howled for what seemed an eternity.

It had been superb advice. I emerged from the room feeling serene and at peace. I subsequently really 'enjoyed' the funeral, keeping a mantra in my head that I had invented from her lest I lose my composure: 'Remember, this is *my* day, not yours.' When I rose to speak about my mother, an incredible sight unfurled in front of me. Because I had been sitting in the front pew dedicated to the immediate family, I had had no real idea of how many people had actually turned up. When I turned round and walked to the pulpit, I could see that not only were all the pews full, but there were also dozens of people crammed cheek by jowl into the choir loft. I surveyed the faces. Many of them were her clients from the shop who'd made the trip to Pendlebury to pay their respects.

In keeping with her express wishes I had also indulged in a spot of subterfuge. The funeral had been planned for a Wednesday. This was no mere coincidence. It was the new parish priest's day off. The service was taken by his predecessor who had always gained Patricia Dowd's approval. After all I didn't want her ghost on my shoulder for the rest of my life. And in the weeks following her death, I was in church practically every day. But this was not some holy explosion of piety and devotion. I just needed to be in the place and setting where I felt closest to her. I found myself comforted by the legions of similar aged women with their 'sensible' overcoats with fur collars, the elderly ladies who spoke with the same northern accent and, when you sat behind them in the church pews, could have passed for her quite easily. The prayers: the *Angelus,* the *Hail Holy Queen* and *Memorare* bound me to my mother. All the rituals and smells of occasional incense gave me a fleeting, transient sense of her presence-absence. On one occasion in particular after Ascension Day mass, a member of the local parish in her early eighties breezed past me with the tell-tale waft of the same scent my mother would ever so occasionally don for special occasions and, for a nanosecond, she was there right beside me. But no sooner had she appeared then she was gone.

The following three months were taken up with two tasks of contrasting but immense importance. I had been commissioned by the BBC to make a personal profile of Pope Benedict XVI, formerly Cardinal Josef Ratzinger, in anticipation of his visit to the UK in September. The documentary production was to be based in the head of BBC Religion on Oxford Road in Manchester, so this was exceptionally convenient for task number two, namely the clearance of the parental home and its eventual sale in late July. After the filming, which included trips to Regensburg to meet Ratzinger's elder brother Georg and an extensive interview with the papal spokesman, Jesuit Father Frederico Lombardi at the Vatican, we got down to the editing. Every day I cycled twelve miles to and from my childhood home to try and construct a fair and informed view of the German pontiff. But living in that near-empty house was weird. It was full of memories and echoes of the past. When I wasn't getting the film into shape, I was trying to recycle possessions (those twelve hundred frocks in the attic kept local charity shops in stock for months on end.) Hidden from public view in my mother's bedroom were a series of statues of saints and the Virgin Mary which were shared out equally among the parish and devout left-footers at the BBC. Tables and chairs went off to a women's refuge. I even managed to sell the family car to the local estate agent who had found us a buyer: a local lad in his twenties who wanted a place with three bedrooms and a garden so he could start a family.

When the day of contract completion came, I did something quite unexpected which I had never envisaged happening. There were three sets of house keys, but I could not bear to part with all of them. I handed over two sets, but that weekend I was due to head north to the annual Quest conference in Lancaster. After our convention ended on the Sunday, I drove to a tiny village in Swaledale where I had passed a few happy days in a rustic property with my parents in the late summer of 1993. I found a wall by a stream just under where the cottage was situated, and inserted the keys in a gap behind a distinct and robust wooden bench. Those keys represent to me an eternal part of a bonding with my parents that I can never part with. I know exactly where they are. When I next visit the most northern of the Yorkshire Dales, rather like the tentative apostle Thomas, I will reach out my hand to insert my fingers in the holes in touch, in hope and expectation.

That autumn, after all the tumult, I needed to flee the UK for a change of space. I chose Madrid. The official version to my chums back home was that it was a linguistic and cultural sabbatical, a chance to really live and breathe Spain and take my workmanlike but imperfect Spanish up a few notches. This was all true. But the reality was that I now resembled a damaged animal which needed to limp off out of public view and attend to some profound wounds. That winter of 2010, as temperatures plummeted down to minus twenty-five back in some parts of Blighty, I wandered around the Spanish capital for weeks on end in a daze. Every now and then I would be taken by surprise and succumb to the juddering, bone jolting grief and run for cover if I was out in public, lest my tears cause me shame and provoke consternation. Yet in some strange way, I turned this energy into something creative. Deep down, the initial curiosity with the Spanish language was metamorphosed into an all-consuming obsession. I enrolled in a seriously academic school and gave myself six to nine months to try and pass the *crème de la crème* of Spanish exams, approved by the government and the prestigious *Instituto Cervantes,* the Diploma de Español Como Lengua Extranjera (DELE) – level superior. My colloquial Spanish and general fluency had been much improved by my years of co-habitation with Pablo. But it was rusty. And the finer points of high level Spanish I had sometimes asked him about had often been greeted with a shrug of the shoulders. The rules of one's own native language end up being known implicitly and not explicitly. I am still not sure how I could explain to a visitor to the UK why we say 'get *on* the plane/train/bus' but 'get *in* the car'. There was still a lot about the tongue of Cervantes I didn't understand.

I don't know where it came from but I became possessed by the idea that this striving had some higher, significant purpose, perhaps an understandable way of working out my sense of loss, who knows? Days and weeks on end reading *El País*, listening to Radio Nacional de España and learning that the verb 'caber', to fit, in the imperfect subjunctive transforms itself into 'cupiera'. Endless lists of idioms. 'Don't count your chickens...' rendered as 'don't sell the bear skin before you've hunted it.' 'You can't make a silk purse out of a sow's ear' became, 'although the monkey's dressed in silk, it's still a monkey' and perhaps my favourite, 'you can't have your cake and eat it,' was 'you can't be at mass in the pews and ring the bells.' How wonderfully, how religiously Spanish.

I think in the run-up to the exam I must have driven my new-found Spanish liaisons mad with my questioning and attention to detail. It bordered on a disturbing mental illness – a form of linguistic ADHD. When exam day came, the oral, a debate with two experts, presented the stiffest test. You had a minute to study the contents of a quotation on a piece of paper and talk for twenty minutes on whether you were broadly supportive or opposed to its content. With my heart thudding inside my chest, I turned my slip of paper over in full view of my two examiners. Here lay a quote from the Chilean poet, Pablo Neruda.

'La timidez es una condición ajena al corazón, una categoría, una dimensión que desemboca en la soledad.'

In English, perhaps imperfectly translated as: 'Shyness is a condition oblivious to the heart, a category and dimension that ends up in the state of being alone.'

One minute only. I spent thirty seconds thinking, 'What does it mean? What would I say in English, dammit?' But I composed myself and opposed its thrust. Most of my shy friends were not loners, they were valiant and full of heart: they just needed time to find their feet and trust people. Try taking ten different ways to say that, over and over again in Spanish. I actually passed this part of the exam convincingly, but came a cropper on the horrendously tricky grammar paper which included a horrible exercise where, in a literary passage of a hundred and fifty words, every lexical unit had a number and you had to spot the five deliberate mistakes: an errant preposition, a stray imperfect instead of a simple past tense. I failed this section by two points. The first exam in my life (apart from my driving test) in which I fell short of the standard required. Blow to the pride. I felt my mother's voice… 'Pick yourself up love … and give it another go.' I did, three months later – and this time I passed.

I departed Madrid with another certificate to my name, still puzzled as to exactly why I had thrown myself into it with such determination. Why had I gone about this with such near religious fervour? Within a year or so, the answer to that question was to become blindingly obvious.

10

Saved by a Saint

I t was 11 February 2013 and an announcement came from Rome that shook the global Catholic community to its foundations. Pope Benedict XVI, the man responsible for the Vatican body in 1986 that described homosexuality as an 'objective disorder', resigned as the Bishop of Rome. In doing so, he became the first occupier of the throne of St Peter to relinquish office since Gregory XII in 1415. The German pontiff's surprise move not only caused shockwaves way beyond the confines of the Church, it also set in train a chain of events for me which made a decisive change of direction. Sceptics will call these a string of coincidences. I call it grace.

Benedict's standing down was surprising enough. But on March 12, the conclave of Cardinals registered another shock. When the white smoke emerged from the Sistine Chapel, the man who appeared on the papal balcony was none of the bookies' favourites. It was the Cardinal of Buenos Aires, one José Mario Bergoglio, a seventy-six year old Jesuit: the first Vicar of Rome from that celebrated and controversial religious order and the first leader of the universal church to emanate from Latin America. Two days after his election, a phone call from BBC Radio 4's *The Report*. Could I possibly hop on a plane at short notice and present an investigation into allegations of one or two aspects of the new Pope's murkier past, namely that he had colluded with Argentina's military junta in the late 1970s in the so-called dirty war against trade unionists and left wing opponents of the regime?

'You speak Spanish don't you,' said the programme editor. 'I mean you'll be working with someone on the ground, but having the language will be indispensable.' All that time immersing myself in grammar and vocab books in Madrid, now seemed to have some obvious outlet.

The subsequent programme was produced and broadcast in the space of two weeks. Evidence of the new Pope's collusion with the torture and violent oppression of the Argentine military was, at best, inconclusive, though our programme far from exonerated him completely. But what stands out now is what happened when we visited the shanty town of Bajo Flores just a few miles from the centre of the Argentine capital. Stories had circulated since the late 1990s that the then Archbishop of Buenos Aires used to travel down *incognito* on public transport. He would be dressed in mufti, sporting his nondescript slacks and cardigan, just to spend time with some of the most impoverished people in the community. Apart from listening to their stories he also put the Church's money where his mouth was: a donation of one hundred and thirty thousand dollars for a new skills and education centre. This was one of the many projects we visited. Accompanying us was the softly spoken yet gently charismatic Father Gustavo Carrara, a worker priest in his early forties. Everywhere we walked, people's faces would light up when they saw him. Elderly women went out of their way to cross the road just to shake his hand. Young kids buzzed around him like bees around early spring lavender. What I was seeing was, in effect, a carbon copy of how Bergoglio had been received on his visits as Archbishop and later as Cardinal. We spent a whole afternoon in Bajo Flores and when we had finished my producer, Charlotte Pritchard, and I bade farewell to Fr Carrara and the community leaders and climbed into our car, ready for the return to the heart of Buenos Aires. As I looked out of the window, I caught a final glimpse of the inspirational priest and then, in a moment so redolent of that trip on the back of the truck in Banda Aceh, I had non-stop tears flowing down my cheeks. I could see the car driver eyeing me in his mirror.

'What is it?' asked Charlotte, 'Has someone upset you?' I

shook my head vigorously and pointed to the priest who had now turned his back on us in order to return to the heart of the shanty town.

'No,' I said, through gentle sobs. 'It's just that...' and I now pointed to him as he grew smaller in the distance. 'I could have done that. I *should* have done that.'

When the words came out, I was startled. As was my BBC colleague. The driver, well goodness knows what he thought. In a remarkable assignment during the early days of Pope Francis' pontificate, it was, for me, the standout moment – and nothing to do with the programme's actual content. And six months later, when I started to recount what had happened, it started up all over again. This time I was in Rome, once again with the BBC for an in-depth investigation into why Pope Benedict XVI had thrown in the towel. We were talking to members of the Vatican Bank, senior princes of the church who had been present at the resignation, such as Cardinal Francis Arinze of Nigeria and the controversial author, Gianluigi Nuzzi, whose writings had unveiled a behind the scenes picture in the Holy See of curia plotting and dysfunction. Many observers concluded that Benedict, aged eighty five when he announced his resignation, had simply lost the willpower to try and manage a series of squabbling factions. He just wanted to retire and read theology and work on some remaining texts of his own.

The new Argentine Pope had wasted no time in bringing in the new broom and was consulting with new people, left right and centre. One of them was my former Dominican Prior, Father Timothy Radcliffe. Helen Grady, my producer, and I took him out to dinner close to the order's HQ at Santa Sabina on the day he had been in for a forty minute session with Pope Francis. All was progressing well until I came to recount the tale of the Argentine trip and the teary remarks inside the taxi – and, would you believe it, the waterworks started up again. Except this time, it went on and on, for the best part of two hours on and off. My former superior was close to tears himself as he saw me constantly wiping my eyes with the serviette. At one point, our waiter had to bring me a replacement.

'What does it all mean?' I pondered out loud. Timothy talked about 'the gift of tears' and said I should drop by the next day to meet Father Brian Pierce OP, a Dominican from Texas, who had founded a community of friars in Honduras.

The following day we convened at Santa Sabina and I related to the priest my summary of what had been happening. 'Tears are a way through defences,' he said. 'What does it mean? I don't know. But I know something. You were with poor people in Argentina and you were moved by one man's work. You are blessed with speaking Spanish, so my advice is this. Don't assume it means you have to be a priest or get ordained. It's far too early to discern that. But what you should do is go and spend some weeks, months if need be, in Latin America with a community of the poor. And *listen*. *Pray*. These tears are trying to tell you something. We're always looking through a glass darkly, but if you trust, something will emerge. The picture will come into focus.'

Following Brian's counsel, I started to examine the notion of tears as a gift and, amazingly, it seems the new Argentinian Pope had been reflecting on the subject at some length (though it had been largely unreported in the press. Not an uncommon development with papal pronouncements).

'Certain realities of life,' he said, 'are seen only with eyes that are cleansed by tears.' For people who are safe, comfortable and loved, he said, learning how to weep for others is part of following Jesus, who wept at the death of Lazarus and was moved with compassion at the suffering of countless others.

'If you do not know how to weep, you are not a good Christian,' Pope Francis was to say much later on a trip to Manila. By all accounts, the founder of the Jesuits, St Ignatius of Loyola, had also frequently been moved to tears when celebrating Holy Mass. I now had an image of myself as some kind of Catholic Gwyneth Paltrow, a film star whose Oscar for best actress in *Shakespeare In Love*, had reduced her to a largely incomprehensible blubbering wreck at the 1999

Academy Awards in Hollywood. So with all this teariness now in some kind of deeper context, I began to follow Father Brian's advice. I put the word out that I was seeking such an opportunity and who better placed to ask around on my behalf than my friend, Julian Filochowski. For two decades Julian had been chief executive with CAFOD (the Catholic Agency for Overseas Development) and was now chair of the Romero Trust, a foundation devoted to the memory of Archbishop Oscar Romero of El Salvador who had been gunned down while celebrating mass in March 1980. Romero's crime? Refusing to keep quiet about the injustices and violence suffered by the innocent poor at the hands of the security government-sponsored forces and their death squads during the period in the run up to the country's civil war between 1980 and 1992.

'I'll put a few feelers out among my contacts,' he said. Within a month he was back in touch. 'There's a Jesuit priest out in northern El Salvador. He's sent me a message about trying to resurrect a radio station that folded at the end of the civil war. They need someone to help train a new team of people and, of course, someone who speaks Spanish and can converse with the people in the local community.'

Within days I was in email contact with Father Miguel Angel Vasquez in the exceedingly remote town of Arcatao, population a mere three thousand citizens. I checked it out on my Times Atlas of the World and could see it was right on the frontier with Honduras, some three hours or so north of the capital, San Salvador. Fr Miguel had been stationed at the parish of San Bartolomé since 1986 in a part of the country that had witnessed some of the most horrendous civil war brutalities. Families had fled from their homes as troops and government-backed militias moved to effectively 'cleanse' the area of opposition. Women and children died wandering the mountainous area around, with scant access to food and water. Some mothers lost husbands and all their sons – volunteers all of the Farabundo Marti National Liberation Movement (FMLN), which took up arms against the cruel excesses of a regime that would stop at nothing to protect the vested interests and privileges of the country's elite group of families – the Salvadorean oligarchy. A fledgling radio station, Radio Farabundo Marti, had operated during the war, moving its infrastructure to what it hoped were hidden points in the mountains, dodging and weaving to avoid detection. Often it was the only source of information which could counteract the propaganda of the dictatorial governing regime, but they were sometimes traced by helicopters and suffered crushing setbacks. It was this station which Father Miguel was now trying to resurrect, as a peace-time community radio outlet. I was a journalist with thirty years' experience and I also had the language. It felt like providence. By November 2014, fulfilling Father Brian Pierce's wise words, I had packed my rucksack and was off to Central America for three months.

The journey there was tortuous. Twenty one hours via Dallas in Texas to San Salvador where Father Miguel met me in his sturdy vehicle to drive up, via Chalatenango, to the mountains of Arcatao, a small town whose name derived from an ancient dialect, *Potón*, and which meant 'house of the serpent'. I had offered to get a series of buses, but was warned off on account of the frequent *asaltos* that take place every year by roaming gangs of people who target travellers. Most are with one of the big drugs gangs, *pandillas*, who divide up large sections of the country between them and operate a seemingly endless turf war with results that have El Salvador now frequently described as the 'murder capital of the world'. The gangs, or *maras* as they are known locally, go by names that often denote their geographical origin: Barrio 18, MS-13, Mara Salvatrucha being the biggest ones. It is estimated that about 60,000 people belong to one *mara* or another, and the homicide statistics tell their own story. Per 100,000 inhabitants, the UK murder rate is 0.9, in the United States it is 3.9, in El Salvador in 2015 the equivalent figure was over one hundred. All this in a country the size of Wales with a population of 6.3 million. On this occasion, I was happy to take the advice and accompany Father Miguel in his robust four by four. Once we left Chalatenango, the road became almost impassable in places. We passed through Guarjila, San José Las Flores and Nueva Trinidad, occasionally picking up and dropping off peasant pedestrians hitching a lift who clambered aboard our pick-up. On the final stretch, we were losing the light and the edges of the setting sun caught the tops of the mountains through the hazy early evening glow. Honduras beckoned just a few miles ahead over the hillside pass. It seemed I was on a totally different planet, even compared with the capital San Salvador. This was, unquestionably, remote.

That first evening I was shown my quarters in the parish convent building of San Bartolomé. There were about six rooms scattered off a central courtyard. Father Miguel had a double for all his belongings, his computer and files, but the rest were all guest rooms. A quick glance made me realise that this was not going to be the Arcatao Hilton Excelsior Suite. Privacy was near non-existent as the dividing 'walls' such as they were, began about two feet off the ground and ended about two feet short of the ceiling. A huge bat flew across above me under the eves of the roof within seconds of me dumping my bags on the bed. As the night fell, a chorus of howling dogs anchored their presence outside in the street. '*Espera los gallos*' … they said: wait for the cocks to crow. They were right. That first night I hardly slept a wink. At two in the morning, a stray homeless man stationed himself outside and began shouting into the convent through windows that contained no glass panes for acoustic protection. Added to the barking hounds and chorus of roosters, they were all beginning to make their very own unique Latin American symphony, 'The Dissonance'.

By three thirty am, Father Miguel's snoring from the next door quarters had stopped. That's because he was now, very audibly, on his first phone call of the day. By five thirty the sun was beginning to clip the mountain peaks and a very friendly woman appeared to begin making *quesadilla*, a cheesy breakfast cake and tortilla bread with *frijoles*. I would eat these red beans for the next three weeks non-stop until the very look of them made me want to run for cover. I confess, in these first twenty four hours, I was starting to regret ever meeting and listening to Father Brian Pierce. But it was my tears that had got me here. Tears which had jolted me out of my comfort zone and here I was *supremely* out of said zone. You couldn't deny there was a certain uncomfortable logic to it all.

By nine o'clock, with my eyes in need of matchsticks to prop them open, I met the local radio team in the presence of the *alcalde*, Arcatao's mayor, José Alberto Avelar. I had arrived with heady notions of doing journalism training, expanding the range of programmes and the like, but I was soon disabused of all that. 'We bought this huge antenna from a local company in the capital which still hasn't arrived via customs, from Italy,' I was told. 'The local transmitter on our cabin is pretty pathetic. We're reaching about two thousand people at most with our output,' explained Rodolfo Rivera, the director of the local school. The immediate goal was to get up to the mountain top, about two and half thousand feet high and build a *caseta*, an expansive hut constructed on a cement base. This is where they hoped to install solar panels and batteries to power the station in the town below and also to locate the still undelivered radio antenna. With this all intact, the signal would be able to reach Chalatenango some twenty five miles away, with a population of thirty thousand and, in time, the capital San Salvador, some seventy two miles south west. So, having thought I'd turned up to impart my knowledge of how to produce a Latino *Desert Island Discs*, it was soon a question of a very rustic version of a cross between *Bob the Builder* and *Grand Designs*. 'We have two major problems,' said Dimas, a prominent local college educator. 'First we have no money to buy all the materials. We need sand, cement, copper wire and gravel. Once we've got all that, we then need to find mules, other *bestias*, and a team of people to get all the materials up there and build the thing. They'll have to sleep up there for ten days or so, work in the heat of the day, and they'll need food and water taken up to them. How long did you say you were here for?'

This was turning out to be more like a scene from Graham Greene's *The Power and the Glory*. By the next day we had made up a shopping list and off we went to secure the materials. The first seven suppliers we came across would only accept cash, so we had a long trip down the road to Aguilares before we succeeded with a credit card. The money issue I had discounted before my departure from the UK. I had just moved from central London back to my native Manchester and saw no inherent reason why a community of Salvadorean campesinos should not profit, indirectly, from the overheating London property market. Father Miguel rang his *albañil*, his construction worker handyman, from across the Honduran frontier. After two weeks, we had assembled a team of beasts and our crack team of labourers who would construct the *caseta*. With miraculous timing, after a seven month delay, the antenna also now arrived having been stuck in customs for an eternity. On the Saturday morning before Christmas 2014, our motley crew met in the town square at 6am with the intention of starting the ascent early to avoid the heat of the midday sun. Despite a few delays due to rebellious mules en route and the hazardous task of locating the mountain path, which had a tendency to disappear into the bushes, we got the first sacks of cement and sand up there just inside two and a half hours. Four such trips were needed that weekend, often in thirty five degree heat. By early mid-January, it was all completed. Stage one was at an end and Radio Farabundo Marti was now set to broadcast to its hugely wider audience.

But broadcast what exactly? The volunteer team was composed of thirty or so members, mostly youngsters, who saw themselves as amateur DJs, playing non-stop music, taking requests on SMS messages or on the radio's Facebook page, but offering little else. 'What's the point?,' asked Vina, a feisty widow in her seventies who had lost a husband and three sons in the civil war. She called me her *hijo adoptivo* (adopted son) and plied me with delicious soup every day. 'I mean I can hear all that music on other radio stations, what are they bringing to Arcatao specifically?' It was a fair point. The station was broadcasting the weekly Sunday mass direct at 8am. This was especially useful for all the infirm and elderly who could not traipse down the valleys to the town square where the elegant church of San Bartolomé stood. (On one occasion, Father Miguel had asked me to preach at the morning mass as he had another commitment in Nueva Trinidad and could not be in two places at once. He was able to comment on the sermon's content having caught it on his car radio. Afterwards, one or two parishioners asked me if I could replace the local clergyman full time – something I dared not share with the Jesuit priest.)

So with the technical challenges surmounted, we now needed a strategy for content. We appointed a young full time director, Felix José Muñoz, who was just finishing a three year course on media studies and broadcast journalism in San Salvador and pledged him a salary of four hundred dollars a month. I also secured the assistance of 'El Chapín', a Guatemalteco by the exotic name of Rudy Renato Chic. I had heard of Rudy's amazing work with Save the Children and other charities in which he had used his formidable range of talents to help youngsters learn about sound editing, scripting *cuñas publicitarias* (publicity and programme jingles) and also marketing. He made the six hour trip down from Guatemala City and implemented a ten day training programme – a feat he has repeated at least twice since.

And the people of Arcatao! What an incredible welcome, right from the outset. As the radio project gathered momentum, my knowledge of the local community grew. And despite their differences in background and education what united them, all, what united us all was the unquestioning dedication to the memory of Oscar Arnulfo Romero – the Archbishop and shepherd who gave up his life for his people. The radio theme was no mere coincidence, for it was Romero's Radio YSAX through which the embattled church leader had spoken directly to the nation and called into question the cruel and unjust actions of the military government. Like

Radio Farabundo Marti, his criticism was met with repeated attempts at sabotage and destruction of the radio, but as he repeatedly pledged, he was the voice of the people who demanded the social justice of the gospels, the poor who merited, glimpses at least, of God's kingdom here on earth. In his sermon in the Cathedral in San Salvador on 23 March 1980, he addressed directly the rank and file members of the army and police who, acting on the orders of their Senior Officers, were massacring their fellow campesinos.

'In the name of this suffering people, whose cries rise to heaven each day ever more tumultuously, I beseech you, I beg you, I order you, in the name of God, stop the repression.'

This was the final straw for the oligarchy and the military high command. The following day he was shot by the single bullet of an assassin at the local hospital chapel of Divine Mercy as he celebrated mass. A quarter of a million people attended his funeral service the following Sunday. Years of behind the scenes obstruction in Rome prevented Romero's case for being considered as a holy martyr of the church being heard at the highest levels, as conservative Cardinals blocked the process fearing the power of his example across the Latin American continent. They called him a communist. But justice has finally prevailed. He was beatified and made Blessed Oscar Romero in 2015 and it is more than possible a date will have been set for his canonisation by the time this set of memoirs hits the printing press. Throughout Latin America he is widely known as 'Saint Romero of the Americas'.

Romero had been murdered during my second year at university. The news, which came out of nowhere, had made a huge impression on me. Like most people, I had to scurry to locate an atlas and check out where El Salvador was. But a man, previously considered a staunch conservative, gunned down at mass after defending his people? What could be more Christ-like than that? And here I was in Arcatao in a community of newly-found friends, sisters and brothers, who quoted his name several times a day, whose homes were decked with his photos. He was everywhere in the physical domain and woven into the soul of the nation. Without doubt, unquestionably a man of God. A Christ-bearer to the world. All this I reflected on during my final week in Arcatao as we savoured how much we had achieved together in the space of five or six weeks. Then, not before time, a familiar question came my way:

'*Señor Marcos, usted está casado?*' The school director wanted to know if I was married. Before answering, I recalled a chat going up the mountain with those mules in which a youngster had started to ask me what the hell was going on in Europe with all this gay marriage business. 'Well it's not just Europe,' I'd said. 'I mean a lot of the USA has it now. And even Mexico, Argentina and parts of Brazil. You never know, they'll be introducing it here next.' The youngster had pulled a face. 'Never,' he retorted. 'This will be the last country.' So I quizzed him more. What would happen if a young man in college, a sixteen or seventeen year old say, declared himself to be gay?

'When you say "gay" you mean "homosexual", right? He'd be mad to do that. He'd be driven out of the village. He'd have to leave Arcatao. It would be a total humiliation for the family.'

It was these words that had me replying a discreet 'no' to the marriage question and then changing the subject abruptly. I thought the cock might crow at any moment, but I was not going to endanger the radio project and any future co-operation with a sudden burst of gay lib. Later that night before I slept, I thought more about it. What a massive irony: here I was probably happier and more fulfilled than at any stage of my life amidst a community of people who didn't even know I was queer. I had spent all my life searching for happiness with 'Mr Right' and seemed to have stumbled across him thanks to the heroic saintliness of Oscar Romero.

When I returned to the UK from Arcatao in March 2015, I narrated this incident to Sir Stephen Wall, a former government diplomat, former adviser to Tony Blair on the European Union. Stephen had also been adviser to the former head of the Catholic Church in England and Wales,

Cardinal Cormac Murphy O'Connor. He had been on his own interesting journey recently, having just declared to his wife and son in his mid-sixties that he was gay. 'You say you chose not to tell them,' he asked quizzically over a spot of brunch on Aldwych in central London. 'Isn't that ... well, a trifle naïve?' I reiterated that it was a cultural backwater, no public sightings of gays and role models, Latin-American machismo, etc. 'Yes, I know all that,' he persisted. 'But they have search engines there like everywhere else.' I took out my Sony tablet and fired it up.

'Type in Mark Dowd/periodista (journalist)/católico,' he said.

Within two seconds up popped the following link as the most frequently cited reference on the Spanish version of Google next to my name.

'la homosexualidad es la bomba de tiempo en la Iglesia Católica dice ex sacerdote.'

Homosexuality is the time bomb inside the Catholic Church, says ex-priest (sic).

On the next line it referred to the fact that I was openly gay.

These diplomats – always going around pointing out unwelcome truths. It was inconceivable that someone in Arcatao had not googled this link. And there was I, deluding myself, yet again, that I was somehow in control. At least this time I didn't do a Gwyneth Paltrow at the dining table.

So within a month I'll be making my third visit to El Salvador, and suspect it may well be time to come out of the closet for the umpteenth time in my life. On this next trip I'll not only be checking on how things are progressing at Radio Farabundo Marti, but also trying to advance another initiative: the Blessed Oscar Romero Solar Park. This is a renewable energy project (inspired by Pope Francis' ground-breaking environmental encyclical, *Laudato Si*) which has already received some considerable encouragement from inside the Vatican and organisations such as the US Catholic Relief Services. On top of this, such is the personal momentum unleashed by my recent involvement in Central America that I recently made an important decision: to redraft my will and make sure my estate is left in favour of the community in Arcatao. This smacks very little of altriusm and has a lot to do with ulterior motives, because I cannot think of anything better as the final days and hours of my life approach than knowing that the shuffling off of my mortal coil will be of considerable financial benefit to that group of people. I have related this news to Father Miguel and informed him that I have now given everyone in the area a cast iron incentive for assassinating me. 'Why would we do that?,' he said. 'We like you and would miss you.' Such charming innocence. British irony does often struggle to be understood once it leaves the shores of Blighty.

I am no saint dear reader. You don't know half of it. And in Matthew's gospel chapter nineteen, Jesus does not say to the rich young man, 'adjust your will and, at the end of your life, having enjoyed your wealth, make sure all your Standard Life pension and ISA plans are in good order and leave what is left to the poor.' No. It's a hundred times, nay a thousand times harder. He says, without compromise, 'If you want to be perfect, go, sell what you have and give to the poor, and you will have treasure in heaven; and come, follow Me.' I am a long way from being perfect, but since making this bond with the citizens of Arcatao I feel different. I feel more settled than ever before. Saint Augustine famously says in his *Confessions*:

'Thou hast made us for thyself, O Lord, and our heart is restless until it finds its rest in thee.'

I think it's an honest admission that the previous nine chapters are witness to Augustine's said restlessness, a unquietness that frequently propels us forward, to keep looking, evaluating lest one becomes one of those people who prefers the comfort of failure to the uncertainty of possible success. Much of the new-found resolution is certainly down to a new sense of purpose and direction that those links with El Salvador have ushered in. But deep down, it is rather more than that.

'Queer and Catholic' is the title of this book. Alas, for many LGBT Catholics in the past, life has framed itself in a stark binary choice, 'Queer *or* Catholic'. Hundreds of thousands have abandoned the faith of their upbringing on account of Church teaching on LGBT issues and its description of homosexuality as an 'objective disorder'. I have been near to throwing in the towel myself at times, but something or someone has always pulled me back from the brink. As my beloved, sadly now deceased Dominican brother, Gareth Moore OP concludes in his masterful *A Question of Truth* written before his untimely early death in 2002:

> *The conclusion of this book is, therefore, not that it is good to be gay, but that it is irrational for serious, reflective Christians … to accept church teaching on homosexuality. … This is not a matter of dissent or materialism; it is simply that the church at the moment produces no good arguments to assent to. Regrettably, in this area, the church teaches badly.*

There will come a day, I am sure (but not in my lifetime) when most if not all Christian churches will accept same sex love and attraction as a totally naturally occurring minority variant of the business of what it means to be human. Just as there are no groups for left-handed Catholics (though there might have been a few centuries ago when it was seen as the calling card of the Devil), in this new world, there will be no groups like Quest and the Lesbian and Gay Christian Movement (LGCM). They will be anachronisms. They will attract purely historical interest in the same way as we still look at Wilberforce and the movement for the abolition of slavery. But what is the gay Christian, the gay Catholic to do in the meantime? Throwing out the toys from the pram is always an attractive option if drama is your thing, but depriving the universal church of a serious, witnessed and well-argued LGBT input would be to deny it the very catholicity which is one of its great hallmarks. Put alongside the central tenets of faith: the Incarnation of God as man in Jesus; the Triune Love of the Father, Son and Holy Spirit; that the pilgrim people of what we call, 'The Church' are guaranteed the accompanying presence of the Spirit to guide it, through all the ups and downs; that Jesus was called to new life in the resurrection and that death can never be the final word – what the Church teaches unconvincingly on matters LGBT can never be a reason for jettisoning those massively higher order truths.

Truths? Or just mere subjective opinions held in fragile hope?

My hunch is that a deeper reason for my new-found deliverance from the rampant Augustinian restlessness is a gradual grounding inside me of the authenticity of the Christian faith. I've stopped fighting because I have actually found myself properly assenting to its truthfulness for the first time in my life. I feel touched by grace, by something that is most certainly not of my own making. This will not be easy to explain, but bear with me because the following words may well be the most important of the eighty odd thousand contained in this book.

When I was eighteen and off to University, I was aware of what might be called *a priori* claims of the Christian faith and of the Jesus story. But I had precious little experience of life to measure them up against: it was a blunt question of: 'you were born here, your parents believed it all, this was and is our culture so get on with it.' Those nagging questions that began at university, and through into religious life and which possibly underpinned the helter-skelter nature of human endeavours in love, have been ever-present. But at the ripe old age of fifty seven, there is now something rather different at work. Take the analogy of a plastic separatory funnel with its wide and narrow ends, the kind one might use to channel liquids. As a youngster, those asserted and unquestioned truth claims were the narrow end. But forty years of life have now allowed me to flip the funnel and turn things on their head. The question I now ask is not principally: 'Is Christianity true?', but 'How do humans behave, fall short of their best and can anything be done about it?'

As a species, our major shortcomings in no particular

order of importance: we demonise strangers, those who do not belong to the pack (of nation, of our gender, of our faith badge.) From time to time we erect tyrannical despotic systems in the name of religious or political ideologies that crush individuals who do not play the passive game of assent. We constantly ignore the golden rule, 'do as you would be done by'. Male dominated structures constantly sideline and undervalue the often superior talents and gifts of women. Hypocrisy, cynicism and spin dominate much of public discourse. Women and men who pursue paths of self-aggrandisement through love of money or power inevitably end up dissatisfied, chasing their tails in pursuit of false gods that never give them rest. If the health of any society is measured by how it treats the weakest and most vulnerable among us, then it must be honestly stated that even our most 'successful' societal constructions are often found wanting. Finally, in the defence of some mythical perfect nuclear family structure, all sorts of people who do not 'fit' are cast off as second class individuals when they are all meant to be seen and treated as children of God. That, if you will, is the summary of my empirically observed input at the wider end of this metaphorical funnel.

Let us now, superimpose over this map of human imperfection, the three year ministry of a man who lived and loved until death two thousand years ago. This rabbi, who said very little about sexual ethics (and not a word about homosexuality) railed against the hypocrisy and smug self-satisfaction of religious leaders. Here was a man who scandalised his own kind by pressing the claims of the hated Samaritans instead of his own stock, the Jews, and urged us to embrace strangers. A man who appeared first to women and not to men after three days of death and darkness. A man who took on organised religious and political power with not one recourse to violence and exposed it as inhumane tyranny. A teacher who threw human short-sightedness on its head by asserting that if we want to save our lives we will lose them, but if they are lost for the sake of others, our lives will indeed be saved. An unmarried man, who warned that he had come to set family members against each other and who also warned that prioritising tribal and family blood ties would lead to factions and violent strife – not a prince, but a son of a humble carpenter who instead called us to a higher ethic of embracing those on the margins. Not a bad match between human shortcomings and the Jesus story. And all that inside three years of ministry. But wait, there is more.

I often hear critics of Christianity lambasting the image of Jesus on the cross. 'It's so bloody and sadistic isn't it? I mean, I don't think little children should be exposed to it. Honestly, when we're trying to bring an end to bloody violence in the world and you have that in front of you.' And another variant on the theme, this one a particular favourite of arch-priest of the new atheism, Professor Richard Dawkins. I paraphrase:

> *Really, why does God think that it was a good idea to have this idea of a tortured, abused body on two planks of wood as the zenith of the salvation story? It only exposes the divine as a really nasty piece of work. God sent his only Son to die for our sins? Such a God, if he is there, must be a sicko.*

Such superficially understandable critiques totally miss the point. If I were God, looking at the way we, as a species, go about torturing and abusing our fellow man, no not just in Aleppo, Srebrenica and Rwanda, but in the massive polarities of wealth and scandalously unequal access to the Earth's resources, and also in the way we treat our Earthly home, then if I took on human form, I'd submit myself to the cruel excesses of human madness *to hold up a mirror to these mad creatures*. I would ask them, is this you? Is this what you do to the most innocent, virtuous and selfless human who ever walked the planet? You kill him because you cannot stand the way his values accuse you by their understated force. The crucifixion and its brutal horror is 'necessary', not because God is some sick sadist on an Atonement binge, it is because this is what we do to one another. God shows us this in the Jesus story and invites us to stop and re-think. This is the nearest I can get to making sense of the phrase, 'saving us from our sins'. It's more like saving us *from ourselves*.

This has been argued out and developed in much more detail and applied to the situation LGBT folk find themselves in by my gay brother, Dominican theologian James Alison, in his many splendid writings. James has been hugely influenced by the works of the French philosopher, René Girard, who wrote extensively about how a historically recurring scapegoating mechanism manifests itself in the realms of violence and the sacred. His arguments revolve around whole societies which project their own unconscious shortcomings onto demonised 'others'. Those who are deemed not to belong are thus silenced and eliminated, buying time before the whole cycle kicks off again. The behaviour and utterances of repressed and self-hating gay men in the church towards their openly self-accepting gay brothers is especially worth considering under this Girardian paradigm.

If the Jesus story maps convincingly onto the chronicle of humanity's collective repeated set of wrong turns, then that, to me, is a convincing argument for being a Christian. But why a Roman Catholic Christian? Especially in a Roman church that currently preaches 'disordered' sexuality and from time to time tells the world that adoption by gay couples is 'doing violence to children'. Why not a neat and opportunistic side step – and become a High Church Anglican or a member of the URC, the United Reformed Church, with its impressive commitment to social justice? Or one of those lovely cuddly, unthreatening Quakers even? Goodness knows, frequently I have looked at not only members of other denominations, but of entire other faiths and thought: 'goodness, those people are a damn sight better specimen and example of decent humanity than my lot.' But there is a global, universal aspect to Catholicism with its top rate intellectual bedrock which keeps me firmly glued. The two thousand year history of the struggles and inspiration of the lives of the saints cannot be swatted aside as mere coffee table reading. And the horrors of the paedophile clerical crisis, ghastly as they are, and recent corruption in the Vatican Bank no more negate the arguments for God and the Truth of the Jesus story, than the boundless kindness of Church agencies in countless schools and hospitals of the developing world clinch the argument in God's favour. The church is a reflection of humanity: a sea of exceptional achievement mixed with the grotesque. But, and this has come especially in my own backyard, I have been privileged to meet a handful of people who possess that unique quality of 'the peace that surpasseth all understanding' that it has and still does touch me to the core of my being. The presence of one, merely one person can answer, through transcendence, the ugly follies of thousands of the tribally religious. It is not a question of counting by numbers but taking a chance on what may indeed be true. Not an 'emotional' spasm, not cowardly 'intellectual' double-think, but that fundamental 'gut' instinct on which in the end we rely as human beings.

As I said in the climax of that *Tsunami: Where was God?* documentary, standing under the huge crucifix suspended over the altar at Westminster Cathedral, if the promise of life beyond the empty tomb is false, it is the biggest hoax ever perpetrated in human history. Such is the near scandalous claim of Resurrection, a truth claim that one flinches away from at times because of its utterly preposterous audacity. But might this be the dark scowl that squints at the brilliance of the early morning sun? 'Do you believe?' I have often been asked. Frequently I have responded, 'it depends which day of the week you ask me.' By grace and sheer gift, those 'No days' are fading more and more, like some distant shore from the liner that speeds on relentlessly out to sea.

I thank God I never had to choose – Queer OR Catholic.

For many many years, I have been proud to state I am Queer AND Catholic.

But now, a small, but deeply important adjustment of inversion:

I am Catholic and (by the way, just more than a little bit) … Queer.

Catholic and Queer!